The World as Metaphor in Robert Musil's
The Man without Qualities

Robert Musil, known to be a scientific and philosophical thinker, was committed to aesthetics as a process of experimental creation of an ever-shifting reality. Musil wanted, above all, to be a creative writer, and he obsessively engaged in almost endless deferral via variations and metaphoric possibilities in his novel project, *The Man without Qualities*. This lifelong process of writing is embodied in the unfinished novel by a recurring metaphor of self-generating de-centered circle worlds. The present study analyzes this structure with reference to Musil's concepts of the utopia of the Other Condition, Living and Dead Words, Specific and Non-Specific Emotions, Word Magic, and the Still Life. In contrast to most recent studies of Musil, it concludes that the extratemporal metaphoric experience of the Other Condition does not fail, but rather constitutes the formal and ethical core of Musil's novel. The first study to utilize the *Klagenfurter Ausgabe* (Klagenfurt edition) of Musil's literary remains (a searchable annotated text), *The World as Metaphor* offers a close reading of variations and text genesis, shedding light not only on Musil's novel, but also on larger questions about the modernist artist's role and responsibility in consciously re-creating the world.

GENESE GRILL (PhD CUNY Graduate Center) is an independent scholar and artist. She has written extensively on Musil and has published the following translations of his works:

Robert Musil: Literature and Politics. By Klaus Amann and Robert Musil. Translation. Contra Mundum Press (2022).

Theater Symptoms: Plays and Writings on Drama. By Robert Musil. Translation & introduction. Contra Mundum Press (2020).

Unions. By Robert Musil. Translation and introduction. Contra Mundum Press (2019).

Thought Flight: The Small Prose of Robert Musil. Translation and introduction. Contra Mundum Press (2015).

She is also the author of a book of essays, *Portals: Reflections on the Spirit in Matter.* Splice (Forthcoming 2022).

T0366771

Studies in German Literature, Linguistics, and Culture

The World as Metaphor in Robert Musil's *The Man without Qualities*

Possibility as Reality

Genese Grill

CAMDEN HOUSE
Rochester, New York

First published 2012 by Camden House
Reprinted in paperback 2022

Camden House is an imprint of Boydell & Brewer Inc.
668 Mt. Hope Avenue, Rochester, NY 14620, USA
and of Boydell & Brewer Limited
PO Box 9, Woodbridge, Suffolk IP12 3DF, UK
www.boydellandbrewer.com

Paperback ISBN-13: 978-1-64014-127-8
Hardcover ISBN-13: 978-1-57113-538-4

Library of Congress Cataloging-in-Publication Data

Grill, Genese.
The world as metaphor in Robert Musil's The man without qualities:
possibility as reality / Genese Grill.
   p. cm. — (Studies in German literature, linguistics, and culture)
Includes bibliographical references and index.
ISBN 978-1-57113-538-4 (hardcover: acid-free paper) —
ISBN 1-57113-538-3 (hardcover: acid-free paper)
1. Musil, Robert, 1880-1942. Mann ohne Eigenschaften. 2. Metaphor in
literature. I. Title.
PT2625.U8M3755 2012
833'.912—dc23

                                                                    2012028705

A catalogue record for this title is available from the British Library.

This publication is printed on acid-free paper.

Printed and bound in Great Britain by
TJ Books Ltd, Padstow, Cornwall

Man könnte tagelang in Gleichnissen fortfahren. Was heißt das? . . .
Gleichnisse gehen mehr an als Wirklichkeit.
Es kommt nicht auf das an, was ich tue, es könnte ebensogut etwas
anderes sein, aber es muss den gleichen Gleichniswert haben.
Obgleich Gleichnis, Gefühl der inneren Notwendigkeit.
Nichts ist fest. Jede Ordnung führt ins Absurde.
Nur hier ist das Gefühl des tiefen Lebens.
Die Kategorien der Welt erscheinen als erstarrte Gleichnisse . . .
Die Welt nur ein möglicher Versuch.
Zugleich mit den Gleichnissen fühlt man, das Leben löst sich in
einem Hauch auf.
Es ist da u[nd] nur bis zu einem gewissen Grad da.

[One could continue all day with metaphors. What does that mean?
Metaphors are more meaningful than reality.
It doesn't depend on what I do, it could just as easily be something
else, but it must have the same metaphoric value.
Despite metaphor, feeling of inner necessity.
Nothing is certain. Every order leads to absurdity.
Yet the feeling of deep life is found here.
The categories of the world appear as frozen metaphors . . .
The world is only one possible attempt.
Along with the metaphors one feels life dissolve in a breath.
It is there a[nd] only there to a certain degree.]

— Musil, *Nachlass*

Contents

Acknowledgments   ix

Abbreviations of Works Frequently Cited   xi

Introduction: Failure to Reconcile as Modernist Success   1

1: Circles   15

2: Repeatability and Crime   49

3: Word Magic   93

4: Still Life: (Not) Doing What Isn't Done   119

Conclusion   157

Works Cited   187

Index   195

Acknowledgments

SEVENTEEN YEARS AGO Burton Pike introduced me to Robert Musil. The 1995 translation of *The Man without Qualities*, which he edited, extended the earlier English translation of the chapters published in Musil's lifetime by including Burton Pike's own translations of the remaining chapters and a great deal of material that had not previously been translated into English. These latter sketches for continuation of the novel, alternative versions of chapters, notes, and thoughts are known as the *Nachlass* (works "left behind," not published during the author's lifetime); and Burton Pike's translation and insightful introduction to the stylistic originality, complexity of themes, and interdisciplinary depth of Musil's thought presented in this volume was my first entrée into Musil's world. From the first moment I heard him speak about Musil and his work on the translation as his graduate student at the City University of New York, I was captivated by the rhythm of the writing in both the German and the new translation, the originality of the images, and the richness and seeming infinity of ideas and correspondences. A short time later I discovered that the astonishing pages of the *Nachlass* translated by Burton Pike were actually selections of thousands more pages of Musil texts. A wealth of poetic prose, philosophy, and intensity of thought was easily accessible only through the *Klagenfurter Ausgabe* (Klagenfurt edition), a searchable and extensively annotated collection of all of Musil's literary and biographical remains and reading texts that I came, in time, to call "Musil's brain." Klaus Amann and Walter Fanta, who edited this edition along with Karl Corino, put the edition into my hands, thereby opening my eyes to the seemingly infinite scope of Musil's web of connected and expanding ideas. For this gift, for the access they gave me to the Musil Institute library in Klagenfurt, Austria, and for their generous welcome into a rich and stimulating society of international Musil scholarship, I am very grateful.

Not only did Burton Pike teach me about Robert Musil, but he also labored to teach me how to read, think, and write clearly and honestly, and to believe in the possibility of language to express complexities and contradictions without collapsing into chaos. Any remaining obfuscation in this book is my own stubborn responsibility, for not only did he train me over many years as a student and long after, but he read and edited this manuscript many times. It is thus no exaggeration to say that I could not have written this book without him.

I have been lucky enough to have other readers as well, friends and colleagues who have read parts of this manuscript and earlier versions. Of these I would especially like to thank Kathryn Barush, who found the time to do close and loving readings, even while in the midst of struggling toward the completion of her doctoral thesis, and my father, Neil Grill, who has been not only an invaluable reader and advisor but also a true kindred literary and poetic spirit for me. Mark Mirsky, novelist and scholar, has been a close colleague in my explorations, particularly of Musil's mysticism and of the connections made in this book between mystical and aesthetic experience. I thank Jim Walker, my editor at Camden House, for his patience, encouragement and guidance, Jim Hardin for his insightful reading and comments, and even my second anonymous reader, who made me do a good deal more work these last few months.

I would also like to thank my friend and colleague Dharman Rice, with whom I had the pleasure of co-teaching a class in transcendentalism and existentialism, where many of the ideas in this book came to life; and also my students in this and all my classes, many of whom have since become colleagues, friends, and fellow conspirators in the continuing quest for meaningful expression and a passionate and ethical life. Of these, I particularly would like to thank Kenneth Harrison, poet, teacher, scholar. I warmly press your hand. I thank my bohemian cohort for keeping me from becoming too dusty and fusty, and especially my many wise women friends (too many to name) for constantly reminding me that of all the obsessions, one's creative and intellectual work is the most fulfilling. Marietta Lutze Sackler started me on my way to learning the German language and has been an inspiration in all ways. I thank my mother, Ruth Grill, for all her loving support and enthusiasm about this project and for the way she taught me to love words, images, and the meaningful patterns they make. I am very grateful for Dr. Sima Gerber, who has been an invaluable friend, support and role-model for how one might combine scholarly rigor with humanistic values. And finally, I thank my best friend and fellow utopian, Stephen Callahan, for the decades of "Heilige Gespräche" (holy conversations) in the red and gold salons of our imaginary and material castles.

Vienna, 15 April 2012,
the 70th anniversary of Robert Musil's death

Abbreviations of Works Frequently Cited

B   *Robert Musil: Briefe, 1901–1942.* Edited by Adolf Frisé with
        help from Murray G. Hall. Reinbek bei Hamburg: Rowohlt,
        1981.

B II   *Robert Musil: Briefe, 1901–1942.* Commentary, Index. Edited
        by Adolf Frisé with help from Murray G. Hall. Reinbek bei
        Hamburg: Rowohlt, 1981.

D   *Diaries: 1899–1941.* Translated by Philip Payne. Edited by
        Mark Mirsky. New York: Basic Books, 1998.

KA   *Klagenfurter Ausgabe: Kommentierte digitale Edition sämtli-
        cher Werke, Briefe und nachgelassener Schriften. Mit Transkrip-
        tionen und Faksimiles aller Handschriften.* (Klagenfurt edition:
        Annotated Digital Edition of the Collected Works, Letters and
        Literary and Biographical Remains, with Transcriptions and
        Facsimiles of All Manuscripts). Edited by Walter Fanta, Klaus
        Amann, and Karl Corino. Robert Musil-Institut, Alpen-Adria
        Universität Klagenfurt, Austria, 2009.

MoE   *Der Mann ohne Eigenschaften.* Edited by Adolf Frisé. Reinbek
        bei Hamburg: Rowohlt, 1970.

MwQ   *The Man without Qualities.* Translated by Burton Pike and
        Sophie Wilkins. New York: Knopf, 1995. Two volumes.

P   *Precision and Soul: Essays and Addresses.* Edited and translated
        by Burton Pike and David S. Luft. Chicago: U of Chicago P,
        1990.

T   *Robert Musil: Tagebücher.* Edited by Adolf Frisé. Reinbek bei
        Hamburg: Rowohlt, 1976.

T II   *Robert Musil: Tagebücher.* Notes, Appendix, Index. Edited by
        Adolf Frisé. Reinbek bei Hamburg: Rowohlt, 1976.

TBAER   *Tagebücher, Aufsätze, Essays und Reden.* Edited by Adolf Frisé.
        Reinbek bei Hamburg: Rowohlt, 1955.

Introduction: Failure to Reconcile as Modernist Success

ALTHOUGH MUSIL OCCASIONALLY FANTASIZED about what he might do after *The Man without Qualities* was finished, there is, in effect, no end in sight — not for the engaged reader who enters into Musil's intellectual labyrinth; not for the scholar who may try in vain to "finish" with Musil and go on to something else; no end to the author's textual variants, to the possibilities, the arrangements and rearrangements; and no definitive solutions to the questions earnestly posed by this sophisticated writer. Musil was halted in the endless task only by his sudden death, in mid-sentence, while re-visioning one of many versions of a chapter he had begun decades before.

This endlessness has often been read as a failure to reconcile, or come to closure, and this reading has often determined assessments of the relative success of important aspects of Musil's experiment. For example the heightened aesthetic and ethical experiences characterized by the exceptional state Musil called "the Other Condition" have been taken by many to be an escapist attempt to achieve a lasting harmonious union, the possibility of which he would later come to reject. This book argues against this view of failure, and contends that Musil's experimentation with narrative non-linearity and metaphor produced an existential model according to which aesthetic experience, as active, participatory word- and world-construction is the fundamental metaphysical and ethical activity of mankind.[1] While many have argued that Musil's utopian projections were bound to fail because they could not last and because they could not be made to correspond with "reality," this book argues that the formal and theoretical bases for all of Musil's work call the criteria of both duration and so-called reality radically into question.

Unlike most other studies of Musil's project, which tend to concentrate on the published sections of the novel,[2] this study engages with the novel project in its total, unfinished state, taking into consideration for the first time the thousands of pages of unpublished material he left behind, the *Nachlass*. It follows Musil into his perspectival displacements and multiplications, and traces within these formal processes the consistencies of his aesthetic and ethical concerns. The *Klagenfurter Ausgabe* (Klagenfurt edition) of the more than ten thousand pages of the entire Musil *Nachlass* has recently made it possible to access this labyrinthine web of correspondences, alternative universes, and their shadows. It also affords the opportunity to access the individual fragments and passages in a non-linear manner that foregrounds the complex cross-referencing and correspondences of Musil's writing process, presenting a new vision of the work. This study takes full advantage of this new resource, closely examining the way in which each of Musil's sentences is haunted by a vibrant palimpsest of choices, perspectives, descriptions, and re-descriptions. A close reading of this sort reveals that Musil's project constituted much more than an attempt at creating a completed, finite work of fiction. The supposedly finished parts (published with Musil's reluctant approval during his lifetime), the not-quite-finished parts (submitted and prepared for publication, but then withdrawn by Musil for more revisions), as well as the thousands of pages of experiments, drafts and revisions that never approached publication, represent more than an interesting artifact or evidence of a writer's method, more even than an astonishing work of art that emerges from the fragments.[3] As the book "progresses" beyond the printed material, particularly as Ulrich retreats further and further into his mystical experiment with his sister, Agathe, Musil's search for answers to the question of "the right life" becomes increasingly serious, and the narrator's irony and intense skeptical analysis is increasingly replaced by an earnest and often rapturous lyricism. While the early published parts of the novel are more tightly wound and plot- and character-driven, the extensive *Nachlass*, thousands of pages of sketches, notes, and alternate versions of thought experiments and thematic questions, may be seen as the real entry into Musil's thought in its uncompromised richness and possibility. Relieved of the pressure, or even the possibility, of publication in the years after his last almost-published proofs were withdrawn from publication and during his years in exile, Musil was free to experiment in earnest, and to expand his thought experiment to infinity.

The *Nachlass* and the published material together project a way of living and being in the world — a method of life in art. A level of engagement, aliveness, and commitment to what Walter Pater called a "failure to form habits"; a hyper-, perhaps even partially pathological consciousness of the role and responsibility of what Nietzsche would call "the creative subject" as word- and world-maker.[4] Not that he was not a consummate artist, striving for perfection in the work itself, but that his painstaking process signals the totality of immersion and attention, the way in which the work, with its many drafts and possible alternatives, threatens (or promises) to take over life itself. Art, and its sources in the world of ideas and imagination, was always much more real and more meaningful to him than anything else.

In the spirit of counterintuitiveness, however, this primacy of art over reality does not constitute the casual disengagement from reality often (and often mistakenly) associated with a devotion to the aesthetic — the exact contrary is the case. When Musil repeats Nietzsche's revolutionary phrase, that "reality and the world are only justified as an aesthetic phenomenon," we would do well to remember that for both of them aesthetics and ethics were one. In a world where reality was thought to be more or less created and perceived metaphorically by the mind, art, for Musil, was part of this process. The mind's perception and contingent relative arrangements were — had to be — ultimately revolutionary processes of engagement.[5] Musil saw all art as a process of disturbance, whereby the current image of the real is broken down and newly arranged (via abstraction, via metaphoric coincidence). In contrast to mimesis, which presupposes a desire to reinforce or celebrate what *is*, Musil's vision of art is as an active and inventive process.

By offering a new reading of the centrality of Musil's concept and use of metaphor as the fundamental building block of multiple decentered worlds consciously brought into being by the "creative subject," I am reading Musil as an exemplary proponent of the modernist aesthetic, which situated the practice of art-making within a broader practice of existential agency, i.e., a way of being in the world wherein personal perception and choice continually create reality. The modernist artists, thus, aware of their role as world-makers, attempted to grapple with the discord and confusion of a loss of communal values, without, however, reducing the terrors of the void to a simulacrum of wholeness or order. In contrast to some interpretations of Musil's work, this study intends to present the notion that the rejection of static truth implied in the novel's form, its lack of an Archimedean fixed point, does not, as might be expected in a dualistic universe, signal meaninglessness, despair, cultural collapse, or the irremediable loss of self, values, or individual agency.

By focusing on the *Nachlass* material and on Musil's metaphysical questions about reality and his ideas about the central role of the artist in constructing our shared reality, I see Musil as a thinker who in many ways challenges current attitudes about the role of art and culture as seen from our postmodern perspective. A broader view of Musil's aesthetic practices and theories might refresh some of the outworn clichés of the contentious attempts to differentiate between modernism and postmodernism;[6] Musil's work is, in fact, a perfect touchstone for discussions about subjectivity, individualism, political and social engagement, aesthetic redemption,[7] and more specifically, the debate about the alleged violence done to reality by the formation of concepts and the use of language altogether. Regarding this latter problem, Musil was deeply engaged with the reality of language's inadequacy and the tendency or even necessity of metaphors, concepts and abstractions to leave out whatever does not fit them; however, he also maintained that this inaccurate metaphor-making brings "Schönheit und Erregung in die Welt" (*MoE*, 573; beauty and excitement in the world, *MwQ*, 625). Hofmannsthal's "Lord Chandos Brief" gave voice to the modernist skepticism about the ability of logical or literal language to express subjective experience; but Wittgenstein provided a theoretical framework for articulating individual emotional and ethical experiences through the poetic image (that is, metaphor) rather than through dialectical rational language.[8] What philosophy and science could not describe or explain might be approximated through the realm of art. The work of art, alongside its associated realm of ethical thinking, is marked out as a realm especially conducive to the expression of particulars, and thus escapes the inherent inaccuracy and generalization of rational and scientific conceptualization or logical abstraction. On the other hand, the selection process necessary for art makes it a form of abstraction as well, and as such it is capable of presenting illusions of completion and harmony. Musil's novel plays with the oscillating figure and ground of union and dissolution, moving in and out of focus and conviction. This oscillation — a movement away from what already *is* toward what *could* and *might* be and then back again — is often overlooked in the enthusiasm to embrace a radical abandonment of formal harmony, unified selfhood, and a faith in some form of *a priori* reality or shared truth. To emphasize only one side of the spectrum is, however, to misread and fatally simplify Musil's more nuanced relationship with the currently maligned "conceptualization" of essence. Musil's Other Condition, for example, is both a singular exceptional experience of "otherness" and a state characterized repeatedly as a return to some form of originary and universal phenomena; it is both an exception from the selfsame and a return to it.

The novel's exploration of a protagonist without qualities makes it a perfect arena for territorial debates about modernist notions of subjectivity, alienation, or "worldlessness."[9] The multiple discourses (of science, philosophy, mathematics, psychology, Gestalt theory, literature, historiography, anthropology, mysticism,[10] sexuality, and art) utilized by Musil make it possible to enter the novel by multiple accesses, and to digress seemingly endlessly along these various rich fault lines without coming to either final rupture or reconciliation. Musil's own resistance to taking a stand, as well as his formal and ideological practice of perspectivism, make a variety of readings possible; and the situation is further complicated by the fact that the novel was left unfinished, with no clear indication of where, or whether, it might have ended had its author lived. While this remains an unresolvable mystery, a wider view of the greater *Gestalt*[11] of the work and its creation can provide us with a more comprehensive view of the inherent tensions and oscillations between the novel's conflicting positions and stances. For despite his famous resistance to fixed positions, Musil did stand firm on a number of central questions, and he took seriously his role as author in helping to shape social and ethical values.

Musil's novel, begun in sketches as early as 1910 and still not finished in 1942, at his death in Swiss exile, naturally reflects the concerns of his times and the stylistic experimentations of his contemporary authors and artists. Yet he often maintained that he was more spiritually connected to his predecessors than to his contemporaries.[12] His most important luminaries were Nietzsche, Emerson, and Dostoevsky, but he devoured books from almost every field of study, finding nourishment and stimulus just as much from works he derided as from those to which he granted his rare approval. He confessed having read no more than ten pages of Proust's work in his life, presumably afraid of being tainted by either the influence of Proust or the rumor of association. The name "Sartre" appears only once in Musil's notes, without any further commentary; and though he mentions Joyce once or twice, rather disparagingly, he does not seem to have been aware of Virginia Woolf. Nevertheless, I will attempt in this book to situate Musil's work within the context of some of the experimental modernists who were his contemporaries, in hopes of illuminating both his work and theirs. Proust, above all, is a significant touchstone for Musil's work. *The Man without Qualities* and *Remembrance of Things Past* share multiple concerns, particularly a theoretical and formal emphasis on the metaphoric, on the tension between universal and particular, and the problem of narrative, time, and deferral. Moreover, French readings of Proust[13] have been of great benefit to my reading of Musil, perhaps because they have tended to be friendlier toward aesthetic concerns than the generally more ethically and philosophically minded Germanist tradition. Despite then his protagonist Ulrich's tendency toward non-participation[14] and Musil's own characteristic resistance to identifying with any group, it would be absurd to insist on uniqueness to such a degree that from this distance we were not able to enumerate some striking similarities between these two novels. While recent books associate him more with the postmodern (Patrizia McBride's *Void of Ethics* and more extremely Stefan Jonsson's *Subject without Nation*) and the "non-modern" (Michael Freed's *Robert Musil and the Non-Modern*),[15] this book assumes that Musil's project, his emphasis on the agency of the subject (however fragmented), his attempt to come to terms with some form of meaning in an increasingly fragmented world, and his own theory and practice of translating ineffable realms via experimentation with language and form place him firmly within the shared trajectory of high literary and artistic modernism of the late 1890s through the first half of the twentieth century. This association with modernism tends, in many readings, to be an association with the alleged failure of the modernist project.[16] Musil, according to a widespread assumption, failed to reconcile oppositions between aesthetics and ethics, reality and the ideal, science and art, the universal and the particular, concept or metaphor and the specificity of truth; failed to find a lasting, enduring solution to the problems posed by and in the novel; failed to bring the novel itself to closure.

Allen Thiher, whose otherwise nuanced and subtle study of Musil elsewhere suggests an understanding of the value of openness, stands for many others when he writes:

> It can be argued that Musil's failure to find a conclusion to his novel demonstrates the difficulty characterizing the modernist project of transforming or, indeed, saving culture through literary discourse. In making this observation, however, we should recall that he mocks the idea of salvation and saving culture as much as any other idea circulating in Vienna before the First World War. . . . At some point during the writing of the novel saving culture became a cliché. . . . From this perspective, if the novel's lack of completion illustrates a failure, it is the failure to create a discourse of salvation, a very modernist failure to create a viable myth."[17]

While it may be true that Musil mocks the idea of saving culture within the novel, it is important that we note Ulrich's proviso referring to the idea of the millennium: "I only make fun of it because I love it" (*MwQ*, 817).[18] Further, we must temper any of Musil's satirical comments on the possibility of creating a literary discourse of salvation in the novel by referring to his essays and addresses, particularly his notes for addresses during the reign of totalitarianism, where we see him engaged in an earnest "defense of culture" with the weapons of art. This is not to imply that he meant that political battles could be fought by or with art. On the contrary, he maintained explicitly that the defense of culture meant that such battles could not be fought with pens and brushes; the best one could do was maintain the free, non-affiliated voice of the artist as the last bastion of critical and non-conscripted thought, and encourage those whose job it was to use other kinds of weapons to understand that a large part of their job entailed protecting the autonomy of culture.[19] Thiher's analysis suggests that the defense of culture was to be somehow better and more successfully waged with some other weapons than the tools the modernists had at hand, and that the "failure" of Musil's novel is indicative of the generally agreed-upon consensus about the failure of modernism to successfully negotiate the problems of engagement with politics, with collectivism and with social issues. While there are other assessments harsher than Thiher's, his exemplifies that even in cases when a critic is not explicitly setting out to argue against modernism or its aesthetic aims, there seems to be a somewhat unexamined assumption about the failure and misguidedness of the project, as if it were a given.

In a fascinating last chapter called "Staging the Failure of an Aesthetic Utopia in The Man without Qualities," Patrizia McBride argues in *The Void of Ethics* that despite Musil's earnest experimentation, he had consistently planned over the course of three decades to depict the failure of the Other Condition and other related solutions, that "he remained fundamentally faithful to the plan of staging the collapse of Ulrich's utopias (130). In her notes McBride persuasively demonstrates this, quoting Musil himself speaking of failure and negative outcome. McBride asserts that the illuminations culled from the Other Condition "remain utterly unintelligible and inconsequential when raised to the level of everyday experience, for they are untranslatable into conventional and conceptual and linguistic structures (141). She acknowledges that "meaning exists and can be irrefutably experienced, yet it is not translatable into the categories of ordinary life and therefore remains inapplicable to it." She then goes on to delineate the two options that present themselves in the face of this conundrum: one is to accept this split between "ordinary and the other condition as irreversible and to develop strategies for making sense of the experience while acknowledging the reality of nonconceptualizable meaning"; the other is to "seek to overcome this split by making the two realms commensurable" (142). The former is obviously supposed to be the mature method, one that a reasonable skeptical modern person would adopt. The latter is Ulrich's project, which is here presented as somewhat adolescent, immature, and bound to be grown out of over the course of the experiment. It is suggested that Ulrich's author had always — at least during his time of writing — been more mature than his character and thus planned from the start to demonstrate the delusionary nature of the experimental attempt of his "friend" and alter ego.[20]

Even Roger Willemsen's defense of aesthetics in *Das Existenzrecht der Dichtung: Zur Rekonstruktion einer systematischen Literaturtheorie im Werk Robert Musils* (Literature's Right to Exist: Toward a Reconstruction of a Systematic Literary Theory in Robert Musil's Work), makes up part of the chorus of voices announcing an "aesthetic of failure and of fragmentariness."[21] While Willemsen's study was published in the 1980s and McBride's and Thiher's in 2010, the same assumption prevails over decades, without any question about its basic premises. Willemsen writes, "The transmutation of life into art and 'nature morte' fails, just as the existence of the novel itself points toward failure along biographical lines." While Willemsen concedes that fragmentariness was inherently the central modality of Musil's stylistic principle even before the novel breaks off, he undermines this positive assessment by concluding that this structure is itself an object lesson telling us that art cannot possibly realize "its utopia, the identification of aesthetic and social completion"; instead, he writes, such a project is bound by its very nature to fail. The novel, he concludes, "sketches typologies of failure, which are guaranteed ahead of time" by the necessary ending in war; there is, he glosses further, a shared meaning to be gleaned from the failure of the sibling lovers and the "negative parallel of the collective" in war.[22] This analysis is similar to, if more subtle than, Lowell Bangerter's assertion in reference to the ending of Musil's novel. Bangerter writes: "Only two things can be determined with relative certainty: First, Ulrich's experiments with both mysticism and love would fail to yield a final satisfying answer, just as attempts to adapt to practical reality had done. Second, his 'vacation' year would end with the protagonists and their world being swallowed up by the war."[23]

Musil studies have consistently argued about Musil's failure to reconcile the realms of art, utopia, or the ideal to something called "reality," often without bothering to negotiate a common definition of essential terms or concepts with which to begin the debate. Thus, before we conclude that Musil's novel presents models that are or are not escapist, utopian, or un-realistic, and whether or not its experimental aims were bound to fail, we must come to some agreement about what, in fact, reality is, or at least was to Musil, and about the role of the individual in perceiving and constructing this reality, the potential of language to communicate perceptions and constructions, and, thus, the role of the work of art as a prime element in this construction.

Insofar as people tend to see only what they already know or only what they expect to see, the "selecting" inherent in the process of thinking means that any reading (of novel, philosophy, world) will be necessarily inadequate and potentially misleading. Subjectivity, with its inherently individualistic and possibly irrational vision, is thus pitted against a rational categorization that itself leaves much to be desired in terms of adequately describing a world of infinite and particular details and relative perspectives. This question of subjective interpretation and its seeming opposite, objective rationality, is inherently related to the specter of a language crisis that haunts most modernist and postmodernist discourse, including Musil's own work. One might ask how, indeed, we can begin to use language to talk about language, when we have arrived at a place where contemporary theory tells us that all systems of explanation, all conceptualizations and categories are misleading or inadequate at best. The important difference between inadequate and misleading is, in a sense, one of the central issues when it comes to tendentious readings of Musil and the modernist project of reinventing and invigorating a worn-out and suspect language system and of negotiating the constructs of reason, science, and morals. Reason, when it is a reduction of the actual complexity of reality in its moving, changing, infinity of causes and effects, probabilities and roundness, to a simple line of determined logic, is hardly "reasonable." Rationality, which reduces multiplicity to abstract formulas and hopeful repetitions is doing very much the same thing as art does, except that art functions by making this process of inaccuracy and selection transparent, thereby making clear the process by which life itself avails itself of such insufficiently descriptive or conceptual frameworks. The central question here is: what can language do and how close can it get to the so-called "real"? To what extent is our reality shaped by our constructions and conceptions of language in the first place? Can concepts, metaphors, categories be meaningful ways to articulate specific and personal experience on some universal level, or are we doomed to choose between a silent solipsism or a hopelessly misrepresentative simulacrum of generality and abstraction?

Different critics reach varying conclusions on these questions. Some, like Stefan Jonsson, argue that Musil rejected all categorization of the subject as an oppression of individual difference,[24] others, like Thomas Harrison and Thomas Sebastian, maintain a more nuanced view of Musil's oscillation between Ernst Mach's functionalist view of reality and a belief in some provisional and qualified substance and essence.[25] While we see Musil oscillating in his notes, diaries, essays, and his novel between a scientist's assessment of what is repeatable, what can be measured and proven to be reliably real, what we only see because we have been trained to see or believe it (social construction, the persistence of habit, lazy acceptance of the status quo), and what we more actively and creatively conceive of ourselves (fruitful metaphor-making, art, existentialism), the latter mode is where Musil's energy is based and where we find the key to the aesthetic redemption sought by Musil and many of his contemporaries.

The metaphoric transparency inherent in an awareness of the way we construct the world through provisional images enables a fruitful resistance to what Musil calls "dead words," in contrast to the "living words" that activate ethics, a sense of temporary meaning, and aesthetic experience. For Musil, the modernist crisis of language and values does not then translate into a canceling out of voices, statements, images, intentions, or author. Instead, his modernist vision, embodied in the form and process of living metaphor, is itself an imperative toward constant proliferation of more and more contingent and shifting realities, all of them potentially meaningful.[26] Thus Musil, although he did not completely reject the existence of a shared, measurable, and to some extent repeatable *a priori* reality, was fascinated by the idea of a magical relationship between human action, thought, artistic creation and the real, physical world,[27] a relation wherein what a person does, says, and even thinks affects and co-creates a shifting reality. While most theorists see the void of a common denominative system as a nihilistic crisis, Musil, following Nietzsche, embraces the challenge of creating the world anew through conception, imagination, and individual perception as a joyful, imperative duty.[28] As such, art-making, far from being an insignificant or escapist indulgence, is raised to a central reality-relevant act of ethical engagement.

Aesthetic experimentation, far from being disinterested, is intrinsically related to political and social liberation, to social ethics as is the experimental novel, perhaps precisely because, as Bakhtin noted, it is inherently anti-canonical. "The novel," writes Michael Holquist in his introduction to *The Dialogic Imagination*, "is the name Bakhtin gives to whatever force is at work within a given literary system to reveal the limits, the artificial constraints of that system."[29] Allen Thiher, in his *Understanding Robert Musil*, puts the case even more directly, when he says that both Musil and Bakhtin "wrote to defend freedom against stultifying dogma and illiberal totalitarianism."[30] Thiher writes that he knows of "no other thinker . . . who stressed with such lucidity that ethical thinking and art are interrelated." Thiher connects this resistance to Musil's "theory of the destruction of forms," invoking the Kabbalistic mystical imperative to continually repair the original vessels of creation, which are said to have burst because they could not "contain the light emanating from God's being." Thiher reminds us that although "the vessels must be continually broken so that the light may be propagated . . . there must also be vessels so that it can be contained. The destruction of the forms of perceived thought and perception is a necessary process, which gives access to a new condition beyond received ideas and their rationality." After the destruction, in other words, there must be new creation, new forms.[31]

In the following chapters I attempt to demonstrate and suggest some new readings of Musil and of modernism. In chapter 1, I present a close reading of Musil's seemingly contradictory uses of the figure of circularity as a sort of object lesson in his characteristic complexity, whereby different concepts (such as qualitylessness, repetition, metaphor) are seen as both positive and negative. Circles are presented by Musil as self-cancelling, as founts of unending originary meaning, as images of creative self-generativity, and as a metaphor for the expanding non-linearity of the novel. In chapter 2, I explore Musil's thinking about what can and cannot be the selfsame (*seinesgleichen*), and the aesthetic and ethical potential activated by exceptions to repetition (criminal acts or taboo forms). This chapter also explores the tension between dead and living words and the way in which metaphor can be both a creative praxis of metaphoric world-construction and a construction or habitual use of ossified concepts. In chapter 3 I return to the question of essence through an exploration of abstraction, primitivism, and the modernist interest in the potential of art and formal arrangement to alter physical reality. This chapter expands on the themes of circling by exploring the concepts of duration, time-lessness, and extra-temporality, and the image of resurrection. In chapter 4, I explore the image and concept of the still-life in Musil's novel as a cipher for aesthetic "disinterestedness" and the problems and pleasures of the eternalization of art. This chapter also features a close reading of the variations in the *Nachlass* of the many versions of "Atemzüge eines Sommertags" (Breaths of a Summer's Day) as illustrative of Musil's obsessive use of metaphor as deferral and resistance to end and death. In the conclusion, I address the question of Musil's engagement with politics, and his commitment to the essential importance of the artists' role as autonomous non-affiliated word- and world-maker. While arguing that conclusions about Musil's intentions for the end of the novel must remain speculative because of his commitment to the novel as an ongoing open experiment and to the "Utopia of the Next Step," I present, in the conclusion, my own reflections on possible endings and on the question of the possibility of ending at all within the context of Musil's endless project.

As Musil wrote in a note found amid an unfinished, unpublished collection of aphorisms, the immortality of works of art is "their indigestibility." This statement is followed directly by another, a challenge as much to Musil himself as to the critics and readers to come. Musil writes simply: "Explicate that!" In this spirit, hopefully rising to the challenge with a good mixture of holy earnestness and necessary irony, we may, in a cosmos where there is no real beginning, certainly no end, and no static center, jump in from where we are.

Notes

[1] See of course Nietzsche's influential definition of art as "the highest task and the truly metaphysical activity of this life" in the preface to *The Birth of Tragedy*.

[2] Stefan Jonsson for example, focuses unapologetically on the first part of the novel (the parallel campaign and Ulrich's lack of qualities) and concludes that "The novel thus reveals the ways in which dominant ideologies of patriarchy, nationalism, and racism reduce the human subject to its cultural origin or sexual disposition by imposing on it an allegedly natural, and hence inescapable essence, coded in terms of ethnicity, gender, and class." Jonsson, *Subject without Nation*, 2. The most recent example of this concentration on the earlier parts of Musil's novel is Norbert Christian Wolf's 1,000-plus page study, *Kakanien als Gesellschaftskonstruktion*. While it certainly ranges far beyond the material in the first part of the novel and explores *Nachlass* material in a deep and enlightening way, its core focus is in the social and political intrigues of the first two books.

[3] See Fanta, "Genesis," 254.

[4] See Musil's "Vinzenz," act 1, where Vinzenz describes himself not as a poet or a user of words but as a "word-maker."

[5] See Wellmer, *Persistence*, 53.

[6] See Wellmer, who suggests that an important difference between postmodernism and modernism is in differing attitudes toward "reconciliation." Wellmer, *Persistence*, 43.

[7] See Rancière in his *Aesthetics and Its Discontents* for a discussion of the contemporary critique of aesthetics and its causes (20–21) and of Schiller's idea of "free play" as a more congenial expression for the postmodern than "autonomy" (27). See also Kern, *Modernist Novel*, on the overturning of outmoded paradigms and "grand narratives," and Weinstein's *Unknowing*, which stresses uncertainty and unknowing as the hallmarks of modernism. Also see Barbara Neymeyr, whose criticism of modernist aesthetics as escapist and dangerous is typical. Neymeyr, *Utopie und Experiment*, esp. p. 83.

[8] See Perloff, *Wittgenstein's Ladder.* "Wittgenstein would have had no answers to these and related questions. On the contrary, his writing of 'philosophy' as if it were 'poetry' dramatizes the process of working through particular questions so as to test what can and cannot be said about literary forms (e.g., poetry), concepts (e.g., barbarism), and facts of life (e.g., death). 'A philosopher,' he wrote in 1944, 'is a man who has to cure many intellectual diseases in himself before he can arrive at the notions of common sense' (C[ulture and] V[alue] 44). And again, 'My account will be hard to follow: because it says something new but still has egg-shells from the old view sticking to it' (CV 44). Perhaps it is this curious mix of mysticism and common-sense, of radical thought to which the 'egg-shells' of one's old views continue to 'stick,' that has made Wittgenstein, who had no interest at all in the 'poetry' of his own time, paradoxically a kind of patron saint for poets and artists" (i).

[9] This was the word used by Lukács in his searing critique of Musil's novel as an exemplum of decadence and disengagement. Bernd Hüppauf concludes that both mysticism and, to a great extent, aesthetics are "distanced from reality." Hüppauf, *Von sozialer Utopie zur Mystik*, 44–47. For an opposing view, see Thomas Sebastian's description of Musil's use of metaphor. Sebastian, *Intersection of Science and Literature*, 46 and Rancière on autonomy and the construction of the world through art, "as the inscription of the unresolved contradictions between the aesthetic promise and the realities of oppression in the world." Rancière, *Aesthetics and Its Discontents*, 129. The phrase "unresolved contradictions" (Rancière also uses the term "dissensus") is reminiscent both of Musil and of Adorno's "extorted reconciliation." See Adorno, "Extorted Reconciliation."

[10] See Dieter Goltschnigg's *Mystische Tradition im Roman Robert Musils: Martin Bubers "Ekstatische Konfessionen" im "Mann ohne Eigenschaften"* for a classic discussion of Musil's mystical influences.

[11] On the influence of Gestalt psychology on Musil see Roth, *Ethik und Ästhetik*, 211.

[12] As scholarship has begun to look into this question more deeply, finding more contemporaries whom Musil appreciated, admired, and supported, the myth, created in great part by Musil himself, shows signs of being broken down.

[13] Particularly Genette's *Narrative Discourse* and Deleuze's *Proust and Signs.*

[14] One of Ulrich's original names in early incarnations of the novel was "Anders" (Other).

[15] McBride, *Void of Ethics*; Jonsson, *Subject without Nation*; Freed, *Musil and the Non-Modern.*

[16] See the introduction to *"Siegreiche Niederlagen": Scheitern, die Signatur der Moderne*, which suggests that the foundation of the currently widespread canard about modernism's inadequacy is based on an association with the failure of the experiment of communism. The editors, Lüdke and Schmidt, quote Franz Fühmann, who they note was one of the leading lights of the literature of the German Democratic Republic: he laments that he has failed "in literature and in the hope for a society of which we all once dreamed" (*"Siegreiche Niederlagen,"* 7). See also Wellmer, *Persistence*, 88–89.

[17] Thiher, *Understanding Robert Musil*, 230. See also See McBride, *Void of Ethics*, 130–42 and Lüdke and Schmidt, *"Siegreiche Niederlagen."*

[18] See also Heinz-Peter Preusser's essay on Musil's use of the model and ideas of Ludwig Klages for an insightful discussion of how isolated readings out of context and assumptions of simplistic ideological allegiances can lead to misreadings of Musil's more complex use of irony and distance. Preusser, "Masken des Ludwig Klages," 224–53.

[19] See Amann, *Musil: Literatur und Politik*, and also McBride's "Utility of Art for Politics," where she makes a case for the viability of Musil's political-aesthetic stance today without, however, conceding that the Other Condition and the Utopia of Essayism succeeded (372, 379). She further argues that Musil's essay writing was a prescient counter to the danger of totalizing systems of war in Musil's and our own time (382).

[20] See also Kermode, *Sense of an Ending*, 128; Moore's comparison of Proust and Musil in his *Proust and Musil* (ii); and Corino's "Der Dämon der Möglichkeit," in which he diagnoses Musil's inability to finish his novels as a neurosis, which he admits was about as creative a neurosis as possible (62–71).

[21] Willemsen, *Existenzrecht der Dichtung*, 248. All translations in this book are my own, unless otherwise credited.

[22] Willemsen, *Existenzrecht der Dichtung*, 248–49.

[23] Bangerter, in "Experimental Utopias," 8.

[24] See Jonsson, *Subject without Nation*, esp. 9, 125, 134.

[25] See Sebastian, *Intersection of Science and Literature*, 35–36 and 41–42, and Harrison, "Suspension of the World," and, for an opposing conclusion, Neymeyr, *Utopie und Experiment*, 69.

[26] See Pike's "Literature as Experience," where he writes: "How can a bridge (a utopian, hence idealistic bridge) be built from this isolated subjective mind to the social, moral, and ethical concerns of society at large? [. . .] There would seem to have been in the early phenomenologists and in Musil an underlying idealism that has since been lost, a belief that in spite of the increasing solipsism and dehumanizing specialization of modern life there is some sphere or level — one hardly knows what to call it — in or on which all the conflicting and apparently unrelated fragments, self and world, feeling and intellect, science and society, skepticism and belief, could somehow be melded into a coherent, ethical whole" (87–88).

[27] See Bouveresse's "Genauigkeit und Leidenschaft," 49; and Agamben, *Man without Content*, esp. 1–5, where he connects Nietzsche's idea of art as the highest metaphysical activity with that of art's dangerous magical powers. See also my essay "The Other Musil," 337. Similarly, Roth, *Ethik und Ästhetik*, 34.

[28] See Josipovici, *What Ever Happened?*, 112–13 and 141. Also see Josipovici's definition of modernism, which seems to describe Musil's attempts as well, as "a tradition of those with no tradition. And it doesn't seem to me that this is wholly tragic . . . neither illustration nor abstraction but the daily struggle of a dialogue with the world, without any assurance that what one will produce will have value

because there is nothing already there against which to test it, but with the possibility always present that something new, something genuine, something surprising will emerge." Josipovici, *What Ever Happened*, 185.

[29] Michael Holquist, Introduction to *The Dialogic Imagination*, xxxi.

[30] Thiher, *Understanding Robert Musil*, 137.

[31] See Harrison's discussion of *Geist* in "Suspension of the World," 44.

1: Circles

Nun ist da ein Mittelpunkt, u[nd] rings umher bilden sich auch lauter Mittelpunkte.

[Then there is a center, and all around it other centers come into being.]

— Musil, *Nachlass*

Die Wege liefen nach kurzem in sich selbst zurück. Der Zustand, in den die beiden auf diesen Weg gerieten, trieb im Kreis, wie es eine Strömung von einer Sperre tut, an der sie hochsteigt.

[The paths soon turned back upon themselves. The state of mind induced in both of them by walking on these paths eddied in circles, as a rising current does behind a dam.]

—Musil, *Der Mann ohne Eigenschaften*

Sie glichen ja zwei Menschen, die Hand in Hand aus dem Kreis, der sie fest umgeschlossen hat hinausgetreten sind, ohne schon in einem anderen Kreis zu Hause zu sein.

[They were like two people who, hand in hand, have stepped out of the circle that firmly enclosed them, without being at home in another one yet.]

—Musil, *Der Mann ohne Eigenschaften*

IN EXILE IN SWITZERLAND, having returned in the last years of his life to working on sections of the novel he had begun decades before, Musil told an inquiring friend that he was not, it was true, moving forward with his work, but that he was, he hoped, moving deeper.[1] This paradoxical deepening is attained by a circular, doubling-back motion that does not move the reader or writer toward a conclusion but rather calls attention to an experience of presence, an aesthetic resistant to progress. This resistance to forward-progression also reflects an ethical imperative based upon the complex analysis of critical scientific and philosophical principles that do not allow for monological vision or unquestioned assumptions about the static nature of reality or values. In his controversial 1937 talk, "Über die Dummheit" (On stupidity), wherein stupidity is equated with, among other things, a wordless brutality reminiscent of the totalitarian regimes in power, Musil reminds his listeners:

> Ich selbst habe vor etlichen Jahren geschrieben: "Wenn die Dummheit nicht dem Fortschritt, dem Talent, der Hoffnung oder

der Verbesserung zum Verwechseln ähnlich sähe, würde niemand dumm sein wollen." Das ist 1931 gewesen; und niemand wird zu bezweifeln wagen, dass die Welt auch seither noch Fortschritte und Verbesserungen gesehen hat! (*TBAER*, 918)

[I myself wrote some years ago that "if it were not so hard to distinguish stupidity from talent, progress, hope, or improvement, no one would want to be stupid." That was 1931; and who will dare question that since then the world has seen still more progress and improvements! (*P*, 268)]

Musil, echoing Erasmus's *Praise of Folly*, which he mentions elsewhere in the speech, refers in passing to another sort of stupidity, one related to that of the holy fool whose conduct in the world is not conducive to worldly success or the efficient attainment of practical goals. This "higher stupidity," he writes, is defined by the psychiatric field as "die Unfähigkeit, sich im Leben zurechtzufinden, das Versagen, vor allen Aufgaben, die es stellt (the incapacity of a person to find himself in life, giving up in the face of all the tasks life poses) and by experimental psychology as "ein Verhalten, das eine Leistung, für die alle Bedingungen bis auf die persönlichen gegeben sind, nicht vollbringt" (*TBAER*, 935; behavior that does not carry out something for which all the conditions except the individual ones are given, *P*, 284.). Although the "higher stupidity" may be characterized as an illness, even by Musil himself, within the larger context of both the essay and of the European world picture at the time of his writing, this inability to complete something or to feel at home in the world may have seemed the only healthy response.

Despite his well-founded suspicion of discourses that promised progress or absolute solutions to complex questions, Musil never at any point during his lengthy experimental project fully abandoned his search for answers to the primary question of what he called "the right life." In the face of contemporary problems, such as subjectivity, uncertainty, relativity, or the bad odor into which wholeness, truth, and beauty had already begun to fall, Musil persisted in his attempts, endeavoring to create new ways of asking the questions and establishing a testing ground more commensurate with the twentieth-century perception of realities. The inherent structure of this experimental realm would destabilize normal valuations of values and posit the possibility of as-yet-unimagined ethical and aesthetic variations to the suspect status quo. The testing ground was to be a novel. And narration in a contemporary novel, according to notes for his essay *Aufzeichnung zur Krisis des Romans* (Notes on the crisis of the novel)[2] of 1930–32, was no longer simply to serve the function of suspense, entertainment, or storytelling but rather that of "die Sinngebung des Daseins, die Gestaltung, die Sinngestaltung" (giving meaning to existence, the shaping, the shaping of meaning). The experimental novelist's task involved a restructuring of form and working methods, one that would favor, particularly in Musil's own kaleidoscopic ever-shifting microcosmos, the circular and unending over the simple straight line toward the end. This circularity is both a problem and a solution for Musil (morally, aesthetically, ethically, and psychologically), but it is, in any case, clearly to be favored over the unexamined and often brutal linearity of "progress" and "improvements." The problem, in its most simplified form, consists at bottom in ascertaining whether, on the one hand, there can be meaning — "giving meaning to existence"— and, on the other, how such meaning that seems to be present in exceptional aesthetic and mystical moments of experience might be translated into the "day-bright" realm of so-called real life, shared experience, and what Emerson, whom Musil greatly admired, called "conduct of life."

Perhaps it is uncertainty in the face of the future, a presentiment of imminent collapse and fundamental instability that calls attention to the moment and away from some promise of future happiness. Emerson, after experiencing multiple tragedies and, perhaps, a loss of absolute faith in "human moral progress," is said to have replaced his previous optimism by an "ecstatic experience of nature"[3] that seems to undo any forward-looking ideal. He suggests, like Nietzsche after him, that philosophers should be "Professors of Joyous Science"[4] and celebrates the experience of the moment in the face of the certain doom of mortality in answer to a revelation from an earlier lecture, wherein he notes (prefiguring Nietzsche again) that "our warm commodious houses and spacious towns are built on a planet swimming unpiloted in the frightful hollows of space."[5] Musil's narrator suggests a similar image, as he calls the solidity of the physical world into question: "Schwebt nicht die ganze feste Welt, mit allen unseren Empfindungen, Häusern, Landschaften, Taten auf unzähligen kleinen Wölkchen?" (*MoE*, 1508; Does not the whole solid world float, with all its sensations, houses, landscapes, actions, upon countless little clouds?).

While a world once conceived of as solid, central, and secure comes to seem just as imaginary and fleeting as any other world, it is only reasonable to turn one's attention away from expectations of future happiness and toward moments of joyful or otherwise heightened experience. This may seem, in such a context, like escapist *ecstasis* in the midst of a pessimistic worldview, or it may delineate an *other* conception of reality altogether, one in which the momentary aesthetic experience of the Other Condition is, in itself, something for which one might trade one's whole life of normal experiences. These moments of exception to the normal condition may become more real than all the rest. In a world where interest takes the form of oppression, ideological *Gleichschaltung*,[6] self-interest or bourgeois comfort, "Kantian disinterestedness" becomes a mode of intensification, a practice of higher wakefulness.

Theodor Adorno, responding a few decades later to a shared historical and cultural catastrophe, writes in his *Aesthetic Theory*: "Artworks imply in themselves a relation between interest and its renunciation. Even the contemplative attitude to artworks, wrested from objects of action, is felt as an announcement of an immediate praxis and — to this extent itself practical — as a refusal to play along."[7] Adorno goes on to propose that all art is naturally a critique of the "rule of brutal self-preservation at the heart of the status quo and in its service." Seen in this light, Musil's rejection of the status quo, his refusal to put himself in service to ideology, society, or any other externally directed requirement, his refusal to bend to the "brutal rule of self-preservation," constituted an aesthetics of resistance and a creative modeling of other paradigms, structures, and ways of thinking about, interacting with, critiquing, valuing, or being in the world. The primacy of the aesthetic and its inviolability takes on a new urgency in a period when totalitarian forces conspire on all sides to usurp art's voice and role as open, experimental, unconscripted. Indeed, as the individual voice is threatened in all realms of society (freedom of press, speech, belief), any realm that maintains independence from the ideological or even merely market-driven utilitarian stronghold constitutes a last refuge of significant thought and action. Musil's aesthetic-mystical concept of the Other Condition of experiencing is thus the opposite of an escapist *vita contemplativa*. Instead, it is part of a "refusal to play along" in a game whose rules are limiting, treacherous, and antiquated; paradoxically, it calls to action, by dissolving the primacy and absolute necessity of the qualities of the social and physical status quo of so-called reality.

This Other Condition, described with increasing frequency by Musil in book 3 of his novel, is primarily an experience of heightened meaning that is often pictured as a circular in- and out-flowing that interrupts the normal condition of dullness and lack of conviction. The latter parts of Musil's novel are mainly concerned with the viability of the Other Condition as a possible model for or solution to the problem of how to live significantly. In one passage, Ulrich reflects:

> "Dass wir immer wieder aus dem Zustand der Bedeutung in das an und für sich Bedeutungslose hinaustreten, um da hinein Bedeutung zu bringen. Wir treten aus dem Zustand des Sinnvollen in den Stand des Notwendigen und Notdürftigen, aus dem Zustand des Lebens in die Welt des Toten." (*MoE*, 1424)

> [That over and over again we leave the condition of significance in order to enter the state of what is in and of itself meaningless in order to bring some significance to it. We leave the condition of the meaningful and enter into the state of the necessary and the makeshift; we leave the condition of life to step into the world of the dead. (*MwQ*, 1717)]

The so-called real world has become the world of the dead; meaning-less, necessary, and needy, which only can be fed by the fruits brought to it from the "condition of significance" or "meaning." This latter condition, Ulrich explains, is accompanied by "einem dauernden Eindruck der Steigerung . . . Aber es ist eine Steigerung ohne Fortschritt. Ebenso ist es ein Zustand des höchsten Glücks" (*MoE*, 1423; an enduring impression of intensification. But it is an intensification without progression. It is also a state of the highest happiness, *MwQ*, 1716). Although Ulrich himself often despairs of being able to make the condition endure in the world of real, measured time, he also maintains that "die Bewegung hört niemals auf, aber sie schwingt auf engstem Raum" (*MoE*, 1423; the motion never ceases, but it oscillates in the smallest space, *MwQ*, 1716). Ulrich is describing, here as elsewhere, an exceptional circle of experience that is alive, meaningful, and eternal, and which, despite all reason and calculation, somehow exists, amid a cosmos of other circles of experience. This "intensification without progression" could be a description of his own working method, as the increasingly expanding bulk of his unfinished novel might be understood as an infinite number of such individual circles, chapters, drafts, and sketches that each vibrate "in the smallest space."

To understand and fairly evaluate the results of Musil's experiment, we must pay attention to this fundamental new aesthetic and ethical proposition, its terms and its basic assumptions. Musil's notoriously philosophical novel deals, of course, with ideas, concepts, and themes; yet its structure and evolution tell us as much about his intentions and purposes as do the images and allegories he uses, if not more. These allegorical strategies function, in turn, as a means of exploring questions about form and method, which, in their turn, circle back to inform *Lebensanschauungen*, or ways of looking at and subsequently *being in* the world. Structure, in other words, is generated simultaneously with the development of ideas and perspectives. In a note for an afterword to his novel,[8] Musil explained that he was an author who wanders from theme to theme, subject to subject as a profligate lover moves from beloved to beloved, never terribly concerned about which are true or which ephemeral loves. This promiscuity is an essential thematic in his work — a thematic that is an object lesson in metaphoric correspondence and multiplicity. Musil wrote many versions wherein characters changed places with each other, and there are moments in the published sections of the novel wherein characteristics, words, sentiments, and ideas travel from person to alien person, mouth to unlikely mouth. Ulrich, for example, finds himself sounding like that "giant rooster" Diotima or, even more disturbingly, like the anemic Germanic anti-Semite Hans Sepp.[9] These variations and strange bedfellows engage in a circling akin even to the unhygienic erotic dance of Schnitzler's *Der Reigen* ((the round), an arc that raises challenging questions about identity, difference, and determinacy.

Structurally Musil's novel is a cosmos of an infinite number of interrelated but separate circles, without center and without circumference.
Implicit in its form is an assumption about the ultimate metaphoric
nature of reality. Each of these circle worlds is a metaphoric variation on
other possible worlds and is created by the temporary conjunction of usually separated elements. It is essential to note that Musil presents different
sorts of circles with often diametrically opposed suggestions about the
possibility of living a passionate life, all existing within the novel's cosmos:
First, a circle of uninterrupted meaning or significance related to the suspicious concept of essence or *a priori* universal reality and truth; second, a
circle that inevitably cancels itself and whatever it proposes out (the circle
of "Seinesgleichen geschieht" ["the selfsame" or "like of it" "happens"
or "pseudo reality prevails" which are different translations of the title of
part 1]); third, a circle made of infinitely proliferating circles without centers, all of which generate new ideas and constantly change their meanings and values in response to relative combination. These different types
of circles, species of similar but different metaphoric correspondences or
analogies, create a metaphor of metaphors. It is a world of circle worlds
that enacts — primarily, but not exclusively — the metaphoric process
called synecdoche, whereby a part of something (one circle; one moment;
one chapter) may represent its whole. Musil, who usually is very precise about definitions, is remarkably vague about observing distinctions
between different types of figurative correspondences. He interchanges
the terms allegory, likeness, simile, metaphor (and its different types: synecdoche, metonymy) indiscriminately. Fundamentally, they are all important to him as processes that *have in common* the tendency to connect,
select, and create correspondences. This lack of distinction or its more
positive counterpart, an ability to see commonality, is itself a process of
metaphor-making. But the confusion of the usually distinct goes a step
further as Musil deranges time, space, and reality with images. While
synecdoche, the term most fitting for much of what he does with metaphor, traditionally assumes a primary tenor or whole that is represented
by a part, metaphoric processes for Musil seem actually to undermine, by
their seemingly boundless proliferation, a belief in any one primary real,
whether part or whole, tenor or vehicle. The metaphoric worlds begin
to take on worlds and realities of their own; they are self-generating and
infinite in their scope, and have the dizzying effect of revealing received
notions of reality to be little more than cardboard mock-ups or "Potemkin villages,"[10] while the "noch nicht erwachten Absichten Gottes" (*MoE*,
16); as yet unawakened intentions of God, *MwQ,* 11), or the author begin
to become more and more life-like or likely. As Nabokov writes about
Gogol's "spontaneous generation" of metaphor, or his tendency to create
peripheral characters through his "life generating syntax": "The peripheral characters of his novel are engendered by the subordinate clauses of

its various metaphors, comparisons, and lyrical outbursts. We are faced with the remarkable phenomenon of mere forms of speech directly giving rise to live creatures."[11]

This sense of irreality and its potential for both creativity and hopelessness is suggested in a passage in which Musil uses images of mechanical-toy worlds to describe the constant movement of feelings, action, and thought as a cycle of rising, development, and decline. In this passage Musil compares the activities of life to building models of *Residenzstädte* (capital cultural centers or cities) or beliefs out of matches and matchboxes, or mosaics of these with stamps. He describes a thought as a toy that recreates reality, or a train of thought as a toy train that drives by pictures of reality:

> Und ähnlich ist es, wenn man einen Gedanken besitzt, der in allen seinen Folgen die Wirklichkeit treu wie ein Spielzeug wiedergibt, oder gar mitsamt seinen Gedankenfolgen gleich einer Kindereisenbahn, deren Feder aufgezogen worden ist, an den Bildern der Wirklichkeit vorbeiläuft. Eine solche Bastelei in Gedanken war auch die Erfindung, sich das geistige und seelische Leben samt und sonders nach dem Muster der Energie als einen Kreislauf des Gefühls zu erklären, das liess sich sowohl auf dem Wechsel und Zusammenhang von Fühlen, Denken, und Handeln des Einzelmenschen anwenden als auch auf den Aufstieg, die Entfaltung und den Verfall des Gemeinschaftsgeistes. (*MoE*, 1249)

> [And it is similar to when one has a thought that describes reality in all its consequences as faithfully as a toy, or even like a child's train along with its train of thought, one whose spring has been pulled so that it rides past pictures of reality. The idea of explaining spiritual and intellectual life, all of it, after the pattern of energy, as a cycle of feeling is just such a thought construction, and could be applied as much to the shift and connection between feeling, thinking, and action of the individual as to the rise, development, and decline of the societal spirit.]

And Agathe, in one passage from the *Nachlass*, exclaims with disgust in response to the seemingly mindless circulation of the natural forces of birth and death and decay, invoking an image of a collection of circles, an apple tree with round, ripening and rotting apples:

> Mein Gott, dieses ganze Werk des Gefühls, sein weltlicher Reichtum, dieses Wollen und Freuen, Tun und Untreuwerden wegen nichts, als weil es treibt; einbezogen alles, was man erfährt und vergisst: es ist ja schön wie ein Baum voll Äpfel in jeder Farbe, aber es ist auch formlos eintönig, wie alles, was jedes Jahr auf die gleiche Art sich rundet und abfällt! (*MoE*, 1244)

[My God, this whole enterprise of feeling, its worldly wealth, this wanting and rejoicing, action and deceit as a result of nothing but drives; including everything that one experiences and forgets; it is beautiful, yes, like a tree filled with apples in every color, but it is formlessly monotonous, like everything that every year in the same way becomes round and drops off!]

Agathe, however, as Ulrich reminds her, had, always "gegen das Ansinnen gewehrt, dass man sein Leben erst rechtfertige, wenn man Bedeutendes tue! . . . Es hat dich nie gelockt, im Herrensattel auf einem Steckenpferd zu reiten . . ." (*MoE*, 1245; argued against the expectation that one justifies one's life only when one does something significant! . . . You were never lured by riding in the master saddle on a hobby horse) . . . He seems to be asking her why she is complaining about circularity now, when she doesn't believe in purpose — even though *he* himself still does to some extent. Never before had she wanted a feeling to last; but now she does — and this lasting, "das unzerstörliche und sich niemals abnutzende Gefühl" (this feeling that is indestructible and that never exhausts itself) is depicted in the novel as the sort of circling that flows timelessly out from its own core and then eternally back in. Ulrich reflects elsewhere: "Die Erregung, in der wir uns befinden, Agathe und ich, drängt nicht zu Handlungen und nicht zu Wahrheiten, das heißt: sie bricht nichts vom Rande ab, sondern fließt durch das, was sie hervorruft, wieder in sich selbst zurück" (*MoE*, 1425; The state of excitement in which we find ourselves, Agathe and I, doesn't urge us to actions or to truths, which means that it doesn't break anything off from the edge, but flows back into itself again through that which it evokes, *MwQ*, 1717).

This sort of circle, the circle of significance, which creates its own self-contained reality outside the "normal condition," becomes more real than the seemingly solid, the sublunary substance subject to time, change, and rotting. This is a challenge to the uncontested reign of the real: it suggests that all experience is metaphorical. Any given superficial reality can be substituted by another when, at the core of an infinite number of descriptions of reality or metaphors, there vibrates a more limited number of lasting essences. On the one hand, then, no particular thing matters. On the other hand, every particular thing, as metaphoric variation, matters extremely, particularly as an object lesson in the way in which the creative imagination engenders our shifting reality. Nihilism thus becomes an imperative of creative responsibility.

Metaphor, in this sense, is a multiplier, but also a diminisher of the primary realm of the real: many circles, many possible worlds, many ways to envision, inhabit, manifest, or experiment with any possible idea. This is the symbolic process whereby any given abstraction, idea, thing, or "tenor" may be described through the representation of an infinity of objects, stories, drafts, or "vehicles," just as long as they have what Musil calls in a note, the same "metaphoric value." Such an infinite proliferation of possibilities presents the reader and the author with a practical problem, to say the least, insofar as we are caught within time or within the paginated leaves of a novel awaited by a publisher. Musil's experimentations with form send him into a sort of M. C. Escher paradox of infinitude and endless spiraling, as the reader follows the narrator and increasingly fragmenting writer deeper into paths that never get anywhere but that point to more and more places. But this circling is the grammar, so to speak, the control of the experiment. It must lead us eternally deeper, and not forward, in order to be aesthetically and ethically true to its purposes, even if that means "failure" in the world of "squares."

Musil, who studied Gestalt psychology, primitive rituals, poetics, and physics, among a multitude of other disciplines with their own discrete languages, image systems, and metaphorical worlds, was well attuned to the powerful effect that our perception of form has on our fundamental conception of values, reality, and meaning. In one diary entry he muses, for example, on the way in which grammar itself determines and limits our ability to see beyond certain fixed endings:

> Punkt u[nd] Strichpunkt sind Stillstandssymptome. Wir machen sie nicht, weil wir es lernten, sondern weil wir so denken. Und das ist das Gefährliche. Solange man in Sätzen mit Endpunkt denkt, lassen sich gewisse Dinge nicht sagen, — höchstens vage fühlen. Unendliche Perspektiven (ins Innere hinein) müsste man wie unendliche Reihen ausdrücken. (*T II*, 822)

> [The period and the semicolon are symptoms of stasis. We don't make them because we learned to, but because that is how we think. And that is the danger in them. As long as one thinks in sentences with end stops, certain things cannot be said, — at most they can be vaguely felt. Infinite perspectives (moving inward) would have to be expressed like infinite rows.]

Breaking out of the established form of infinite rows, Musil conceives of a cosmos with a new grammar composed of circles: circles into which and out of which the protagonists may walk; circles that sometimes seem to whirl around pointlessly, canceling everything out with their wheel-of-fortune-like spinning; or mystical circles of eternal oneness that send out energies from their cores, energies that flow back in and then out again like a fountain. Focusing for a moment just on the latter two types of circles, we confront a paradox. A circling that cancels itself out and seems to connote meaninglessness exists right alongside a circling that is the cipher for the highest possible contact with essence, with a mode of experiencing that has always been the "Mark unserer Moral und Idealität" (*TBAER*, 673; measure of our morality and ideality).

The *Kreis der Bedeutung* (circle of meaningfulness or significance),[12] in its smallest and paradoxically infinite form, is also a metaphor for Musil's recurring fascination with "the mystical moment" as shimmering frozen-fluid substance. Moment, then, is synecdochally related to the all, just as the word is related to chapter, chapter to part, part to whole of the unfinished novel. In Musil's novel each moment is metaphor for an infinity of other possible moments, written or not yet actualized. This attention to the momentary thus reflects the philosophical and aesthetic experience of multiple and relative realities that Musil and his contemporaries were just beginning to feel uneasily at home in at the turn of the Einstein century. This is the world wherein the subjectivity first revealed by Kant in the eighteenth century was being revived over a hundred years later by the empiricists, whom Musil literally went to school with as a student of philosophy, physics, and behavioral psychology in Berlin. Contemporary scientific, philosophic and psychological insights were naturally reflected in artistic representations of fragmentary personal realities, of non-linear consciousness, of often incomprehensible attempts to express the ineffable in some still communally recognizable form, language, or idiolect.

Burton Pike, making connections to Musil's scientific and philosophical background, stresses the essayistic as a possible structure to replace forward-moving linearity: "In Musil's novel," he writes, "deferral is privileged, and its primary mechanism is essayism."[13] Certainly, essayism is a central structural element in Musil's novel, manifestly in harmony with the experimental and open-ended nature of its themes. But how, indeed, is an essay structured? The answer, for Musil, is that an essay is made up of many related but individual attempts, almost aphoristically erupted, not necessarily immediately developed or followed up upon. An essay is a world of circles, in other words, without a significantly motivated beginning or end. And if this sort of non-linear trajectory swirls and sputters within a single essay, how many more single but mutually interrelated sparks are thrown out into the infinite world of an unfinished novel containing over 3,000 pages of possiblities — including the development of characters, intrigues, attractions, crimes, fascinations, and love affairs? Indeed, while Musil does defer philosophically (particularly in the challenging late chapters, in which Ulrich's notebook analyzes the nature of feeling), he also defers via aesthetic-mystical description of internal states, descriptions of his characters' subjective experience of the internal and external world. His most powerful method of deferral, moreover, is through emphatically non-didactic lyricism and metaphoric poetic prose, which serves not to explain, analyze, or describe, but to make present and palpable that which cannot be communicated any other way. This prose frequently stops time, pulling the reader increasingly deeper into any number of possible or impossible realities, roads, and states of mind, and off the fast track to worldly success, plot, or determined end. It is essential to remember that Musil chose to write a novel and not a philosophical treatise precisely to avail himself of these latter supra-rational modes of expression. Indeed, recounting his youthful discovery of the essential difference between what he would come to call dead and living words, Musil writes that he was "von einer tiefen Verachtung für den Verstand erfüllt" (filled with a deep contempt for reason).[14] "Zur gleichen Zeit" (at the same time), he continues, he began to throw himself into his fresh enthusiasm for logical and mathematical studies, in order, he explains, "um sie zu besiegen" (to conquer them).[15] An attempt to conquer logic and reason and a favoring of the type of knowledge just barely graspable by exploration of the "living word" or image would require different criteria and processes than those normally reserved for science (repeatability, consistency, determinacy, mathematics), criteria and processes that have more in common with aesthetic experimentation than scientific or philosophical analysis.

It is not, then, essay alone that stops the narrative, unless we think of essay *as form*, that is, the fragmented and more or less interrelated conglomeration of open-ended representations, instead of as philosophical or logical content — the formal attempt at fruitful "unsettling" modeled by Emerson. In this case, we may see all the individual parts of this great novel — whether philosophical arguments or exempla, or aesthetic representations of states of being — as structured by Musil's essayistic *form*, if not by exclusively essayistic content. This form is perhaps best described by Ulrich's characterization of his own notebook jottings as "eine Sammlung von Bruchstücken, deren innere Verbindung nicht gleich zu erkennen war" (*MoE*, 1138; a collection of fragments whose inner coherence was not immediately apparent, *MwQ*, 1239). Moving from the concept of essay, Pike suggests that the answer to the question of non-closure in Musil's novel might be best understood by looking at "the notion of the fractal in contemporary mathematics." "A fractal," he continues, is a "curve or surface having the property that any small part of it, enlarged, has the same statistical character as the whole (New Oxford Dictionary). Fractal geometry, as in Mandelbrot sets, posits a potentially infinite series of identical units, potentially multidimensional in both space and time." Referring, then, to a proposition raised in my doctoral dissertation, he comments that "the novel as a whole exists in every one of its parts."[16] This concept, inspired by Nicholas of Cusa's *de docta ignorantia*, further envisions all lines reduced or extended to circles. The infinite line, according to Cusa, is made up of an infinite number of dots, which each contain expanding infinite potential worlds; and the line itself, as it stretches around the universe, becomes a circle.[17] The synecdochal moment, the dot, the fragment of infinite potential, is also a cipher for an experience of heightened meaning that stands out within a structure usually conceived of as linear and purpose-driven, against, furthermore, a "normal condition" usually characterized as indifferent, lukewarm, even dead. The question becomes not so much "does meaning exist" but rather "is it possible to translate or salvage the meaning of these moments into the realm of the normal condition?" Musil writes about the incommensurability of different states of being: "Zitiere leise für dich ein Gedicht in der Generalversammlung einer Aktiengesellschaft und diese wird augenblicklich ebenso sinnlos werden, wie es das Gedicht in ihr ist" (*KA*;[18] Softly quote a poem to yourself on the floor of the stock exchange, and the stock exchange will become for a moment just as meaningless as the poem is in it, *P*, 197). That the moments of meaning are not easily transferable into the status quo or into lasting, measurable time is not reason enough to abandon their significance. We might, rather (if we are forced to make a choice), abandon the significance of the so-called real world for them. But which world is the really real one?

The shift to a heliocentric model of the universe had involved ideological revolutions, as humans took a century to begin to accept not being the immobile center of a fairly consistent system of concentric circles imagined thousands of years earlier. Similarly, in Musil's day new scientific beliefs and visions about the organization of the universe challenged people to think about new philosophical, social, or metaphysical structures. The concept of an infinity of multiverses, which had already been discussed in different language in the late Middle Ages and the early Renaissance by Nicolas of Cusa and Giordano Bruno (both of whom Musil mentions in his diaries), is only now beginning to be seriously entertained by the scientific community. Einstein's theories of relativity, as well as dialog about whether the universe was made up of waves or particles, certainly allowed people to dream about less contained cosmologies, mostly tending away from determinism and linearity and toward decentralization and subjectivity, even if they were not fully able to understand the consequences.

Cusa, in his *De docta ignorantia* (among other things a treatise on how to know the world through metaphor and comparison) had argued: "The universe can have no circumference and no centre, for if it had . . . it would be constrained within a limit, and this is totally impossible. Just as the earth cannot be the centre of the infinite universe, so neither can the sphere of the fixed stars nor any other sphere be its circumference." Prefiguring Einstein by four centuries, Cusa's theory maintained, "Nor indeed is the very centre of the universe more within our earth than without it . . . wherever the observer is placed in the universe, that will appear to him the centre. . . ."[19] And Bruno, in his *De l'infinite universi et mondi*, continues where Cusa left off, declaring: "there is a single general space, a single vast immensity which we may freely call void; in it are innumerable (*innumerabili et infiniti*) globes like this one on which we live and grow. This space we declare to be infinite, since neither reason, convenience, possibility, sense-perception or nature assign to it a limit. In it are an infinity of worlds (*infinity mundi*) similar to our own, and of the same kind."[20] And, as if he were talking about Musil's novel, Bruno writes:

> [Individual matter] whether corporeal or incorporeal, is never completed, and among eternally pursuing individual forms, seeking eternally nevertheless those to pursue, never resteth content . . . Thus the infinity of All is ever bringing forth anew, and even as infinite space is around us, so is infinite potentiality, capacity, reception, malleability, matter.[21]

In their own time these terrifying ideas went mostly unheeded or censured (Bruno was burned at the stake); but they became even more frightening when, as Nietzsche's Madman cried, we had wiped "away the entire horizon with a sponge"[22] or killed off the authoritarian father God. People, understandably, preferred to believe in centrality and purpose. If only, Musil suggested, we could find the Archimedean point, we could move the world (*P*, 63). But modern man had to come to terms with the probability that there was no single point to be found, no absolute truth or goodness, no strictly determined cause and effect, no necessity determining our actions and their results. Erwin Schrödinger, in a 1956 lecture on the effect of Einstein's theory of relativity, suggests that the fall of Time as absolute ruler was related to other revolutions which undermined linearity and the control of external forces: "I suppose it is this, that [relativity] meant the dethronement of time as a rigid tyrant imposed on us from outside, a liberation from the unbreakable rule of 'before and after.' For indeed, Time is our most severe master by ostensibly restricting the existence of each of us to narrow limits. . . ."[23]

Musil embodies this contemporary refiguration of time, space, and reality in his differentiated but coeval circle images. His cosmos of circles becomes not only a multivalent metaphor for his conception of time and its relationship to human values and history (purposeful purposelessness), but also the abiding structure of the novel itself— a structure built on small circles of metaphoric potential. The circle of meaning is constantly called into question by the competing tendency of the circle of self-cancelling, which destroys or at least changes everything that comes into being. Meaning, however, is not definitively disposed of in what remains a necessarily incalculable system composed of both "die Leere [eines] sich dauernd fortsetzenden sinnlosen Kreislaufs" (*MoE*, 1244; the emptiness [of an] eternally continuing meaningless rotation) and moments of "Lust ohne Ausweg" (*MoE*, 1204; desire that could not find expression, *MwQ*,

1192) that sink in a circle "wieder in den Körper zurück und erfüllte ihn mit einer Zärtlichkeit, die so unbestimmt war wie ein später Herbsttag oder ein früher Frühlingstag" (*MoE*, 1204–5; back within the body, filling it with a tenderness as indefinable as one of the last days of autumn or first days of spring, *MwQ*, 1193).

The difference between these two sorts of circles is further conceptualized by Musil through discussion of the "two different ways" of living passionately in the world. These he calls in some discussions "appetitive and non-appetitive"; at other times, "egocentric and allocentric"; and in other passages, the difference between living "in something" and "for something." Preparations for "the right life" require choosing, for example, between living "for" or "in" something. Ulrich explains to Agathe that there are

> zwei Möglichkeiten, leidenschaftlich zu leben, einfach die appetithafte, und ebendann auch als deren Gegenteil die nicht-appetithafte . . . In jedem Gefühl ist ein Hunger, und verhält sich wie ein reißendes Tier; und ist kein Hunger, sondern etwas, das, frei von Gier und Sattheit, zärtlich wie eine Traube in der Herbstsonne reift . . . Was ich den appetitiven nenne, drängt zum Handeln, zur Bewegung, zum Genuss; durch ihn verwandelt sich das Gefühl in ein Werk; oder in eine Idee und Überzeugung, was alles Formen der Entspannung, aber auch der Umspannung und Neukräftigung sind. Denn indem das geschieht, nützt sich zugleich das Gefühl ab, verläuft sich in seinem Erfolg und findet darin ein Ende. . . . Und nicht zu vergessen, und unvoreingenommen beurteilt, diesem appetitiven Teil des Gefühls, oder unserer animalischen Anlage, wie du ihn lieber genannt hast, verdankt die Welt alle Werke und alle Schönheit; aber auch alle Unruhe und Unverlässlichkeit, und zuletzt die Leere ihres sich dauernd fortsetzenden, sinnlosen Kreislaufs! (*MoE*, 1244)

> [Two possibilities to live passionately, simply the appetitive, and then its opposite the non-appetitive . . . In every feeling there is a hunger, and it behaves like a devouring animal, and there is no hunger, rather something that, free from greed and satisfaction, ripens tenderly like a grape in the autumn sun. . . . What I call the appetitive urges toward action, toward movement, toward enjoyment; through it feeling is transformed into work; or into an idea and a conviction, all of which are forms of release but also of tension and re-energizing. For, as the transformation happens, the feeling uses itself up, proceeds to a success, and finds therein an end. . . . And not to be forgotten, to judge without bias, it is this appetitive part of feeling, of our animalistic tendency, as you [Agathe] preferred to call it, that the world has to thank for all works and all beauty; but also all unrest and all deceit, and, ultimately, the emptiness of its eternally continuing meaningless rotation![24]]

While living "for something" seems to be an all too systematic process,

> Ein Leben ohne Sinn, eines, das nur den sogenannten Erfordernissen gehorchte und ihrem als Notwendigkeit verkleideten Zufall, somit ein Leben der ewigen Augenblicklichkeit . . . ein solches Leben war ihm einfach eine unerträgliche Vorstellung! Nicht weniger aber auch ein Leben "für etwas," diese von Meilensteinen beschattete Landstrassendürre inmitten undurchmessener Breiten. Das alles mochte er ein Leben vor der Entdeckung der Moral heißen. (*MoE*, 1413)

> [A life without meaning, a life that obeyed only the so-called necessities, and their contingency disguised as necessity, in other words a life lived eternally moment to moment . . . such a life was for him a simply unbearable idea! But no less unbearable than a life "for something," that sterility of highways shaded by milestones amid unsurveyed expanses. He might call all that a life preceding the discovery of morality. (*MwQ*, 1534)]

Living "for something" is purpose-driven, forward moving, whereas living "in something" is eternal, reverberating, and somehow paradoxically related to the discovery of "morality." Morality in this case, should probably be understood to be the living kind, that is, a reverberating ethics rather than a rigid *a priori* system. However, Musil's own inconsistency with regard to the use of the word morality might be another clue to the complexity of the question. On the one hand, he is often very clear: "Ich unterschied damals zwischen Moral und Ethik, wobei ich der Moral die toten Vorschriften überließ, während mir die Ethik als ein bewegtes Strahlen erschien" (*KA*;[25] I differentiated in those days between morality and ethics, whereby I relegated morality to the dead prescripts, while ethics appeared to me as a living radiance). On the other hand, he just as often uses the words "moral" or "morality" in contexts that make it clear that by his own definition he means "ethics." The Other Condition, as a suspended realm where opposites can meet, contains both a sort of morality and a sort of ethics. It seems to embody both the realm of originary ideas *and* the free open realm of play that is prerequisite for creation. But it is not ever a realm of dead precepts. It is the realm of "living in," beautifully figured by the fountain around which the young Germanic anti-Semite Hans Sepp circles in a late sketch. He is oddly caught by Agathe's useless beauty in this endless turning, in embarrassing contradiction to his purposeful political program:

> In einem fürstlichen Park stand eine Fontäne. Schlank bewegt, wiegend im Wind fiel ihr Strahl in ein Marmorbecken. Unendlichkeit des Auges und des Ohrs. Der kleine Proletarierknabe hatte damals die Fingerspitze auf den geglätteten Rand gelegt und war rund um den Kreis gegangen, marmorn gleitend, immer wieder, ohne satt werden zu können, wie Tantalus. (*MoE*, 1634)

[In a magnificent park there stood a fountain. In slender motion, waving in the wind, it flowed into its marble basin. Infinitude of eye and ear. The little proletarian boy then laid his fingers on the smooth edge and went round and round the circle. Gliding on marble, over and over, not able to become full, like Tantalus.]

As Sepp (Schmeisser in this version) fantasizes about Agathe putting her arm around him, his sense of space warps even further: It was "ihm Zumute wie einem Wesen, das bisher nur in einer Fläche gelebt hat und zum erstenmal das Geheimnis des Raums kennen lernt" (*MoE*, 1635; like a creature who had had up until that moment lived only in flatness and who had come to learn for the first time the secret of space). Musil further explores the experience of living "in something" through a novel note entitled "Valerie," a name Musil used to refer to his own seminal experience of mystical longing and romantic love. Musil's so-called "Valerie experience," also referred to in his notes as "the affair with the Frau Major," illustrates the mysterious role played by metaphor in this sort of love without conclusion. Musil's experience is reminiscent of Goethe, another great devotee of the metaphor, who, as Julius Bab writes, allowed "no individual event to become more than a metaphor," fleeing any binding force that would threaten the constant openness of Becoming.[26] Metaphor, a metaphysical means of "living in" rather than for, is a universalizing process whereby the individual free spirit, in the Nietzschean sense, does not imprison himself to any individual actual or specific idea, person, or happiness. Goethe's danger, Babb writes, "may appear as 'house and hearth, as wife and child, as fire, water, dagger or poison'; the sweeter the physical lure, the greater the necessity to flee to 'higher' ground." Musil, telling his story in the third person as Ulrich, reports that he experienced the retreat "fast wie eine Lösung . . . Er reiste von einem Tag auf den nächsten ab; sagte, wir werden uns wenig schreiben. Schrieb dann Briefe, die wie die Offenbarung einer Religion waren, und zögerte, sie abzusenden" (*MoE*, 1636; almost like a breaking up. He left from one day to the next; said, we won't write much. Then wrote letters that were like a revelation of religion, but hesitated to mail them, *MwQ*, 1442). Despite his inexperience, Musil continues, he realized, "dass sie nur der Anlass, aber nicht der Inhalt seines plötzlichen Erlebnisses war" (*MoE*, 1637; that she was only the impetus, but not the content, of his sudden experience, *MwQ*, 1443). As this became clearer to him, he packed his knapsack and traveled far away from the specific person and any possible consummation, and closer "ins Herz der Welt" (*MoE*, 1637; into the heart of the world; *MwQ*, 1443). There he was free to participate in an ecstatic experience of metaphoric union, of living "in," which dissolves space, time, and self:

Von ihm zur Geliebten war es ebenso weit wie zu dem Grashalm bei seinen Füssen oder zu dem fernen Baum auf der himmelskahlen Höhe jenseits des Tals. Seltsamer Gedanke: Raum, das klein Nagende, Entfernung ent-fernt, löst den warmen Balg ab und lässt einen Kadaver übrig, aber hier im Herzen waren nicht mehr sie selbst, sondern wie der Fuss vom Herzen nicht weiter ist als die Brust, war alles mit ihm verbunden. [Ulrich[27]] fühlte auch nicht mehr, dass die Landschaft, in der er lag, außen war; sie war auch nicht innen; das hatte sich aufgelöst oder durchdrungen. (*MoE*, 1637–38)

[From there it was as far to his beloved as to the blade of grass besides his feet or to the distant tree on the sky-bare heights across the valley. Strange thought: space, the nibbling in little bites, distance distanced, replaces the warm husk and leaves behind a cadaver, but here in the heart they were no longer themselves, everything was connected with him the way the foot is no farther from the heart than the breast is. Ulrich also no longer felt that the landscape in which he was lying was outside him; nor was it within; that had dissolved itself or permeated everything. (*MwQ*, 1443–44)]

In contrast to this almost embarrassing rapture of union, Musil writes in another passage entitled "On: For — In":

Alle guten Menschen leben für etwas . . . so viele interessante, ehrenvolle, befriedigende Berufe. Dann die Liebe. Die Vereine. Die Hühnerzucht. Das Schwergewichtsheben. Den Fussball. Das Tennis. Die Politik. Die Heilsarmee. Das Markensammeln. Die Suppenanstalten. Das Stenographiesystem Öhl. . . . Das gemeinsame Symbol, das sie besitzen, ist ein Notizbuch mit sehr vielen energischen Eintragungen; Erledigtes ordentlich ausgestrichen . . . Die Hauptsache ist, dass das, wofür ein Mensch lebt, einen Magnet bildet, der durch das, was er anzieht, immer weiter vergrössert wird. (*MoE*, 1635)

[All good people live for something . . . so many interesting, honorable, satisfying careers. Then there is love. Organizations. Breeding chickens. Lifting weights. Football. Tennis. Politics. The Salvation Army. Stamp collecting. Soup kitchens. The Öhl stenographic system. . . . The common symbol that all of these possess is a notebook with many energetic entries; things done crossed out in an orderly fashion. The main thing is, that for which a person lives is a magnet which always grows larger and larger through everything it attracts.]

The novel's "progress" itself swings back and forth between living for and in, between appetitive and non-appetitive, as it moves forward and then stands still, reaches for an idea and then doubles back, suggests and then takes back the suggestion. Musil's novel resists the attraction of such monolithic goals, denies the single Archimedean point its centrality, and refuses the fetishism of taking only one fascination as the whole. In short, although the forward-moving, progress-oriented, animalistic tendency of appetitive, egocentric living, and living *for* something, are credited by Ulrich as being responsible for all inventions and progress in the world (as well as all war and destruction) it is clearly the other tendencies (non-appetitive, allocentric, and living *in* something) that determine the novel's structure as novel — "ein Geschehen, ohne dass etwas geschah" (*MoE*, 1245); a happening without anything happening). This animalistic/appetitive principle might even have something to do with Aristotle's poetic explanation of man's natural desire for mimesis. If we take this analogy further, we see that the allocentric and non-appetitive correspond to the metaphoric abstraction of non-linearity favored in Musil's novel. Abstraction, insofar as it is connected to universal forms, is always closer to timelessness and further from utility than representation, which is drawn from and comments upon particularities of place and moment.

Notes on his book of aphorisms, "Aus einem Rapial" (translated by Burton Pike as Arrows from a quiver), which he compiled and tried to publish during his exile as an antidote to the slowness of his novel ("Rapio = auch rasch, eilig, hastig, ausführen, benützen, angreifen" [*Rapio* = also rash, hurried, hasty, complete, utilize, grasp]) reveal the lack of appetitive energy that challenged Musil as author:

> Die Notizen zur aktuellen Kapitelgruppe und die Aphorismen zeigen die gleichen Schwierigkeiten der Ausarbeitung. Über beiden waltet kein Wille, Entschluss, Affekt, der zur Wahl nötigt. Ein Gedanke schließt sich an den anderen, und das geht nach vielen Richtungen. (*TBAER*, 558)

> [My notes to the current chapter groups and the aphorisms present the same difficulties for completion. There is no will ruling over either of them, no decision, no emotion, that would necessitate a choice. One thought attaches itself to another, and that goes in many directions.]

In his preface to a new edition of *Morgenröte* (Dawn), Nietzsche writes that he should be read "rück- und vorsichtig" (backward- and forward-looking).[28] In a note to his translation, Walter Kaufmann draws attention to this pun on the more common meaning —carefully — of these words in German: carefully means looking backward and forward. What Nietzsche seems to mean here is that he does not want to be read in a straight line, without looking back, but in a kind of a circular motion, whereby all new utterances or phrases are considered in relationship to those which have come before, and, presumably, all earlier entries or thoughts in relation to what comes after. While one might argue that all good writing considers what has come before, Nietzsche's method is particularly fitting for reading Musil's work. Reading backward and forward is a necessity considering

Musil's obsessive a-chronological writing of drafts and versions, his revising and thinking processes, which seem to continually circle forward and backward, shifting events and circumstances in and out of linear narrative and simultaneity. This process is even philosophically motivated by one of Musil's many utopian conceptions, "the Utopia of the Next Step," which considers every action (entry, version, excerpt) by the result that it engenders, that is, how it alters or inspires other entries, excerpts and versions. Another comment by Nietzsche, from the preface to the *Genealogie der Moral* (Genealogy of morals), wherein he mentions that he is returning to aphorisms and ideas he had written in earlier books, speaks to the circular process by which the development of thoughts and beliefs, our "ifs and buts," "yeas and nays," "grow out of us with the inner necessity with which a tree bears fruit — related and each with an affinity to each . . . not as isolated, capricious, or sporadic things, but from a common root."[29] And this idea is echoed by Musil, as Ulrich wonders about the suspicious circularity of his thought — "dass sich in allem, was ich bis jetzt zu sehen vermeine, ein Zirkelschluß verbirgt" (that there is a vicious circle lurking in everything that I think I have understood up to now), continuing:

> Denn ich will nicht — wenn ich nun auf das ursprüngliche Motiv zurückgreife — aus dem Zustand der "Bedeutung" hinaus, und wenn ich mir sagen will, was Bedeutung sei, so komme ich immer wieder nur auf den Zustand, wie ich bin, und wie ich jetzt bin, das ist eben, dass ich aus einem bestimmten Zustand nicht hinaus will! (*MoE*, 1429)

> [For I don't want — if I now go back to my original motif — to leave the state of "significance," and if I tell myself what significance is, all I come to again and again is the state I am in, which is that I don't want to leave a specific state! (*MwQ*, 1721)]

And further, when he doubts his condition because of his inability to stand outside it and judge it or resist it, he concludes, "Aber kann etwas eine Suggestion sein, dessen Vorankündigung, dessen erste Spur ich beinahe mein ganzes Leben zurück zu verfolgen vermag?!" (*MoE*, 1429 But can something be hypnotic (suggestion[30]) whose premonitions, whose first traces, I can follow back through almost my entire life? *MwQ*, 1721). A reader of Musil's novel, following the modernist injunction to read deeply in such a way that a novel might change one's life, may find herself wondering why it seems that the narrator and his characters are always discussing ideas and problems that she herself is currently just on the verge of considering, until she realizes that indeed, the circularity of Musil's ideas has been preparing, in premonitions and traces, the very ideas which she mistakes as solely her own fresh thoughts. An earlier passage in this chapter from Ulrich's notebooks comments on this confusing condition (a confusion that the reader of the novel also experiences) as he muses: "Allerdings gehört es zu den Eigentümlichkeiten unseres Zustands, dass jede neue Betrachtung alle älteren in sich aufnimmt, so dass es unter ihnen keine Rangfolge gibt, sie scheinen vielmehr unendlich verstrickt zu sein" (*MoE*, 1427; Of course it is part of the peculiarity of our condition that every new observation assimilates all the earlier ones, so that there is no hierarchy among them; they seem, rather, to be infinitely entangled, *MwQ*, 1719–20). This circling is the fountaining kind, which supposes some sort of fundamental core or source, Nietzsche's "common root," to which we return, over and over. It is reminiscent of the Nietzschean imperative "Werde wer du bist!" (Become who you are!) and also of Ulrich's surprising admission that he had always believed that morality was not *made* by humans, but *discovered*, "that morality itself must have a morality." This confession seems to contradict the radical open-endedness of the other sort of possibilitarian generation of infinite circles and to raise the question: is anything at all possible? Or are there, indeed, certain limitations — of character, nature, probability, that determine to some extent the distance or depth to which any given beginning or being may attain? This might be something like the acrostic, to speak with Emerson, of a person's character, which, no matter which way we read it, comes out the same. Musil notes that this idea is as unfashionable as it is fashionable. It certainly does not fit easily into the overall summary we try to make of Musil's philosophical stance as modernist — or even postmodernist — innovator who eschewed belief in absolute values or truths. Yet if we ignore this persistent and incongruous tick in Musil's text, this recurrent mention of some essential something, and its almost rapturous representation in the scenes of mystical ecstasy shared by the siblings, we are clearly not reading faithfully but skipping over the little pesky parts which do not fit smoothly into a simple category. As Moses Maimonides suggests in his *Guide for the Perplexed*, the fervent, devoted reader looks *more* closely wherever there is a discrepancy, wherever something does not seem to be consistent. In that careful looking is to be found — for a moment only, non-translatable, not to be held on to or brought up into the light of day perhaps — the most important part of the text.

How, then, does the idea of a timeless core, an eternal essence fit in with the competing structure and idea of non-determined infinite possibility? How, indeed, does Emersonian self-reliance and repudiation of tradition and slavish conformity exist alongside the idea of an eternal pre-established "over-soul"? How do the Kantian categorical imperative — to act as if what is true for you is true for all men — and the radical idea of the subjective experience of reality coincide with a belief in some unknowable but present *a priori* Beauty or Truth? Why does Dostoevsky's underground man seem at times to actually long for the "Crystal Palace" of absolute beauty and goodness at which he so crudely thumbs his nose?

How does the Nietzschean trans-valuation of values and smashing of traditions compute into worship of the ancient Greeks and of Goethe? How
again should we understand Nietzsche's contempt for otherworldliness
and celebration of the earthly and physical alongside his reduction of the
whole world to a metaphor, its justification purely as an aesthetic phenomenon? How, indeed, are we to understand the connection between
Emerson — the philosopher of transcendence — and Nietzsche — the
precursor of existentialism?

Answers to these perplexing questions can only be approached
through an understanding of the coincidence of opposites present in
these comprehensive thinkers, only by not rushing to categorize into
dualistic camps. A beginning of an answer will only be glimpsed, I would
further suggest, if we begin to take seriously the process and experience
of metaphor — as an infinite proliferation of possible variations on a
theme or group of themes, as a world of self-generating but connected
circle-worlds. Once we accept that our perceptions and descriptions of
the world are metaphors for something that cannot be described, we may
learn to see them as illusions, but also to value their constant creation and
re-creation as one of the most meaningful activities of the human mind.

In a cosmos wherein "a belief cannot be an hour old" or wherein
a feeling ceases to be itself in the moment that it changes, the written
word is constantly subject to revision. The multiple perspectives of the
author without qualities ensure that any progress or action is undermined
by the narrator's consciousness of the inevitable process of cancellation,
that spinning wheel-of-fortune whereby whatever was at the top at one
moment is now at the bottom, and vice versa. This hyperconsciousness
does not allow for any glib satisfaction or simple solutions, but rather
instantly calls up an opposing opinion or reason whenever it appears that
we might be getting somewhere. Thus the active, animalistic drive for
creation and destruction is revealed to be an impulse that does not stand
up under the scrutiny of reason or practical purpose. On the other hand,
instances and examples of mystical, aesthetic, allocentric, non-appetitive
moods, and tendencies toward life "in something," are depicted increasingly in the most favorable light as Musil's narrator abandons the world
of activity to explore the Other Condition of love, of mysticism, of the
"millennium." The only non-ironic portions of the book — and its most
beautiful passages — are celebrations of this sort of experience. Countless critics have argued that Musil did not intend to favor this mystical
and aesthetic consciousness, because Ulrich and Agathe's idyll in paradise
did not last, further arguing that Musil failed to integrate the mystical,
aesthetic experience of the Other Condition into "real life." I suggest, in
response, that we examine this paradigm of lasting and of reality under
the glass of Musil's overall synecdochal structure of infinitely separated
but related metaphorical moments. Success, under such terms, must be

gauged according to an entirely different conception of Time and Reality. In an experimental system, in other words, wherein the primary reality of the world of the normal condition is called into question, the "failure" of alternate modes of experiencing and alternate modes of time to fit into this largely discredited system is only to be expected. It may even be viewed as a sort of success, rather than a failure; a sort of "higher stupidity."

As such, the normal measurements of time and space, of completion and efficiency are clearly overcome by utterly different means of gauging success in life. To not finish, to avoid completion, is freedom, if only of the negative kind. As Emerson writes in "Circles," an essay from which Musil took another line for his novel,

> I no longer commute my possible achievement by what remains to me of the month or the year; for these moments confer a sort of omnipresence and omnipotence, *which asks nothing of duration*, but sees that the energy of the mind is commensurate with the work to be done, without time.[31]

Deeply digesting the possibility of a universe or multiverses of limitlessness, decenteredness, relativity of time and space, and the shifting nature of the subjective perception of center means to ask nothing of duration, to dwell in timelessness. It means to deeply reconsider the paradigms of social, moral, and aesthetic success that prevailed under other models. Musil's novel, its structure as well as its recurring metaphoric attention to circles and moments, challenges the reader to do just that. It took at least a century after Copernicus before people really stopped imagining they were at the center of everything (in some ways, we still believe we are); it has been about a century since Einstein declared the relativity of time and space, yet we still cling to linear and measurable securities such as goal and closure and duration, as if we were still living under the Ptolomaic system. As Michael André Bernstein put it, "The problem in the modern world, as Robert Musil so clearly understood, is that at the level of epistemology, historiography, and logic we have long since ceased to believe in the authority of precisely the explanatory principles that we nonetheless continue to rely upon to structure our narratives of historical causality and personal development."[32]

The chapterlets of Musil's novel, which careen ever more out of linear or chronological order as the novel "progresses," are each their own more or less self-contained but interconnected circle of reality. They are formal experiments with Musil's concerns about time, durativity, and action (conduct of life), as well as more directly with the nature of metaphoric variations on themes, the nature of alternate worlds, possibilities, variables, and, by extension, the existential "what if" of the subjunctive case. In a modernist novel that has lost what Musil's "friend" and protagonist Ulrich calls the "elementary, narrative mode," one can see the function of metaphor as the creation of an almost infinite number of expanding thought moments, decentralized centers within the "infinitely interwoven surface," which present convincing alternatives to the comforting illusion of the "thread of the story." The structure of infinite circles, like the new grammar that Musil suggests we might employ to begin to think in new ways, allows the narrator to "say certain things" and to think certain things that he would not have been able to say or think within a different sort of structure. These "endless perspectives" travel "in toward the interior" rather than in one linear direction, and shimmer thus as Other Conditions and alternatives to a world structure of progress, linearity, and mono-direction.

While Musil speaks of grammar, he might also have been thinking of Nietzsche's discussion of the uses of polytheism in *Die fröhliche Wissenschaft* (The gay science), which stresses the defining function of form or *Gestalt* in establishing our ways of looking at the world. For Nietzsche, polytheism was important, because it taught people how to see a "plurality of norms" instead of being mono-centered. This variety, although nominally about "gods, heroes, and overmen of all kinds, as well as nearmen and undermen, dwarfs, fairies, centaurs, satyrs, demons, and devils," came to be, says Nietzsche, a structural model of seeing individually and of establishing the rights of the individual, "free-spiriting" and "many-spiriting." Polytheism became a prototype for the individual's "strength to create for ourselves our own new eyes — and ever again new eyes that are even more our own; hence man alone among all the animals has no eternal horizons and perspectives."[33] No eternally fixed horizons or perspectives, in other words, but, rather, as Musil would have it, "infinite[ly changing] perspectives (moving inward)."

The many new eyes that are eternally created and recreated are also present in Rilke's "Archaischer Torso Apollos," where the headless sculpture shines like a candelabra of individual candles: "denn da ist keine Stelle die dich nicht sieht" (For there is no place that does not see you).[34] The many points of decentered seeing tell the viewer, the reader, the poet, "Du musst dein Leben ändern" (You must change your life), circling us back to the connection between the formal/aesthetic and the ethical/worldly. A body that sees — breaking out of all bounds like a star with many points — is a body made entirely of eyes; multiple circles without one center. But even one eye can multiply into a world of circles.

The first sphere in Emerson's essay "Circles" is the human eye, this "primary figure," this "first of all forms," reminding us of the core at the heart of Musil's mystical, fountaining circling. Though this primary figure is, in the Emersonian sense, self-reliant and experimental, it is also connected to some notion of timeless truth, morality, or goodness: to what Emerson would call the "Over-Soul." And Emerson states that "Augustine described the nature of God as a circle whose centre was everywhere, and its circumference nowhere."[35] Musil seems to refer to this image when he writes of the difference between what he calls "allocentric and egocentric," remarking in a passage from the draft chapter "Sonderauf-gabe eines Gartengitters" (special mission of a garden fence): "Egozen-trisch sein heißt fühlen, als trüge man im Mittelpunkt seiner Person den Mittelpunkt der Welt. Allozentrisch sein heißt, überhaupt keinen Mittel-punkt mehr haben . . ." (*KA*;[36] Being egocentric means feeling as if one were carrying the center of the world in the center of one's self. Being allocentric means not having a center at all anymore, *MwQ*, 1528). To have no center is to have centers everywhere.

Patrizia McBride's excellent book *The Void of Ethics* concentrates on the centerless circle as cipher for the problem of a lack of values in modernity, and concludes that Musil would have us "acknowledge the ethical void as constitutive for the human condition and to cherish it as an opportunity for rethinking ethics in modernity."[37] This centerless circle is for McBride a reminder of "the violence lurking in all endeavors aimed at surreptitiously filling this void with yet another absolute vision of the good life." Therefore she deems that Musil's experiments with the Other Condition (an attempt in her definition to fill the void with unending meaning), are doomed to failure. But while it is certainly true that Musil rejected the idea of filling the void with superficial images of absolute goodness or truth, there is no inherent reason why the void of ethics could not be filled with constantly changing, renewing, self-generating possibilities — and fresh, living metaphors, instead of frozen, calcified prejudices and unexamined assumptions. The Other Condition, by its very nature momentary and fleeting, but also paradoxically infinite and eternal, is the perfect fluid medium with which to fill such a void. This process illustrates the paradoxical connection between transcendentalism and existentialism, as the experience of mystical otherness or ecstatic Dio-nysian dis-individuation translates into active and conscious ways of being in and creating the shared world with every action and thought. *The void of ethics, in other words, is filled, over and over again: with aesthetics, with aesthetic experience.*

This aesthetic experience leads to flexible ethical aliveness, to existen-tialism, which actively resists the freezing and calcifying of momentary met-aphorical images into realities and facts. Having no center, then, does not mean being empty, but rather having many centers. Much like being with-out qualities, having no center is both positive and negative. On the one hand, being without qualities is a disease of the times, a "Zeitkrankheit," demonstrative of a lack of conviction, aesthetic characteristics, and desire; on the other hand, it can be viewed as the only possible reasoned response to a world wherein everything cancels itself out and wherein marrying one's self to any one decision or opinion is to deny the moving, changing sub-stance of conscientious aliveness, to sink into the dull habit or "wretched contentment" of Nietzsche's despised bourgeois. Being without qualities is being open, single, unattached to any one limited outcome, answer, or opinion; it is being open to an infinity of possibilities; it is the experimental mode.[38] Being without center holds the same dichotomous valuation. It is a sickness, a stupidity, a higher wisdom, a challenge to the persistence of the basic purpose-centric model of the universe.

Prince Myshkin, the "holy fool" of Dostoevsky's *The Idiot*, describes the moments before his epileptic attacks in a way that suggests deep kinship with Musil's Other Condition. Like the exiled Musil, this fictional character ends up in Switzerland; and like Musil, he is unable ultimately to function in the corrupt and foolish world of linear time and social expectations. Myshkin thinks to himself of the moment before his attacks, "that all these gleams and flashes of the highest sensation of life and self-consciousness, and therefore also of the highest form of existence, were nothing but disease, the interruption of the normal condition."[39] This distinction between the "normal condition" and disease and exceptional moments is echoed by Musil's novel continually, as he speaks of "genial Augenblicke" (genius moments), "ausnahme Zustände" (exceptional conditions) and the normal and "other" conditions that oppose them. Myshkin, like Musil, describes these abnormal moments as "the acme of harmony and beauty" as "completion," as "proportion," and concludes that "For this moment one might give one's whole life." These "higher moments" contain "infinite happiness," he continues, making the connection between these small units of interruption to the normal flow of time and infinity or timelessness: "At that moment . . . I seem somehow to understand the extraordinary saying that there shall be no more time."[40]

In one draft passage Ulrich considers the failure of his adventure with his sister, but finds ultimately that the alternative to all "that was best in his life" is not something he could ever fully embrace. The phrase that begins this passage, "Looked at in this way," signals that there are other ways of looking at it, too, that this perspective is just being tried out, essayed, subject to rejection.

So war das Beste in seinem Leben immer ein Unsinn gewesen, der Schimmer des Denkens, der Hauch von Übermut, diese zarten Boten einer besseren Heimat, die zwischen den Dingen der Welt wehen. Es blieb nichts übrig als vernünftig zu werden, er musste seiner Natur Gewalt antun u[nd] sie wahrscheinlich nicht nur in eine harte, sondern auch von vorneher langweilige Schule nehmen. Er wollte nicht geboren sein zum Müssigänger u[nd] würde es jetzt sein wenn er nicht bald anfinge, mit den Folgen dieses Fehlschlags Ordnung zu machen. Aber wenn er sie prüfte, lehnte sich sein Wesen dagegen auf, u[nd] wenn sich sein Wesen dagegen auflehnte, sehnte er sich nach Ag[athe]. (*MoE*, 1565)

[Looked at this way, what was best in his life had always been an absurdity, the shimmer of a thought, a whiff of bravado, these tender harbingers of a better homeland that hovers between the things of the world . . . There was nothing left but to become reasonable, he would have to do violence to his nature and take it under not only hard but also boring tutelage. He didn't want to be a born idler and would become one now if he didn't begin soon to make sense of the consequences of this failure. But when he considered it, his being rebelled against it, and when his being rejected it, he longed for A[gathe].]

Ulrich ends in this instance by rejecting the world of reason and the "things of the world" as against his nature, despite his admission that the other pockets of shimmering meaning in between had in some ways failed to endure. He says a bitter goodbye to his sister in another draft passage, parting as well from the utopian dream of establishing a millennium of love on earth from the union of their two persons. And yet he tells Agathe, half disdainfully, that she will love again, some art historian or banker, someone other than himself, thereby affirming the continuation of the cycle and movement of these circles of meaning (however illusory, however fleeting) as the "best of life" that there is. In a metaphoric universe, in other words, it is not important whom one loves or for how long, but simply *that* one loves. In accordance with Goethe's model of the *Urpflanze*, a particular flower or feeling dies, and another intrinsically related new flower and feeling appear in its place, necessarily exceptional, necessarily not to be translated into normal time, normal space.

Furthermore, as Prince Myshkin associates these moments of beauty, harmony, and infinite happiness with a disease or sickness, we might note that they are defined as sickness only insofar as the normal condition of non-ecstatic moments is considered the rightfully prevailing condition. Dostoevsky's novel, like Musil's, raises the question of whether, instead, such "fools in the eyes of the world," such "men without qualities" (that is, qualities that might aid them in becoming successful, efficient, functional), might not be, in their idiotic momentary trances and timeless aesthetic ecstasies, closer in fact to the more "really real" and "essential" experiences of existence. Clearly, Dostoevsky's hero is singled out as exceptional in a society wherein, as the narrator writes, people are successful, become generals, and so forth, as a rule, precisely by being as ordinary and unoriginal as possible. Against this "seinesgleichen geschieht" Musil will contend that the exceptional moments, the "genius moments" are the only ones wherein truly moral, that is, ethical, activity can take place.

Burton Pike offers an illuminating parallel in an essay on *The Man without Qualities* and Isaiah Berlin's idea of negative and positive freedom.[41] While the positive freedom associated with the force and power of Arnheim, the successful businessman/author, appear in the novel as hollow simulacra to Ulrich, negative freedom is fostered in the vacuum of values left by a crumbling external society. The man who, like Ulrich, enjoys his positive freedom as opposed to the status quo of "seinesgleichen geschieht," may seem to remain outside reality, or in a realm outside meaningful action, unless one views this state within a Nietzschean context as a necessary preparatory stage on the way to creating a new world. Pike writes:

> Musil would agree with Isaiah Berlin that "the struggle for freedom . . . is a struggle not for a positive goal but for conditions in which positive goals can be fulfilled." Indeed, in his novel Musil states the same thing: Ulrich says that "we really shouldn't demand action from one another; we should create the conditions that make action possible." [II, 805] Negative freedom is the space of potentiality, and for Musil, potentiality remains the motivating force. To actually act in society, positive freedom, would mean the end of possibility, of potentiality. The ideal of a society in which the individual could transform his negative freedom into positive freedom remains at the other end of the unfinished bridge that was the most suggestive of Musil's metaphors: "The goal to be reached by those who will come after." [I, 43]

Negative freedom may also be related to the "most advantageous advantage" expounded by Dostoevsky's underground man, a sort of freedom to not participate in a corrupt system even at the expense of personal success and comfort in that world. The underground man, in his ironic but partially heartfelt evocation of the "crystal palace," as perfected goal, as wholeness, as absolute beauty, explains:

> Man is predominantly a creating animal, doomed to strive consciously towards a goal and to occupy himself with the art of engineering — that is, to eternally and ceaselessly make a road for himself that at least goes somewhere or other. But sometimes he may wish to swerve aside, precisely because he is doomed to open this road, and also perhaps because, stupid though the ingenious figure generally is, it still sometimes occurs to him that this road almost always turns out to go somewhere or other and the main thing is not where it goes, but that it should simply be going . . ."[42]

If this place the stupid ingenious man is doomed to attain to is death, it would be quite natural to veer off the road as much as possible, and to attempt, as long as possible, to create byways, to keep going, to not arrive. "Can it be," he continues,

> that he has a love of destruction and chaos . . . because he is instinctively afraid of achieving the goal and completing the edifice he is

creating? How do you know, maybe he likes the edifice only from far off, and by no means up close; maybe he only likes creating it, and not living in it . . .

Discussing "the All-Loving as the Eternal Artist" in his notebooks, Ulrich gives us an insight into his own creator's psychology of completion:

> Er liebt die Schöpfung, solange er sie schafft, von den fertigen Teilen wendet sich seine Liebe aber ab. Denn der Künstler muss auch das Hassenswerteste lieben, um es bilden zu können, aber was er bereits geschaffen hat, mag es auch gut sein, erkaltet ihm; es wird so liebeverlassen, dass er sich darin selbst kaum noch versteht, und die Augenblicke sind selten und unberechenbar, wo seine Liebe wiederkehrt und sich an dem weidet, was sie getan hat. Und so wäre denn auch zu denken: Was über uns waltet, liebt, was es schafft; aber dem fertigen Teil der Schöpfung entzieht und nähert sich seine Liebe in langem Abfließen und kurzem Wiederanschwellen. Diese Vorstellung passt sich der Tatsache an, dass Seelen und Dingen der Welt wie Tote sind, die manchmal für Sekunden auferweckt werden. (*MoE*, 1125)

> [He loves creation as long as he is creating it, but his love turns away from the finished portions. For the artist must also love what is most hateful in order to shape it, but what he has already shaped, even if it is good, leaves him cold; it becomes so bereft of love that he hardly still understands himself in it, and the moments when his love returns to delight in what it has done are rare and unpredictable. And so one could also think: What lords it over us loves what it creates; but this love approaches and withdraws from the finished part of creation in a long ebbing flow and a short returning swell. This idea fits the fact that souls and things of the world are like dead people who are sometimes reawakened for seconds. (*MwQ*, 1224)

And a few lines later, the conclusion: "Die fertige Welt[:] Sünde! Die mögliche: Liebe!" (The world as it is [or: the finished world], sin! The possible world, love!). In order for the creator to continue to love the work, it must remain always unfinished, potential, infinite, a continual work in progress.

"I am only an experimenter," writes Emerson in his essay "Circles," sounding very much like Musil: "Do not set the least value on what I do, or the least discredit on what I do not, as if I pretended to settle anything as true or false. I unsettle things. No facts are to me sacred; none are profane; I simply experiment, an endless seeker, with no past at my back."[43] And again, linking his essayistic patterning and dissolution of pattern with the forms of nature, Emerson continues to discredit permanence and construct another organizing principle:

In nature, every moment is new; the past is always swallowed and forgotten; the coming only is sacred. Nothing is secure but life, transition, the energizing spirit. No love can be bound by oath or covenant to secure it against a higher love. No truth so sublime but it may be trivial tomorrow in the light of new thoughts. People wish to be settled: only as far as they are unsettled, is there any hope for them.[44]

Possibility, experimentation, continual circling and outgrowing of the circumferences and the temporarily drawn limits are all actions whose carrier is metaphor. Metaphor, as the process and product of transformation, gives glimpses of other worlds, thereby radically unsettling what was, moments before, certainty and truth. Such metaphor, like the works of art that it occurs in, creates alternative realities that — for an indefinable duration only — redescribe and revivify normal existence. Thus time, as timelessness, fleetingness, and distention, is, also in the realm of the novel, the fundamental fourth dimension by virtue of which all our perceptions of space, story, and any possible interpretations of reality exist. Time within a modernist novel fluctuates, depending upon relationships, on relativity. Metaphors may be seen as little more than relative relations of one thing to another, or of one reality with another; as temporary means to see qualities in new ways, to open up possibilities, to provide a glimpse of what might be. They are tools of experimental hypothesis and of the subjunctive mode.

As such, metaphor functions in *The Man without Qualities* on many levels. The narrator constantly makes us aware of the tension between fiction and reality, and of fiction's role as metaphoric, utopian, as an Other Condition, and repeatedly elucidates the ways in which novels are metaphors for reality. In addition, the actions and "qualities" of characters are themselves metaphorically in friction with each other, further complicating any attempt to define or determine characteristics or expectations. Finally, metaphor on the sentence or word level functions as an a-logical means of communicating, using what Musil, taking a cue from Ernst Kretschmer's terminology in his study of dreams, refers to as the realm of the "sphärisch" (spherical).[45] Metaphors — on the level of the word, the action, or the world(s) of the novel— function, in short, as decentralizing alternative realities, interrelated but separate spherical worlds. These new worlds continually call the supremacy of traditional values, purposes, and structures into question. Metaphors, deviating, displacing, seemingly self-generating, further serve to resist the all-too-common reduction of literary texts to transmitters of information or data. They insist upon an indeterminate communication of "something else," something that manages to distract the reader and the author from any expectation of a given goal or purpose, from any simplistic or easily translatable linear narrative.

This emphatically non-linear, non-literal structure should be the starting point for any speculation of the novel's final purposes, intentions, or meanings, or, indeed, our evaluation of its failure or success in attaining these. If we take the structure of circles seriously, considering deeply what it has to say about alternate realities, the creative regeneration of worlds, and infinity, our usual paradigms of success (duration, progress, end, centrality) must be reexamined. Any one of the fleeting, incommensurate, non-translatable moments of experience that evanesce throughout the novel may be enough to justify all of existence or, indeed, the success or successful failure of a novel, finished or not.

Notes

[1] "Von mir läßt sich nicht mehr sagen, als dass ich noch immer den *MoE* wie ein Paar Handschellen an mir hängen habe; ich bin auch gar nicht weitergekommen mit dem Buch, doch hoffe ich: tiefer." Letter from Musil to Victor Zuckerkandl, 22 Dec. 1940. *KA*: Lesetexte: Schweizer Korrespondenz, 1939–43.

[2] *KA*: Nachlaß: Mappen. Mappen Gruppe IV, IV/3 "A" Aufsätze. IV/3/379: Aufzeichnung zur Krisis des Romans.

[3] Richardson, *Emerson: The Mind on Fire*, 354.

[4] Emerson, *The Later Lectures of Ralph Waldo Emerson*, 84.

[5] Emerson, *Early Lectures*, 1838–1842, 378.

[6] Two aphorisms by Musil defining this Nazi neologism: *Gleichschaltung*: "Another measure of the strangeness of what is happening today with the German spirit is that a word has come into usage for a large part of these happenings, a word that presents the native speaker with no less difficulty than it does a foreigner. 'Schalten,' the action word at its foundation, belongs to the older history of the German language and had possessed in the present day only a weakened life, so that there were indeed many derivations of it in use, while it itself was somewhat petrified and only used in specific situations. So one can say, for example, that someone *schaltet* free (disconnects or isolates) from something, but the simple sentence one *schaltet* no longer carries a complete meaning. On the whole, the word is most often seen in the formula 'schalten und walten,' which means something to the effect of to manage and to have a free hand, but which is spun with a bit of poetical moss. One grasps that there is some Romanticism behind the idea of using the word *schalten*. Its original meaning signifies to push, tow, set in motion, force. This Romantic word has the most modern of children. A *Schalter* is something at the train station, namely a ticket office, and something having to do with electrical room lighting signifies a little window that one can push open and closed, but also there is, in an electric power station, something called a large '*Schalt*-board.'" *KA*: Lesetexte aus dem Nachlass. Band 14: Gedichte, Aphorismen, Selbstkommentare. Aphorismen aus dem Nachlass: "Ich stelle zusammen". *Gleichschaltung* 1). "The word: It marks the strangeness (it will be difficult for foreigners to understand it) of what is happening today in Germany, that this word *Gleichschaltung*, which plays such a large role in it, cannot be directly translated into other languages. This word was suddenly there one day out of nowhere for the not-yet-National Socialist Germans. Lamps, machines are *gleichgeschaltet* (switched into conformity) — and Germans. Difference between norms and similarities. It has active and passive meanings in psychiatry. Levers and similar mechanisms, electric currents *ein- und ausschalten* (switch on and off). *Schaltwerk* (control unit). *Schalthebel* (switching lever). In general: *Gleichstrom* (co- or parallel current): a current whose direction remains the same. There is a *Batterieschaltung* (accumulator switch) for galvanic elements, next to and following one another. One speaks of (different) modes of *Schaltung* in dynamo machines. Likewise in an electrical lighting system. *Schalten*, Middle High German. To push, tow (esp. a ship), into movement, to force. In New High German becomes = to steer; Old High German *scaltan* = to push, New High German. Schalter = sliding sash from middle high German

schalter (*schelter*) = bolt. *Schaltjahr* (leap year) already in old high German because of the day that is pushed forward. (to push is also a basic meaning of *schalten*) [*walten* really = being strong] see *Gewalt* (violence)." "*KA*: Lesetexte. Band 14: Gedichte, Aphorismen, Selbstkommentar. Aphorismen aus dem Nachlass: "Ich stelle zusammen".

[7] Adorno, *Aesthetic Theory*, 12.

[8] *KA*: Transkriptionen und Faksimiles. Nachlass: Mappen. Weitere Mappen. Vortrag. Vortrag/68.

[9] See Ulrich Schelling's "Das analogische Denken bei Robert Musil," which outlines what he calls Musil's "constructive irony" as a "system of mirrorings and ironic fractures". Schelling elaborates on what he calls the "magic wand of analogy" that enables Ulrich to be "the one who is the secretary of the failed 'parallel action'; that Tuzzi calls him his 'cousin and that he feels himself a deep sympathy for Tuzzi; that Moosbrugger is more important to him 'than his own life that he leads'; that he spends time with the Christian Germanic Nationalist and has 'a taste for Gerda's strange friends'; that the expressions of the crazy Clarisse are 'considerably similar' to his own and that even Lindner sometimes speaks like Ulrich. That Musil understood these configurations and partial harmonies as analogies too is proven directly by the following: 'Everything that we do is only metaphor. That is: analogy . . . our whole existence is only analogy.'" Schelling, "Das analogische Denken," 179.

[10] "Potemkin village" refers to purportedly fake facades of buildings set up by Grigory Potemkin in 1787 to present a shining front for Catherine II's visit to the Crimea.

[11] Nabokov, *Lectures on Russian Literature*, 19–21.

[12] *KA*: Lesetexte. Band 3: Der Mann ohne Eigenschaften. Die Fortsetzung. Fortsetzungsreihen 1932–1936. Erste Fortsetzungsreihe. 51. Das Ende der Eintragung.

[13] Pike, "Unfinished or without End?," 366.

[14] In this fragment, the "I" is both himself and Ulrich, as often happens in Musil's notes.

[15] *KA*: Ulrichs Tagebuch. Die Utopie der Höflichkeit.

[16] Pike, "Unfinished or without End," 368.

[17] Grill, "Ecstatic Experience," 289.

[18] *KA*: Lesetexte. Band 12: Essays. Ansätze zu neuer Ästhetik, 493.

[19] Cusa's influential ideas are paraphrased by Dorothy Waley Singer in *Giordano Bruno*, 56.

[20] Bruno, *Giordano Bruno: His Life and Thought with an Annotated Translation of His Work "On the Infinite Universe and Worlds,"* 363.

[21] Bruno, *Giordano Bruno*, 75.

[22] Nietzsche, *Gay Science*, 181.

[23] Clark, *Einstein*, 310.

²⁴ My translation; but see *MwQ*, 1331–32: "I'll simply use a familiar example and call the two kinds of passionate existence the appetitive and, as its counterpart, the nonappetitive, even if it sounds awkward. For in every person there is a hunger, and it behaves like a greedy animal; yet it is not a hunger but something ripening sweetly like grapes in the autumn sun, free from greed and satiety . . . he went on to speak only of what he understood by the appetitive. It urges to action, to motion, to enjoyment; through its effect, emotion is transformed into a work, or into an idea and conviction, or into a disappointment. All these are ways in which it discharges, but they can also be forms of recharging, for in this manner the emotion changes, uses itself up, dissipates in its success comes to an end . . . 'The world has the appetitive part of the emotions to thank for all its works and all beauty and progress, but also all the unrest, and ultimately all its senseless running around!' he corroborated."

²⁵ *KA*: Ulrichs Tagebuch. Die Utopie der Höflichkeit.

²⁶ Bab, *Das Leben Goethes*, 29–30.

²⁷ In this early version Ulrich is still called Anders. The text reads: "A. fühlte auch nicht mehr . . .".

²⁸ This important aside was pointed out to me by my esteemed colleague Dharman Rice. Nietzsche writes: "Gut lesen, das heißt langsam, tief, rück- und vorsichtig, mit Hintergedanken." *Basic Writings of Nietzsche*, 458n5.

²⁹ Nietzsche, *Basic Writings*, 452.

³⁰ Pike's translation of the German word "Suggestion" in this isolated phrase is "hypnotic," which does not include the secondary meaning of some external and possibly untrustworthy influence that becomes clear when reading the whole translated passage. Musil muses on the difference between the casual understanding of the word "hypnosis" and the scientific meaning of "affective suggestion."

³¹ Emerson, *Essays*, 188.

³² Bernstein. *Forgone Conclusions*, 124.

³³ Nietzsche, *Gay Science*, 191–92.

³⁴ Rilke, *Gedichte*, 483.

³⁵ Emerson, *Essays*, 179.

³⁶ *KA*: Lesetexte. Der Mann ohne Eigenschaften. Die Fortseztung. Fortsetzungsreihen 1934–36. Neuansätze [Grundentwurf]. 49. Sonderaufgabe eines Gartengitters.

³⁷ McBride, *Void of Ethics*, 8.

³⁸ See Schmidt's *Ohne Eigenschaften* for a discussion of what Schmidt sees as Musil's appropriation of Meister Eckhart's phrase "âne eigenschaft," connoting a positively valued state of being without possessions. Eckhart transformed the phrase's meanings to include not only a release from material possessions but also a release from spiritual possessions or attachments in the form of beliefs, habits, preconceptions or hopes, an extreme state of spiritual, material, and moral vagabondage related to Eckhart's other central terms "Ledigkeit" (singleness) and "Abgeschiedenheit" (separated non-attachment).

³⁹ Dostoevsky, *Idiot*, 224.

[40] Dostoevsky, *Idiot*, 225.

[41] Pike, "Negative Freedom in the Man without Qualities," unpublished paper delivered at "Recontextualizing Robert Musil," International Robert Musil Society Conference (Lancaster, England, 2007).

[42] Dostoevsky, *Notes From Underground*, 31.

[43] Emerson, *Essays*, 188.

[44] Emerson, *Essays*, 189.

[45] See *T*, 838: "6. April 1930. Frühling — Brüder Čapek — Prag — diese drei Worte verbunden durch ein ziemlich unsinniges Zeitwort bildeten meinen Bewusstseinsinhalt beim Aufwachen nachmittags. Ich hatte die ganze Zeit über geglaubt, nicht zu schlafen, sondern wach zu denken. Es wäre eine Art gestörtes Denken, das mit der Freudschen Traumtheorie nichts zu tun hat. Aber etwas später kam mir doch vor, ich hätte ein ähnliches Bild vor mir gehabt, wie eins einmal in der Prager Presse war, einer der Čapeks ein Blumenbeet gießend. Das wäre dann wohl ein Bilddenken, 'sphärisch' in Worte übersetzt." [6.April 1930. Spring—Čapek brothers—Prague—these three words bound together by a seemingly meaningless verb constituted the content of my consciousness upon awaking in the afternoon. The whole time I had thought that I had not been sleeping, but rather had been thinking while awake. It would have been a kind of disordered thought quite different from Freud's theory of dreams. But later it occurred to me that I had had seen a picture before me, similar to one I had seen once in the Prager Presse, of one of the Čapeks watering a bed of flowers. That would be rather a thinking in pictures, "spherically" translated into words.] And: "Nur habe ich das früher durch eine Art Anklingen (assoziativ oder 'sphärisch') zu erklären versucht. Es ist aber wohl so, wie beim Schreiben selbst: wenn aus einer Leitidee Gedanken hervorgehn, die man unmöglich wissen konnte" (*T*, 862). [But in the past I have attempted to explain this as a kind of suggestion (associative or "spherical"). It is, however, the same with writing itself: when ideas arise from out of a main theme, ideas that one could not have anticipated.]

2: Repeatability and Crime

HUMANS BOTH DESIRE AND TIRE of the security and inevitability of *seines-gleichen geschieht* (the selfsame happens) and long for and fear its equally inevitable interruption. This tension is palpable, again and again in seemingly infinite variation, in both the themes and the experimental techniques of Musil's novel. Its complications are expressed only in part by Ulrich's confession to his sister Agathe, "Ich habe auch das unstillbare Streben in mir, die Erlebnisse wiederholbar zu machen. Aber in dem Augenblick, wo sie es sind, ist die Welt materiell und langweilig. Du hast gestern ein Wort gesagt, das mich ergriffen hat: Alles, was wir tun, ist unwiederholbar . . ." (*MoE*, 1645; I also have this irrepressible striving in me to make experiences repeatable. But in the moment when they become repeatable, the world is material and boring. Yesterday you said something that moved me: everything that we do is unrepeatable . . .).

One may agree with Agathe that nothing we do is repeatable. Or one may believe that there is nothing new under the sun, while still believing that human innovation or choice and will can contribute something to the status of reality; or believe that at bottom "*das Ding an sich*" is *a priori* constant but also acknowledge that human subjectivity inhibits a communal agreement on what any given thing is. As is philosophically current, one may argue instead that any seemingly common or shared truth, essence, or experience is nothing but a social construct, invented by the "power elite" to enforce conformity to a value system "privileging" its own interests. From this perspective, repeating patterns are usually seen as outmoded and reactionary conventions, which serve to inhibit new seeing or new ideas. This attitude often results in a contention that everything cancels itself out and/or that the individual cannot be the author(ity) embedded in his or her life, world, or even work of art. Another just as reasonable "next step" to this philosophical stance, however, would be that humans have both the agency and the responsibility to break out of such repeated patterns and create new forms (new metaphors) after their own consciences and evolving ideals. To complicate matters further, still others may contend that certain repeating patterns, like archetypal mythologem, are indeed integrally and continually important to human kind, precisely because their very symbolic nature reminds us of the impossibility of ever actually reducing reality down to a set system or pattern. This sort of repeating pattern raises the question of which myths are genuinely bound to human or even divine experience and which are artificially and arbitrarily embedded into our group consciousness. Indeed, even as the modernists were casting away most comforting crutches of commonality, the primitivism in vogue from the early 1900s on reinstated a sense of a small world, as theorists spoke of "significant form" and the universal language of abstraction, which leaves out details, differences, and specificities that might inhibit common understanding, thereby possibly connecting us to the contemplation of something otherwise inexpressible but possibly universal.[1]

To sum up the positions: repeatability is what we find in nature; it is what we find inside our minds; it is an invented and arbitrary attempt to socialize and delimit imagination; it is the residue of unexamined received ideas; it is the echo of reverberating mythic truths; it is the starting point for experimental reinvigorating of the status quo through art and existential creativity; or it is a means of understanding the ineffable. Put yet another way: repeated forms are tiresome, excruciatingly boring, always the same; or deviations from these necessary constants can be conceived as crimes, crises, aberrations, or possible means of unraveling and rearranging all previously known forms and ideas. Musil entertained most — if not all — of these theories at various moments within the pages of his novel. The first part, *Seinesgleichen geschieht* (the like of it or selfsame now happens/pseudo reality prevails) and the second part *Ins tausendjährige Reich (die Verbrecher)* (Into the millennium (the criminals)), can be seen, respectively, as explorations of the way things repeat themselves (*seinesgleichen geschieht*) and the exceptions (conceptualized as crimes) to repeating or maintaining the status quo. Yet once this approximation is looked at more closely, a secondary question arises. *Which is the crime: the process of forcing individual entities into the (possibly artificial) constructs of repeatable patterns? Or deviating and breaking out of these set structures?*

According to some careful observers (such as Ernst Mach and Friedrich Nietzsche), nothing in nature ever exactly repeats itself. No two things are so like each other that they could be called by the same name or placed in the same category. It is only by leaving out or ignoring differences that we arrive at similarities, concepts, metaphors, categories. It is only by pretending that things and events repeat precisely that we can even begin to give experiences and objects names. As "belief," in Ulrich and Agathe's contention, "cannot be an hour old," all "living" or meaningful entities or states of being are fleeting, eluding definition and denotation, mocking our attempts to describe and contain. The moment we have assigned a name to a feeling, a condition, or a characteristic to a person or a relationship, it has become something else altogether, something we may not even recognize. And yet we proceed, necessarily, as if things and persons and experiences were similar, same, like, predictable; as if they will act and feel and be more or less as they have acted and felt before.

While this necessarily imprecise vision or description of the world as a reassuringly constant (or frustratingly tedious, or mystically archetypal) cycle of repeatability may constitute a sort of crime against science and reason, radical deviations from these repeating patterns and expected cycles constitute another sort of crime or taboo-breaking. This transgression is thematically represented or enacted in Musil's novel by deviations from the norm, "exceptional moments," non-participation (as in the man without qualities), anti-social behavior (incest, forgery of a will, "dropping out" — all committed by the sibling "criminals"); and formally enacted by the novel's inherent resistance to closure, by its "crimes" against linearity, plot structure, and a dependable sense of reality within the fictional world.

Repeatability and crime are relevant terms when we talk about aesthetic questions such as rhythm, dynamics, tempo, harmony, and discord. Yet, again, they are central terms for questions of ethics, action, *laissez-faire* conformity and revolutionary deviation or perversions. Musil's stance as a "Möglichkeitsmensch" (man of possibility) may seem to place him soundly in the camp of existentialist agents of individual creation. But his perspective — based as much on his commitment to scientific principles as on philosophical or mystical and aesthetic presentiments — may actually be surprisingly more like that of Kant, who, as A. N. Wilson explains in his book *God's Funeral*, "was trying to marry the twin truths: namely, that by the very process of perceiving and knowing, we invent our world; and also that this world has a reality of its own."[2] In a note, Musil summarizes the paradox: "Kant: Begriffe ohne Anschauung sind leer. Anschauung ohne Begriff ist blind" (*MoE*, 1820; Kant: Concepts without observation are empty. Observation without concepts is blind). In another formulation he explores the question of how the phenomenological world interacts with the human mind: "In Wahrheit ist das Verhältnis der Aussen- zur Innenwelt nicht das eines Stempels, der in einen empfangenden Stoff sein Bild prägt, sondern das eines Prägstocks, der sich dabei deformiert, so dass sich seine Zeichnung, ohne dass ihr Zusammenhang zerrisse, zu merkwürdig verschiedenen Bildern verändern kann . . ." (*MoE*, 1435; In truth, the relationship between the outer and the inner world is not that of a stamp that presses into a receptive material, but that of an embosser that deforms itself in the process so that its design can be changed into remarkably different pictures without destroying its general coherence). The paradox is also finely stated by Nietzsche, who characterizes the "challenge of every great philosophy": "which, when taken as a whole, always says only: This is the image of all life, and from this learn the meaning of your life! And conversely: Read only your own life, and from this understand the hieroglyphics of universal life."[3] As already discussed, Musil even describes an Ulrich who believes that humans do not create morality but uncover it:

Denn auch das war eine seiner Ansichten, dass die Moral nicht von den Menschen geschaffen wird und mit ihnen wechselt, sondern dass sie geoffenbart wird, dass sie in Zeiten und Zonen entfaltet wird, dass sie geradezu entdeckt werden könne. In diesem Gedanken, der so unzeitgemäss wie zeitgemäss war, drückte sich vielleicht nichts als die Forderung aus, dass auch die Moral eine Moral haben müsse, oder die Erwartung, dass sie sie im Verborgenen habe, und nicht bloss eine sich um sich selbst drehende Klatschgeschichte auf einem bis zum Zusammenbruch kreisenden Planeten sei. (*MoE*, 1413)

[For that too was one of his views, that morality is not made by people and does not change with them but is revealed; that it unfolds in seasons and zones and can actually be discovered. This idea, which was as out of fashion as it was current, expressed perhaps nothing but the demand that morality, too, have a morality, or the expectation that it have one hidden away, and that morality was not simply tittle-tattle revolving on itself on a planet circling to the point of implosion. (*MwQ*, 1534)]

This may, however, indicate more a species of wishful thinking that vainly hopes to salvage meaning for what might really be a planet spinning toward implosion. Perhaps, then, trying to ask whether Musil believed that the mind makes the world or the world the mind, or, to pose the question another way, whether individual subjective experience de-forms or in-forms the basis of reality or our functional human relation to the physical world, is simply the wrong question.[4] As Antonio Porchia wrote, "Not believing has a sickness which is believing a little";[5] and with Musil, and his "friend" and protagonist Ulrich, we would do well to be sensitive to the almost constant fluctuations between the longing for solidity, repeatability, and significance, the fear of flux and meaninglessness, and the dread of monotonous, petrified dead words and experiences. Instead, then, we might look at Musil's observations about and experiments with repeatability, *mutatis mutandis, seinesgleichen geschieht,* and the exceptions and interruptions to these recurring forms, in order to ask the question, not whether or which, but *how*, or by what process, does the human mind negotiate between these two extreme poles. How is the making of art, the writing of a novel, an especially fertile ground for practicing or carrying out this process? How, further, is this larger process repeated in all of our everyday choices, reflections, and impressions?

Significantly, this complex set of questions cannot be answered in a static context, that is, from any single or time-bound perspective. Instead, an understanding of Musil's findings about repeatability, about its positive and negative possibilities and relationship to both art and life, to both aesthetics and ethics, is contingent upon two defining elements. These are the element of time (duration and fleetingness) and an element that I call

"metaphoric transparency," that is, the awareness of the necessarily metaphoric process of perception and description of reality. At one moment,
in one form or context, a metaphor may be a cliché; at another it may be
a tool for new seeing. If seen as durative fact, and not symbol, a repeated
form is rigid and limiting. If understood as metaphor, it is a means to virtually infinite possibility.[6]

A pattern that endures and repeats is usually one that has outlasted
its initial purpose; hence it is relegated to Musil's realm of dead words
or dead thoughts. For it is sure to always mean and be the same thing,
no matter what the circumstances. A pattern that is fleeting, or experimental and not repeatable, is seen as fresh, utopian, creative, and invigorating, and belongs in the realm of living words and living thoughts so
long as it does not try to last: "Worauf es ankommt, das lebendige Wort,
das in die Seele greift: Voll Bedeutung u[nd] Beziehung im Augenblick,
von Wille u[nd] Gefühl umflossen; im nächsten nichtssagend, obgleich
es noch alles sagt, was sein Begriff enthält" (*MoE*, 1645; The point is,
the living word, that takes hold of the soul: filled with meaning and
relationship in the moment, surrounded by will and feeling; in the next
moment saying nothing, although it still says everything that is contained in it conceptually). We might also consider that the living word
and the ecstatic experience it accompanies is a sort of absence of pattern, as it is characterized by a lifting of boundaries and categories, and
by a Dionysian mixing of normally discrete elements. These exceptions,
however, to *seinesgleichen geschieht* also seem to constitute a repeating
pattern of their own. That pattern is dependably one wherein distinct
patterns that have already been accepted are dissolved. They are, in a
sense, un-moored moods, wherein the usual securities of definition and
category are suspended or dissolved, but others are temporarily played
with, arranged, and imagined.

In order to describe his Other Condition Musil thus gathers together
examples of what Martin Buber, in his famous and popular anthology of
eclectic mystical testimonials, called "Ecstatic Confessions," finding their
commonalities. Musil moves beyond even Buber's mix of Eastern, Western, Sufi, Christian, Judaic, Protestant, and Buddhist mysticisms, associating these similar but also distinct narratives with other examples of such
experiences from the realms of madness, child psychology, love, creative
states, patriotism, war, the experience of art, nature enthusiasm, primitive
ritual, ancient magic, Dionysian *ecstasis*, and more. While some may disap-
prove of such imprecise miscegenation of different cultures and concepts,
especially under the hand of a writer and thinker valued for his precision
and scientific accuracy, this "leaving out" of differences to arrive at a commonality or abstracted formal likeness is, of course, a necessary compo-
nent of the metaphoric process. Finding commonality or correspondence
between disparate entities, ideas, or images is precisely the criminal act of

metaphor-making — an act whose processes and potentials are explicitly explained and modeled by Musil in his notes and novel.

Associated with these *other conditions* of experience are those other types of anciently repeating patterns (mythologems, archetypes) that recur along recognizable lines (that is, Isis and Osiris as outline of brother and sister union; crime as holy ritual; naming as power and danger; conversion experience, eternal recurrence, and so on). These mythologems or archetypes are to be found repeatedly in Buber's *Ecstatic Confessions*, along with the more personal and individual experiences described by the mystics, and Musil finds them in his studies of mental illness, love, primitive magic, social movements, nature mysticism, and art as well. They somehow seem not to lose their freshness and significance, perhaps because of the consciousness that they are to be understood as symbols (via metaphoric transparency). They invite infinite interpretation and they do not pretend to be substitutes for reality, remaining instead durative images or stories for contemplation and reverberating echo. These patterns may also endure by virtue of the action of the motif: "Motiv," Musil writes, "ist, was mich von Bedeutung zu Bedeutung führt. Es geschieht etwas oder es wird etwas gesagt, und das vermehrt den Sinn zweier Menschenleben und verbindet sie durch den Sinn" (*MoE*, 1425; motif is what leads me from significance to significance. Something happens, or something is said, and that increases the meaning of two human lives and unites them through its meaning, *MwQ*, 1718). It recurs in different shapes, in infinite forms that share certain common themes or cores, which, however, by virtue of their changing, underline, rather than obscure, their symbolic nature and, along with this, the symbolic nature of all attempts to define and represent reality.

A posthumous early essay of Nietzsche's, "Über Wahrheit und Lüge im außermoralischen Sinn" (On truth and lying in a non-moral sense), seems to clearly elucidate the theory of metaphoric deviation and repeatability expressed in *The Man without Qualities*. This essay, which passages in Musil's novel explicitly echo in both concept and phraseology, describes Nietzsche's genealogy of the human development of values, as a belief that all knowledge and representation of the world is metaphoric. Truth, he writes, "is a mobile army of metaphors, metonymies, anthropomorphisms, in short a sum of human relations which have been subjected to poetic and rhetorical intensifications, translation, and decoration."[7] Humans are constantly creating reality, constantly constructing edifices of concepts upon which really airy unstable things we foolishly rest our lives. Nietzsche writes:

> Let us consider in particular how concepts are formed; each word immediately becomes a concept, not by virtue of the fact that it is intended to serve as a memory (say) of the unique, utterly individualized, primary experience to which it owes its existence, but because

at the same time it must fit countless other, more or less similar cases, i.e. cases which, strictly speaking, are never equivalent, and thus nothing other than non-equivalent cases. *Every concept comes into being by making equivalent that which is non-equivalent.*[8]

He then gives the example of the concept of leaf, "which is formed by dropping the individual differences" between one leaf and another, and points out that the word "snake" only designates one of the snake's attributes, leaving out many other important characteristics, and could just as easily be used to describe a worm, whose movements also "snake." Thus all words, when they are taken as absolute descriptions and not metaphors, are confining categorizations which threaten to limit our understanding and perception of individual objects or ideas. We use words to describe the world to ourselves and each other. Inasmuch as these words dissolve rather than illuminate differences, language becomes a force of depersonalization and conformity. As Musil laments,

> Das Leben wurde immer gleichförmiger und unpersönlicher. In alle Vergnügungen, Erregungen, Erholungen, ja selbst in die Leidenschaften drang etwas Typenhaftes, Mechanisches, Statistisches, Reihenweises ein. . . . Der Kunstwille war sich schon selbst beinahe verdächtig geworden. (*MoE,* 1093)

> [Life was becoming more and more homogeneous and impersonal. Something mechanical, stereotypical, statistical, and serial was insinuating itself into every entertainment, excitement, recreation, even into the passions. . . . The will to art had already become more or less suspicious. (*MwQ,* 1189)]

This conforming, mechanizing, force is, of course, related to the problem of being "without qualities," a "*Zeitkrankheit*" (an illness of the times) which, like metaphor and pattern, can be both a formula for atrophying and losing of individuality and creativity, *or* a possibility, an openness that allows for infinite variations. The language crisis of the turn of the last century, characterized by Hofmannsthal's "Lord Chandos Letter," by philosophical skepticism about the relationship between words and the things they purported to signify, tended to place language under suspicious scrutiny, often culminating in a judgment of wholesale bankruptcy of language's ability to communicate, express, or bridge the hopelessly subjective idiolect of each individual mind.[9] At the same time, however, modernist authors, Musil in the forefront, were actively working to reenergize this suspect language. Writers and artists used the non-didactive aesthetic means at their disposal to effectively communicate subjective experience, all-too-literal, non-transferable ideas and experiences, via metaphor, image, and formal arrangement. Language can, and all too

often does, enable clichéd seeing, and, indeed, a realization of the distance between words and "true" things (whatever those might be) often
does create a sense of disturbance or existential nausea. Yet it is also the
case, despite alienation and clear-seeing, that language has the capacity to
be one of the most powerful existentially charged means of reestablishing
a sense of oneness with the world and some sense of meaning. Why else
does Sartre's Roquentin decide that his only possible path to a purposeful
life lies in writing a novel? Why else does Ulrich lay out his possibilities
similarly under the trio: suicide, going to war, writing books?

All too often Nietzsche's epigones seem to have listened to only the
first part of his message, and are so excited by the destruction of values
and traditions and the thrill of the imminent abyss that they do not stay
long enough to take in the all-important next step after the iconoclastic
orgy. After the idols are smashed, Nietzsche encourages us to create more
forms — forms that, as long as we constantly remind ourselves that we
have created them ourselves, do not become idols but are, nevertheless,
beautiful and meaningful in their very affirmation of creative energy.

While our vision of the world as solid and fixed is, according to
Nietzsche, a devolution, on the one hand, from fruitful conscious
metaphor-making to forgetful and rigid concept acceptance or *idées
reçues*, he emphatically celebrates the persistence of artistic re-forming
and reinventing of living metaphors that are irrepressibly at odds with
the con-forming, atrophying tendency of comfort-seeking society. This
creative work is — more than the deconstructing necessary before the
lifetime of rebuilding — the point of Nietzsche's critique of truth and
lying. Another significant parallel to this theme is Oscar Wilde's essay
"The Decay of Lying," which celebrates the artistic lie within the context of the reign of naturalism and realism. Artistic lying becomes, in
Wilde's hands, a form of higher truth-telling, insofar as it subtly undermines the credibility of so-called truth by its emphasis on perception,
imagination, and subjectivity. Thus one of the artist's tasks is to expand
our seeing of individual objects or experiences by deliberately dissolving
the boundaries or limitations of dead words or designations. As Proust's
narrator declares while speaking of Elstir's paintings in *Remembrance*,
he was able to discern that

> the charm of each of [the seascapes] lay in a sort of metamorpho-
> sis of the objects represented, analogous to what in poetry we call
> metaphor, and that, if God the Father had created things by nam-
> ing them, it was by taking away their names or giving them other
> names that Elstir created them anew. The names which designate
> things correspond invariably to an intellectual notion, alien to our
> true impression, and compelling us to eliminate from them every-
> thing that is not in keeping with that notion.[10]

REPEATABILITY AND CRIME ♦ 57

Emerson, in his journal, writes similarly of how language, specifically naming, emphasizes at will various attributes of reality:

The metamorphosis of nature shows itself in nothing more than this; that there is no word in our language that cannot become typical to us of nature by giving it emphasis. The world is a Dancer; it is a Rosary; it is a Torrent; it is a Boat, a Mist, a Spider's Snare; it is what you will; and the metaphor will hold. . . . Swifter than light, the world transforms itself into that thing you name.[11]

While language can indeed work to obscure the very large gap between things and words, it can also bring that distance into fruitful relief. This more positive process is the part that informs Musil's life's work as a "*Wort-macher*" (word-maker)[12] and leads him to employ the designation Vinzenz, in Musil's farce, uses to describe his career and the creative aspect of naming described by Emerson. A word-maker, emphatically not a person who uses words already made by others, is explicitly engaged in the modernist project of reclaiming language for meaningful use. New repeating patterns are needed, new patterns that call attention to the fact that they are not to be "taken at their word," or literally, but that they are provisional, changing, never meaning exactly the same thing to all people at all times. As Musil writes, "Gott meint die Welt keineswegs wörtlich" (*MoE*, 570; God doesn't mean the world literally at all, *MwQ*, 388), which in no way necessarily devalues the world.

In his essay "The Poet," Emerson makes a distinction between the mystic, who nails a symbol to one meaning, and a poet, who knows that every sensuous fact (that is, empirically perceived element of the physical world) has multiple meanings. The "poet," in other words, knows that each individual thing can be described by a multitude of words and each word can be said to describe a multitude of things. Ulrich explains to an advice-seeking Diotima that the process of metaphor-making, described elsewhere by Proust as "eliminating from [things] everything that is not in keeping with" a chosen notion,[13] is, indeed, the basis of literature. But, he continues, it may not be a dependable way to understand the world or how we should live, or, rather, it cannot be read as a system with consistent results in every situation:

"Haben Sie schon ja einen Hund gesehen?"fragte er. "Das glauben Sie bloss! Sie haben immer nur etwas gesehen, das Ihnen mit mehr oder weniger Recht als ein Hund vorkam. Es hat nicht alle Hundeeigenschaften, und irgendetwas Persönliches hat es, das wieder kein anderer Hund hat. *Wie sollen wir da je im Leben 'das Richtige' tun?*" (*MoE*, 572, emphasis mine)

["Have you ever seen a dog?" he asked. "You only think you have. What you see is only something you feel more or less justified in regarding as a dog. It isn't a dog in every respect, and always has some personal quality no other dog has. *So how can we ever hope, in this life, to do 'the right thing'?"* (Emphasis mine, *MwQ*, 624)]

This surprising juxtaposition of an analysis of language with a question of right conduct is a flagrant revelation: form, words, and their relationship to our perception and our modes of expression have everything to do with ethics. As Musil repeatedly notes: aesthetics and ethics are one. The seemingly harmless process of synecdoche, taking the part for the whole or the whole for the part, is thus oddly inhibiting to discovering a right conduct of life — "how can we ever hope, in this life, to do 'the right thing'?" — because we can never know, by observing generalizations, what will be the most important element in a particular case. Ulrich continues:

> Oder man findet gewisse Steine und nennt sie wegen der ihnen gemeinsamen Eigenschaften Diamant . . . Alles hat Teil am Allgemeinen, und noch dazu ist es besonders. Alles ist wahr und noch dazu ist es wild und mit nichts vergleichbar. Das kommt mir so vor, als ob das Persönliche eines beliebigen Geschöpfes gerade das wäre, was mit nichts anderem übereinstimmt. (*MoE*, 572)
>
> [Or else you find certain stones, and because of the properties they have in common they are all regarded as diamonds . . . Everything partakes of the universal and also has something special all its own. Everything is both true to type and is in a category all its own, simultaneously. The personal quality of any given creature is precisely that which doesn't coincide with anything else. (*MwQ*, 624)]

Further, he compares the process to that of literature reception and literature construction. When you read, he tells his cousin: "Ihre Auffassung lässt aus, was Ihnen nicht passt. Das gleiche hat schon der Autor getan" (*MoE*, 573; You leave out whatever doesn't suit you. As the author himself has done before you, *MwQ*, 625). Moving back and forth from literature to life (ironically on another level as well, since the conversation takes place within a work of literature), he concludes, saying: "Wenn wir also, wie ich gesagt habe, in der Dichtung einfach auslassen, was uns nicht passt, so tun wir damit nichts anderes, als dass wir den ursprünglichen Zustand des Lebens wiederherstellen" (*MoE*, 574; when we simply leave out in art whatever doesn't suit our conceptions, we're merely going back to the original condition of life itself, *MwQ*, 627). He adds that this process is true for all the concepts "auf die wir unser Leben stützen . . ." (*MoE*, 574; on which we base our lives, *MwQ*, 627). All these concepts, he writes, "sind nichts als erstarren gelassene Gleichnisse" (are no more than congealed metaphors, *MwQ*, 626). "Congealed metaphors" are certainly cousin to what Nietzsche calls in his essay the "residue of metaphors," warning that "the fact that a metaphor becomes hard and rigid is absolutely no guarantee of the necessary and exclusive justification of that metaphor."[14]

In precisely a "moment" within *The Man without Qualities*, wherein two concepts, "Gewalt und Liebe für Ulrich wieder nicht ganz die gewöhnlichen Begriffe [haben] (*MoE*, 591; violence and love do not have quite their conventional meaning, *MwQ*, 645), it occurs to Ulrich that "das Leben — zum Platzen voll Einbildung auf sein Hier und Jetzt, letzten Endes aber ein sehr ungewisser, ja ausgesprochen unwirklicher Zustand! — sich in die paar Dutzend Kuchenformen stürzt, aus denen die Wirklichkeit besteht" (*MoE*, 591; life — bursting with conceit over its here-and-now but really a most uncertain, even a downright unreal condition — pours itself headlong into the few dozen cake molds of which reality consists, *MwQ*, 645). The fact that two concepts temporarily lose their conventional meaning here, and that they do this *within a moment*, is another reflection of the fruitful and extratemporal nature of some types of metaphor. Paradoxically, the insight that is born is that metaphor can be reductive as well as rich in possibilities. These few dozen molds, which constitute one way in which people and authors metaphorically translate reality, are clearly somewhat restrictive; they seem to limit rather than expand imagination and, by association, the possibilities of literature and life. We have to differentiate however, between these "congealed metaphors," which Ulrich mocked in his discussion with Diotima, metaphors that are more like clichés or tired concepts, and another fresher, more immediate species of newly minted juxtapositions.

Proust's narrator, Marcel, famously, in the waiting room at the Guermante's mansion, is inundated repeatedly by a series of metaphoric correspondences and sense-memories (paving stones, clanking spoons, textures of cloth) that make him believe for the first time that he can write. Marcel notes the sudden transmutation from real world to the realm of fairy tale after wiping his mouth with a napkin that reminds him of a towel from his past life: "Immediately, like the character in The Arabian Nights who unwittingly performs precisely the rite that calls up before him, visible to his eyes alone, a docile genie, ready to transport him far away, a fresh vision of azure blue passed before my eyes. . . ."[15]

The sudden perception of a fresh correspondence between two separate entities transports Proust's narrator — and Ulrich as well —from their present time-bound world into the extra-temporal like magic. Such correspondence cannot, according to both theorists of metaphor, be bidden, it cannot be logically prepared for, but when it comes, it comes with a beatific force that temporarily blots out everything else. While there may be only limited petrified realities (heavy and fixed as stone) or formal arrangements invented out of the pragmatic necessity of the pursuance of normal life and the continuation of some semblance of narrative, there seem to be infinite possibilities for the extra-temporal legerdemain of metaphoric displacement — to effortlessly topple centuries of tradition, discombobulate time lines, or to magically translate a dreamer from a post-First World War Parisian drawing room to a hovering trans-historical magic carpet.

Metaphor— the act of making equivalent that which is not equivalent — is a sort of category mistake, a deviation. More importantly for the creation and valuation of literature, metaphor, as Paul Ricoeur writes, "bears information because it 'redescribes' reality." "Thus," he continues, "the category mistake is the de-constructive intermediary phase between the description and the redescription."[16] Metaphor, in other words, being inherent in the creation of any fictional world, involves a critique of the "real" world as prerequisite to a redescription. The destruction (as with Nietzsche) is, however, only the preliminary to re-creation. By connecting Ricoeur's work on metaphor with his work on narrative and time, we may note that fictional time, in his conception, is a metaphoric redescription of cosmological and historical time, which explores "the resources of phenomenological time that are left unexploited or are inhibited by historical narrative . . . These hidden resources of phenomenological time," Ricoeur continues, "and the aporias which their discovery gives rise to, form the secret bond between the two modalities of narrative [fictive and historical]. Fiction," he concludes, "is a treasure trove of imaginative variations applied to the theme of phenomenological time and its aporias."[17]

While all novels thus bear a metaphoric relationship (as imaginative variation) with reality, in *The Man without Qualities* and in *Remembrance of Things Past* we are presented with more than just two simple or self-contained redescriptions of the world. In addition to performing the normal metaphorical function vis-à-vis reality, metaphor in these works takes on a more specialized role, that of presenting further imaginative variations to the basic imaginative variation of each fictional world itself. This multiple undoing reflects strikingly back upon life from the realm of literature by its explicit questioning of all attempts to make order and to tell stories in a strictly linear order. As Musil wrote in response to a criticism leveled against the relative plotlessness of his novel, "Das Problem: wie komme ich zum Erzählen, ist sowohl mein stilistisches wie das Lebensproblem der Hauptfigur . . ." (The problem: how shall I come to narration, is as much my stylistic problem as it is the life problem of the main character).[18] Both novels wage their own wars on normal reality: Ulrich, when asked what he would do if he could rule the world for the day, announces, "Es würde mir wohl nichts übrigbleiben, als die Wirklichkeit abzuschaffen!" (*MoE*, 289; I suppose I would have no choice but to abolish reality, *MwQ*, 312); Marcel, for his part, declares that art alone can reveal to us "our life, life as it really is, life disclosed and at last made clear, consequently the only life that is really lived. . . ."[19]

Metaphoric thinking is thus an alternative to what Ulrich describes as longing for

die einfache Reihenfolge, die Abbildung der überwältigenden Mannigfaltigkeit des Lebens in einer eindimensionalen, wie ein Mathematiker sagen würde, was uns beruhigt; die Aufreihung alles dessen, was in Raum und Zeit geschehen ist, auf einen Faden, eben jenen berühmten "Faden der Erzählung," aus dem nun also auch der Lebensfaden besteht. (*MoE*, 650)

[the simple sequence of events in which the overwhelmingly manifold nature of things is represented, in a unidimensional order, as a mathematician would say, stringing all that has occurred in space and time on a single thread, which calms us; that celebrated "thread of the story," which is, it seems, the thread of life itself. (*MwQ,* 709)]

Although, he continues to muse, people love the illusion of this logical ordering of cause and effect, and look to it "im Chaos geborgen" (as their refuge from chaos), he notes that "ihm dieses primitiv Epische abhanden gekommen sei, woran das private Leben noch festhält, obgleich öffentlich alles schon unerzählerisch geworden ist und nicht einem 'Faden' mehr folgt, sondern sich in einer unendlich verwobenen Fläche ausbreitet" (*MoE*, 650; he had lost this elementary, narrative mode of thought to which private life still clings, even though everything in public life has already ceased to be narrative and no longer follows a thread, but instead spreads out as an infinitely interwoven surface, *MwQ,* 709). In a modernist novel that has lost that "elementary, narrative mode," one can see the function of metaphor as the creation of an almost infinite number of expanding thought moments, decentralized, non-repeating nodes, within the "infinitely interwoven surface," which assert convincing alternatives to the comforting illusion of the "thread of the story."

In an early *Diary* sketch from somewhere between 1899 and 1904, Musil, echoing in subject and some central phraseology Dostoevsky's underground man, imagines walking onto the street, among "Lauter 2x2 Menschen" (nothing but 2 x 2 people) and asking one of them, "Bitte was ist eine Strasse?" (Excuse me, what is a street?). The answer: "Strasse — Strasse, Schluss, bitte stören Sie mich nicht weiter" (Street — street, period, please don't disturb me any further).[20] In Dostoevsky's earlier version, we find the underground man introducing the 2x2=4 motif, which continues to be essential throughout his rave, and beginning, but never developing, the example of not a street but a wall:

"Upon my word," they will shout at you, "it is no use protesting: it is a case of twice two makes four! Nature does not ask your permission, she has nothing to do with your wishes, and whether you like her laws or dislike them, you are bound to accept her as she is, and consequently all her conclusions. A wall, you see, is a wall . . . and so on, and so on."[21]

Musil takes the discussion further into the realm of metaphor, as if he were speaking to the same pedestrians as the underground man:

> Aha Strasse [die Leute sagen] etwas gerades, taghelles, dient um sich darauf fortzubewegen. Und Sie empfinden plötzlich ein kolossales Überlegenheitsgefühl, wie ein Hellsehender unter Blinden. Sie sagen sich: Ich weiß ganz bestimmt, dass eine Strasse nichts gerades taghelles ist, sondern dass sie vergleichsweise [ebensogut] etwas Vielverzweigtes, Geheimnis- und Räthselvolles ist [sein kann], mit Fallgruben und unterirdischen Gängen, versteckten Kerkern und vergrabenen Kirchen. (*T*, 9)

> [Aha street [the people say] something straight, day-bright, serves for moving oneself along on. And you immediately experience a colossal sense of superiority, like a [clear-seer] visionary among the blind. You say to yourself: I know most certainly that a street is not something straight and day-bright, but rather that it [can just as well be] in comparison something with multiple branches, filled with secrets and riddles, with traps and underground passageways, hidden prisons and buried churches.]

The narrator continues with an explanation of why the first person addressed in this sketch sees differently from the 2x2=4 people, concluding that:

> Zieht das Auge der Andern die Erscheinungen zu geläufigen Begriffen zusammen, seinem Bedürfnis nach Messbarem folgend, so zerstreut das Ihrige, löst, kraft der gewonnenen Erfahrungen, in *Unwägbares . . . Ungreifbares* auf. Bei allen Dingen sehen Sie über die Form hinweg, in die gekleidet sie erscheinen und wittern die geheimnisvollen Vorgänge einer Hinterexistenz. (*T*, 9)

> [While the eye of the others brings all appearances together under common concepts, following its need for the measurable, yours disperses, dissolves, by virtue of its earned experiences, into *the imponderable . . . the ungraspable*. In all things you see beyond the form in which it is disguised and sense the mysterious happenings of a hidden existence.]

The "clear-seer" or visionary recognizes, in other words, that behind the varied forms (words and images) in which things and ideas are "clothed" there is some other mysterious existence, an existence that, as suggested by the imagery he uses, is dark, underground, many-branching, subconscious, and somehow threatening to the "day-bright" security of the 2x2=4 people.

The experience of metaphor can help a person discover a conduct of life or the right way to live, but only by encouraging him to rediscover and reinvent, rather than to return to previous already used findings or definitions from some other situation. Still, even a daring seeker like Ulrich may occasionally crave the temporary harmony of designations and words, just as Agathe, in a moment of extreme disconnection from everyday reality craves the security of her brother's pocket watch.[22] One draft chapter demonstrates how returning the names, or finding the right names for things, in this case flowers, is also a powerful magical process, a process that seems to save Ulrich from a temporarily terrifying infinity by ordering (albeit arbitrarily and temporarily) the world into categories:

> Wenn Ulrich eine Blüte betrachtete — was nicht gerade eine alte Gewohnheit des einstmals Ungeduldigen war —, so fand er jetzt manchmal des Ansehens kein Ende und, um alles zu sagen, auch keinen Anfang. Wusste er zufällig den Namen zu nennen, so war es Rettung aus dem Meere der Unendlichkeit. Dann bedeuteten die goldenen Sternchen auf einer nackten Gerte "Goldbecher," und jene frühreifen Blätter und Dolden waren "Flieder." Kannte er den Namen aber nicht, so rief er wohl auch den Gärtner herbei, denn dann nannte dieser alte Mann einen unbekannten Namen, und alles kam wieder in Ordnung, und der uralte Zauber, dass der Besitz des richtigen Wortes Schutz vor der ungezähmten Wildheit der Dinge gewährt, erwies seine beruhigende Macht wie vor Zehntausenden Jahren. (*MoE*, 1088)

> [When Ulrich looked at a blossom — which was not exactly an ingrained habit of this once impatient man — he now sometimes found no end to contemplation and, to say it all, no beginning either. If by chance he could name it, it was a redemption from the sea of infinity. Then the little golden stars on a bare cane signified "forsythia," and those early leaves and umbels "lilacs." But if he did not know the name he would call the gardener over, for then this old man would name an unknown name and everything was all right again, and the primordial magic by which possession of the correct name bestows protection from the untamed wildness of things demonstrated its calming power as it had ten thousand years ago. (*MwQ*, 1183)]

Repeating, categorization, naming, is thus salvation from the terror of the possibility of nothingness and randomness, related to Apollo's role as orderer, as a veil through which we may safely look at the true Dionysian chaos. Exceptions to the repeating patterns, like Dionysian union, the dissolution of the boundaries between persons and objects, can thus be seen as moments when the rigid and artificial differentiation between things has been temporarily lifted. We name and categorize in order to keep at bay the realization that we cannot really ever definitively know the world. Or, alternately, if we create repeating patterns and use names and words in a way that explicitly engages in a consciousness of metaphoric transparency, we remain aware of the provisional symbolic nature of human perception and description of reality. Out of this awareness we unravel and reweave the possibilities for meaning(s) and human experience. As such, art's role is, in part, to plumb the depths of this meaning and meaninglessness, constantly asking questions about received representations and positing ever-new narratives.

If we remain unmoved by the investigations of art, metaphysics, and aesthetic experience as explorations of reality, relegating these experiments to the realm of frivolous play or entertainment or — perhaps more damagingly — to the realm of dry scholarly non-attachment, it is probably out of a fear of facing up to the abyss of the probable errors upon which all of our daily requirements and assumptions are based. If there is nothing behind it all, if there is no purpose or truth, or ultimate form, then we don't want to know. If there is, we also do not want to know, because it would most likely mean changing our lives entirely. As Ulrich notes, the "primitive Forderungen der Realität [sind] nicht im Einklang mit den luftigen Konsequenzen der Moral" (*MoE*, 1858; primitive requirements of reality [are] not in harmony with the airy consequences of morality). So Ulrich asks himself whether the history of the rise and fall of civilizations, fashions, and inventions might be nothing more than

> ein Herausklettern aus dem Nichts, jedesmal nach einer anderen Seite versucht . . . die Unruhe eines Mannes, der sich bis zu den Knien aus einem Grab herausschaufelt, dem er doch niemals entrinnen wird, eines Wesens, das niemals ganz dem Nichts entsteigt, sich angstvoll in Gestalten wirft, aber an irgend einer geheimen Stelle, die es selbst kaum ahnt, hinfällig und Nichts ist?" (*MoE*, 1745)

> [a climbing up out of nothingness, each attempt on a different wall? . . . the restlessness of a man shoveling himself down to his knees out of a grave he will never escape, a being that will never entirely climb out of nothingness, who fearfully flings himself into shapes but is, in some secret place that he is hardly aware of himself, vulnerable and nothing? (*MwQ*, 1557–58)]

To fearfully fling one's self into shapes, or to pour one's self into "the two dozen cake forms" of which life is made, is presumably an attempt to escape infinity, circularity, or the possibility of purposelessness. Like Nietzsche's Madman who careens through the streets, where his fellow humans are blithely snickering at the death of God, not perceiving the cataclysmic shock waves of the massive still-unfathomed transformation of society, Musil is still grappling with the psychic consequences of humans having wiped away the horizon (of values, of God, of common truth), and observing the process by which humans must create limitations for themselves in order not to go mad.

The escape into form may, however, be the only possible answer to the question of meaning: the world and existence, as Nietzsche repeats, are only justified as an aesthetic phenomenon. Musil notes:

> Bereits im Vorwort an Richard Wagner [in *The Birth of Tragedy*] wird die Kunst — und nicht die Moral — als die eigentliche metaphysische Tätigkeit des Menschen hingestellt; im Buch selbst kehrt der anzügliche Satz mehrfach wieder, dass nur als ein ästhetisches Phänomen das Dasein der Welt gerechtfertigt ist. (*MoE*, 1779)

> [In the Preface [to *The Birth of Tragedy*] addressed to Richard Wagner, art — and not morality — is already posited as the real metaphysical activity of mankind; in the book itself, the pertinent sentence that the existence of the world is justified only as an aesthetic phenomenon recurs several times. (*MwQ*, 1583)]

This "aesthetic," connoting both the sensory and the artistic, speaks to the difficulty or impossibility of making direct contact with either the world as it is or a viable explanation of the world (either morally or rationally). As such, it should not be a surprise when Musil writes that "Schönheit oder Erregung kommt in die Welt, indem man fortlässt" (*MoE*, 573; by leaving things out, we bring beauty and excitement into the world, *MwQ*, 635) — by precisely the process that he criticizes as imprecise. Proust's definition of Beauty, provided in a letter to Madame de Noailles, describes this optical illusion similarly: "It's a kind of blending," he writes, "a transparent unity in which all things, having lost their initial aspect as things, have lined up beside each other in a sort of order, are instilled with the same light and are seen within each other. I suppose," he concludes, "this is what is called the gloss of the old masters."[23] And, in *Remembrance*, the narrator admits the necessary reduction and abstraction that takes place in the translation of reality into fiction, confessing that he has reduced the whole environs of Combray to a few outlines, "like the decor one sees prescribed on the title page of an old play, for its performance in the provinces." "As though," he continues, "all of Combray had consisted of but two floors joined by a slender staircase, and as though there had been no time there but seven o'clock."[24]

While selecting is imprecise, or even irrational, it has the potential to serve a higher purpose. As Ulrich says, "Jede Ordnung ist irgendwie absurd und wachsfigurenhaft, wenn man sie zu ernst nimmt, jedes Ding ist ein erstarrter Einzelfall seiner Möglichkeiten. Aber das sind nicht Zweifel, sondern es ist eine bewegte, elastische Unbestimmtheit, die sich zu allem fähig fühlt" (*MoE*, 1509; Every order is somewhat absurd and like a wax figure if one takes it too seriously; each thing is a petrified singular case of its possibilities. But that is not doubt, but a moving, elastic uncertainty that feels itself capable of everything). Once the horizon is wiped away with a sponge, in other words, one may turn either to nihilism and doubt, on the one hand, or to a creative possibility that feels itself "capable of everything."

This "moving, elastic uncertainty" is the other, the fruitful side of the metaphorical process. While, according to Nietzsche, humans are

> not defeated, indeed hardly even tamed, by the process whereby a regular and rigid new world is built from its own sublimated products — concepts — in order to imprison it in a fortress. The drive seeks out a channel and new area for its activity, and finds it in myth and art generally. It constantly confuses the cells and the classifications of concepts by setting up new translations, metaphors, metonymies; it constantly manifests the desire to shape the given world of the waking human being in ways that are just as multiform, irregular, inconsequential, incoherent, charming and ever-new; as things are in the world of dream. Actually, the waking human being is only clear about the fact that he is awake thanks to the rigid and regular web of concepts, and for that reason he sometimes comes to believe that he is dreaming if once that web of concepts is torn apart by art.[25]

This process of waking up the consciousness to the fact that we are dreaming is described by Ulrich as the "tear in the paper" of normal experiencing that makes us aware that our usual relationships with and designations of things are insufficient or even misrepresentative. When the illusion of the paper or smooth surface of reality is temporarily torn, the names of things, the boundaries that separate them from each other, dissolve and allow one to see through the *"Bildfläche"* (pictorial plane) that usually masquerades as reality. In such a mood,

> Du kannst nicht einmal mehr die Worte grasen oder weiden bilden, weil dazu eine Menge zweckvoller, nützlicher Vorstellungen gehört, die du auf einmal verloren hast. Was auf der Bildfläche bleibt, könnte man am ehesten ein Gewoge von Empfindungen nennen, das sich hebt und sinkt oder atmet und gleisst, als ob es ohne Umrisse das ganze Gesichtsfeld ausfüllte. Natürlich sind darin auch noch unzählige einzelne Wahrnehmungen enthalten, Farben, Hörner, Bewegungen, Gerüche und alles, was zur Wirklichkeit gehört: aber das wird bereits nicht mehr anerkannt, wenn es auch noch erkannt werden sollte. Ich möchte sagen: die Einzelheiten besitzen nicht mehr ihren Egoismus, durch den sie unsere Aufmerksamkeit in Anspruch nehmen, sondern sie sind geschwisterlich und im wörtlichen Sinn "innig" untereinander verbunden. Und natürlich ist auch

keine "Bildfläche" mehr da, sondern irgendwie geht alles grenzenlos in dich über. (*MoE*, 762)

[You can't even form the word "grazing," because a host of purposeful, practical connotations go along with it, which you have suddenly lost. What is left on the pictorial plane might best be called an ocean swell of sensations that rises and falls, breathes and shimmers, as though it filled your whole field of view without a horizon. Of course there are still countless individual perceptions contained within it: colors, horns, movements, smells, and all the details of reality; but none of them are acknowledged any longer, even if they should still be recognized. Let me put it this way: the details no longer have their egoism, which they use to capture our attention, but they are all linked with each other in a familiar, literally "inward" way. And of course the "pictorial plane" is no longer there either; but everything somehow flows over into you, all boundaries are gone. (*MwQ*, 827)]

What is counterintuitive about this break, tear, exception, is that it seems to reveal a world more in harmony with itself, and enable a relationship of perceiver and world more fluid and unified than normal. The exceptions to arbitrary repeating patterns, enabled here by the separation of things from their names or limiting designations, may be glimpses into what is "really real," either by virtue of a patternless boundary-lessness that terrifies because of its limitlessness, or by allowing us ingress into states of being or vision that threaten to unravel and devalue our everyday concerns to such an extent that we must ignore or trivialize them in order to function in the "real" world.

Without subscribing to the Platonic school of Essences or absolute Goodness, Truth and Beauty, even Existentialist thinkers may speak of an attention to what is "essential" in the sense of important or fundamental rather than *a priori* determined (knowledge of death, Time, limitation, choice, self-responsibility, aesthetic or mystical experience, ethics). This essential is functionally at odds with the norming pattern of oblivious worldliness and social expectations. To pay attention to such things may be allowed on Sundays or on short holidays, but to take, as Ulrich does, a "vacation from life" in order to discover "the right life," or attempt to live life "like the character in a book," removing the "fatty tissue" and doing only what is absolutely "motivated" or essential, is clearly anti-social. While the bourgeois may appreciate art on his "days off," the devotion and commitment necessary for the artist to create is certainly borderline insane. Art, if it is not considered entertainment or frivolous, can shatter the glass, tear the paper, or as Nietzsche writes, tear the web of concepts, that rigid "columbarium" or "burial place of perception" through which we usually comfortably see a reality rigidly diagrammed into categories and definitions.[26] Paradoxically though, as is becoming increasingly clear here, art-making consists almost by definition in making (and unmaking) such patterns. As such, the existentialist and his seeming opposite, the transcendentalist, are both "fools in the eyes of the world," whose choices, actions, lack of action, and utterances are exceptions, and when effective, obstructions to the mindless flow of progress of *seinesgleichen geschieht*. The question of repeated patterns (as predetermined essence, rigid but random habits, or actively created experimentations) cannot be reduced for Musil to any strict dualistic system such as metaphysical vs. materialistic. He allows for both kinds (as do his luminaries Nietzsche, Emerson, and Dostoevsky), aware of their necessity and differing functions in human perception and activity. But the exceptional and deviating patterns (motifs, interruptions, recurring ruminations) are clearly the favored ones for Musil, just as the Dionysian lifting of distinctions is, for Nietzsche, the more essential state, which the Apollonian order seems to merely serve or make possible. The exceptional states are amenable to an openness of interpretation, a "possibility sense," and, above all, a fluid, shifting, creative interaction with received or ancient patterns that continually eschews petrification and the congealing of any given metaphoric description of "reality." The Other Condition, in its usual role as container of coincidence of opposites, embraces both sides of this tension, temporarily suspending the flow of normal moments to enable the creative and self-generative contact with whatever it is that is eternal, without being bound by it.

The transcendentalist rejects the unconsidered patterns of received tradition (morals, religion, social customs) as a means to return to what are deemed more essential patterns or core truths. This is actually not so different from what existentialist philosophy encourages. The existentialist credo, "existence precedes essence" is, in this sense, a temporal disordering that does not necessarily cancel out the possibility of essence (in the sense of central or first things). It allows for such essentiality only as it is *metastable* (to use Sartre's word for this species of constant ethical changing), only as it responds to and reinvents itself from the ever-new creative energy — the primary existence — of the individual.

Any form, once it loses its freshness and forgets that it is only a metaphor, becomes a cliché, a congealed dead thing, a received custom, a social or aesthetic convention; in short, a very undesirable and reactionary sort of soporific. In a scene already described above, Ulrich confronts the beauty of an old church and with it the tension between petrified forms, traditions, definitions, and the creative energy of a fluid force he calls "mist." He delineates two sorts of metaphors whereby we creatively de- and re-construct the fixed meanings and historical course of the world: "Nebel" (mist) and "Erstarren" (petrifact) (*MoE*, 132; *MwQ*, 139). Ulrich models freshly misty metaphor-making by imagining seeing the church as an old matron, wondering what he would think if instead of a church: "da im Schatten eine riesige Matrone gesessen wäre, mit großem, in Treppen fallendem Bauch, den Rücken an die Häuserwände gelehnt" (*MoE*, 129–30; it had been an old matron sitting here in the shade, with a huge belly terraced like a flight of steps, her back resting against the houses behind her, *MwQ*, 135). But his creative metaphor is a description of petrification, as the moments of his looking, "preßten sein Herz mit dem ganzen Urwiderstand, den man ursprünglich gegen diese zu Millionen Zentnern Stein verhärtete Welt, gegen diese erstarrte Mondlandschaft des Gefühls hat, in die man willenlos hineingesetzt wurde" (*MoE*, 130; rooted in him and compressed his heart with all the resistance of primal instinct against this world petrified into millions of tons of stone, against this frozen moonscape of feeling where, involuntarily, he had been set down, *MwQ*, 136). What, however, a careful reader has to ask, is this "primal instinct" of rebellion? Is it not its own sort of prefiguration or archetype, a part, perhaps, of the larger pattern of oscillation between fixed forms and the energy of change? Neither stone nor mist, therefore, is alone the true element, but rather, they work together to satisfy our shifting human instincts and desires for oscillation — oscillation between freedom and necessity, or perhaps freedom and an artificially imposed set of limitations.

Art necessarily requires limitations, "selecting" and an imprecise representation that ignores or represses more details or truths than it can possibly express. George Steiner in *Grammars of Creation* uses Hölderlin's *Über die Verfahrungsweise des poetischen Geistes* to discuss the tension between the universal (that repeats) and the particular (that deviates), but he could also be talking about Musil:

> If the creative Geist is boundless (unendlich), what relates it to the necessary limitations of all articulate and performative signs? . . . Hölderlin defines the function and aim of art as "'Die Vergegenwärtung des Unendlichen" (the making present, the making contemporary of the unbounded). How, he asks, can that which is in incessant motion, as are thoughts and all vital processes, be made "punctual" (. . . Punkt is a key term)? . . . [The poet] seeks mediation between a child's indiscriminate identification with the wholeness of the world — the Wordsworthian intimation of unboundedness — and the willed abstraction which, ineluctably, chooses an expressive but bounded form.[27]

By calling attention to the "Punkt" or point and its relation to time (punctual), Steiner elucidates the association between creative selection and Time. The unbounded, in other words, is not just a spatial but also a temporal term, and the limited realm of the work of art is paradoxically momentary *and* lasting, limited *and* infinite by virtue of the "willed abstraction" that

expresses unboundedness even as it chooses a limited form. Steiner continues, illuminating the "paradox of the 'momentarily lasting'":

> The infinity of potential content has been trapped, as it were, in the
> limited configurations of conceptual and aesthetic statement. But
> language generalizes, negates individuation . . . that which executive
> form had made bounded and momentary, now radiates toward its
> own kind of open-ended universality (Allgemeinheit). By virtue of a
> "magic stroke," Zauberschlag, poetry restores to life, to the incom-
> mensurability of "the lived," that which abstraction and reduction
> to local and temporal form had taken from it. . . . The poet's lan-
> guage . . . its determinate of elements, clarity and opaqueness, swift-
> ness and retardation, abstraction and concreteness, conjoin in that
> "Stillstand der Bewegung" (that standing still of motion) which
> matches the universal to the particular.[28]

This "*Stillstand der Bewegung*" is for Musil, too, a recurring motif, which
we will return to more deeply in chapter 4 in the discussion of still lives.
But for now let us merely note the importance of the "apparent contradiction" that Steiner describes, the fruitful tension, in other words,
that he reveals to be at the heart of the "magic stroke" that turns universal into particular and particular into universal. How is it that poetry
restores — through abstraction — that which abstraction has taken from
it, if not, indeed, by the two elements of time and metaphoric transparency; by, in other words, calling attention to the infinite contained within
the part — synecdoche — and to the ultimate metaphoric nature of all
perception and experience?

Musil makes this tension even more literal when he continually stresses
the relationship between our experience of life and that of literature. Not
only should art select the most essential or representative moments, but
life might do this as well. He speaks, in this context, about our life's work:
"Das Lebenswerk soll nur aus 3 Gedichten oder 3 Handlungen bestehen,
in denen man sich aufs aüsserste steigert; im übrigen soll man schweigen, das Nötige tun u[nd] gefühllos bleiben, wo man nicht schöpferisches
Gefühl spürt"[29] (Life's work should consist of only 3 poems or 3 actions,
in which one strains oneself to the utmost; in general, one should stay
silent, do what is necessary a[nd] remain without feeling, where one does
not sense creative feeling). This seems to contradict his own narrative
style, which tends to spread out rather than concentrate itself. But his
intention is, perhaps, to approximate in the novel this proportion, since
amid the pages and pages of musings, the heightened events or actions are
relatively few. He continues in this note: "Man sei 'moralisch' nur in den
Ausnahmefällen u[nd] norme das Übrige wie Bleistifte oder Schrauben.
M[it]a[nderen] W[orten] die Moral wird auf die genialen Augenblicke
reduziert u[nd] im übrigen bloss vernünftig behandelt . . ." (*MoE*, 1878;

one is only "moral" in exceptional cases and normalizes what remains into things like pencils or screws. In other words, morality is reduced to the moments of genius a[nd] in general one should just act rationally). Once again, aesthetics, or the ability to orchestrate and understand patterns or perception and creation, is inextricably related to a living morality, that is, a personal, ever-shifting, responsible ethics. Ulrich asserts repeatedly through the novel that he wants to live life like a character in a book, removing what he calls "the fatty tissue of life"; and likewise Proust's narrator describes a state of mind wherein a supposed real character, his lost love Albertine, is perceived as a fictional personage. He posits a world "in which Albertine counted so little . . . perhaps an intellectual world, which was the sole reality," and a world in which his grief would be, "something like what we feel when we read a novel [wherein we would] think no more about what Albertine had done than we think about the action of the imaginary heroine of a novel after we have finished reading it."[30] In *La Nausée* as well, Sartre's Roquentin muses on the tension between real life, narration, and non-linear suspension of time, concluding that there is something significant about the process of conscious arrangement of the otherwise insignificant moments of our lives:

> Nothing happens when you live. The scenery changes, people come in and go out, that's all. There are no beginnings. Days are tacked on to days without rhyme or reason, an interminable, monotonous addition. From time to time you make a semi-total: you say: I've been traveling for three years. Neither is there any end: you never leave a woman, a friend, a city in one go . . . There are moments — rarely— when you make a landmark, you realize that you are going with a woman, in some messy business. The time of a flash. After that the processing starts again, you begin to add up hours and days: Monday, Tuesday, Wednesday. April, May, June. 1924, 1925, 1926. That's living. But everything changes when you tell about life . . .

This *telling*, Sartre implies, is connected to the impulse for making meaning, for gathering incidents into repeated patterns and purposes, however artificially. "There are days which pass in disorder," he continues, and then comes the sudden ecstasy:

> Nothing has changed and yet everything is different. I can't describe it; it's like the Nausea and yet it is just the opposite . . . I see that it happens; that I am myself and that I am here; I am the one who splits the night; I am as happy as the hero of a novel . . . I do not know whether the whole world has suddenly shrunk or whether I am the one who unifies all sounds and shapes.[31]

Like Musil's nocturnal alter ego *Monsieur le Vivisecteur* (*D*, 2–3), Roquentin splits the night, feels as happy as a hero of a novel, and then becomes author of the whole universe, unifying all sounds and shapes together through a suspension of narrative time, through focus, attention, repeated patterning and deviations, which lend meaning to an otherwise endless procession of randomness. The arrangement of something as seemingly trivial as Mrs. Dalloway's dinner party might also be an allegory for this constant tension between form and randomness, as Woolf's heroine struggles to believe that the party — her work of art — has meaning: "She did think it mattered," the narrator writes, "her party, and it made her feel quite sick to know that it was all going wrong, all falling flat."[32] Cataclysm, crime, danger are all preferable to the randomness of "seinesgleichen geschieht," to dullness without formal dynamics. As Woolf's narrator continues: "Anything, any explosion, any horror was better than people wandering aimlessly. . . ."[33] And it is the presentiment of death, which seems somehow to actually lend her the purpose and meaning she seeks. Death is what provides her with the formal boundary; death: "a thing, wreathed about with chatter, defaced, obscured in her own life, let drop every day in corruption, lies, chatter . . . an attempt to communicate; people feeling the impossibility of reaching the center which, mystically, evaded them."[34] With the help of this formal essentiality, Mrs. Dalloway pulls herself together to return to her guests: "But she must go back. She must assemble," as if the activity of arrangement, assembling were the only possible defense against the abyss.

How might this call to abstraction or reduction down to essential things relate to the open-ended variations, digressions, and divagations approaching infinity in Musil's novelistic experiment? How, in other words, does this reduction relate to its seeming opposing force of eternally exponentially evolving possibilities? How, further, does the injunction to concentrate the episodes in one's life and in a novel down to those most heightened and essential events correspond to the relative uneventful nature of Musil's novel, and of modernist novels in general? How, for example, does a chapter wherein the action consists of Ulrich "thinking," or one in which the narrator concludes that "not doing" is as "glühend" (flaming) as doing, constitute a reduction to the three essential events of a life, except by a consideration that what is essential is, in fact, something quite different from what might be expected?[35]

When the narrator of a novel suggests that the people in the novel should live life like characters in books, we are right to pause, for, of course, they already are, in fact, characters in books! But — and this is the important question here — what sort of books? Books that stress what for Proust was the "sole reality" or for Musil a life without the fatty tissue, books wherein the thread of the story, otherwise known as the plot, is very tenuous amid the heady atmosphere of swirling timelessness and the dense non-action of thinking, amid the constant distention of extended metaphors and recurring metaphoric moments of mystical aesthetic experience. The books in which these characters would live if they were real are, presumably, the sort of books they do live in as fictional, books rather more like those favored by Virginia Woolf in her famous essay "Modern Fiction." Rather than recording plot, tragedy, love interest, or catastrophe, modern fiction is said to describe life "as it really was" after the turn of the century, as a subjective experience of "myriad impressions — trivial, fantastic, evanescent, or engraved with the sharpness of steel. From all sides they come, an incessant shower of incomparable atoms; and as they fall, as they shape themselves into the life of Monday or Tuesday, the accent falls differently from of old; the moment of importance came not here but there." "Life," Woolf continues, "is not a series of gig-lamps symmetrically arranged; life is a luminous halo, a semi-transparent envelope surrounding us from the beginning of consciousness to the end" (106). Presumably those most essential activities, those "moments of genius" wherein true morality exists, those "exceptional cases" must be imbedded in hours, years, and thousands of pages of less intensely motivated experience and must function as revolutionary tears in the paper of normal consciousness, status quo, and expected pattern. As such, the pages and moments wherein the patterns seem to cancel themselves out because their counter-forces push and pull in an already regulated measure of good, bad, growth, petrification, birth, death, novelty, tradition, desire, repulsion ad infinitum are periodically interrupted by the secondary pattern of critical questioning and re-creation of new patterns that continually resists the falling into sleep of the moral and aesthetic conscience and consciousness. This new imperative required a new way of narration, one which was, in fact, deemed to be even more naturalistic than the reportage of nineteenth-century realism. Musil, seemingly unaware of or unimpressed by the experiments of his near-contemporaries, writes of the challenge:

> Das Kunststück hat aber noch Keiner zuwege gebracht, das wirkliche, naturalistische Leben umher, dieses in zusammenhanglose Stunden — in eine erbärmliche Gleichgültigkeit zerfallene Leben so darzustellen, dass es nicht über uns hinausgeht und doch schön ist." (T, 118)

> [But no one has yet successfully developed a facility for presenting the real naturalistic life around us — this life that fragments into hours without any context and into pitiable indifference — in such a way that it does not reach way beyond us and is yet still beautiful. (D, 74)]

Judith Ryan, in *The Vanishing Subject: Early Psychology and the Modernist Novel*, suggests that modernist novelists called attention to the expanding moment in their long narratives as a reflection of the real significance they attributed to momentary exceptional experience amid the previously more privileged force of linearity. She writes: "The early 20th century writers' attempt to embed depictions of such moments into the novel, rather than reserve them for lyric poetry as the Romantics had done, was symptomatic of their view that these special states were part and parcel of reality, not something beyond it."[36] The modernist novelist, informed by perception science and empowered by the science of subjectivity, continued to undermine the primacy of the prosaically objective and linear "real." By daring to expand the moment in prose, they made claims for the significance of the fleeting, the uncertain, and the irreducible, and implicitly all tried to find the bridge that Musil was explicitly seeking: a bridge from such evanescent experiences to everyday reality and conduct of life. As such, the many subtly same but slightly different versions of normal reality, narrative and chronological time, of *seinesgleichen geschieht* serve a purpose — if only as backdrop for the radical deviations or "crimes" that syncopate the general norm.

In an ironic twist however, the so-called normal is itself revealed to be terribly variegated, as contemporary science reveals that no two things are exactly equivalent. The very reality of *seinesgleichen geschieht* is called into question by the very act of its depiction. By describing the many persons, events, ideas, places, that are like but not like, Musil calls attention to the process by which even supposedly consistent life proliferates itself in metaphoric variations on themes. The novel's form itself continually returns to these repeating patterns and seemingly essential motifs, as chapter after chapter explores similar questions and presents similar experiments in different contexts, with different players or characters and in different arrangements. This very proliferation of slight differences, however, begs the question of sameness. A reader may trace the repeating themes, but both the narrator and Ulrich also continually point out the repetitions (as Musil himself does in his notes on the novel). Musil writes, for example, that Anders (an early name for Ulrich) is to be understood as "Repräsentant dieser Zeit mit seinen Konflikten, wenn auch ein begabter" (*MoE*, 1995; a representative of this time with his conflicts, if a talented one), reminding himself, "Dann muss man das Typische mehr betonen" (*MoE*, 1995; Thus one needs to stress the typical more). "Auch was A[nders] tat, war aus dem gleichen Grunde oft nur der Stellvertreter von etwas anderem und hatte mehr symbolische als wirkliche Bedeutung" (*MoE*, 1996; Also, what A[nders] did was for the same reason often only a stand-in for something else and had more symbolic than real meaning). In another note Musil comments that Ulrich criticizes Arnheim for his behavior with Diotima: "Ist es erlaubt, der Seele einer Frau mystische Gefühle einzuflössen u[nd] ihren Leib ihrem Gatten zu überlassen? Mut[atis] mut[andis] wiederholt sich das eigentlich auch zw[ischen] U[lrich] und A[gathe]!" (MoE, 1934; Is it allowed to inspire a woman's soul with mystical ideas and leave her body to her husband? Mu[tatis] mut[andis] that repeats itself actually between U[lrich] and A[gathe] too!). To cite a few more examples when there are so many, Musil takes the pattern of retreat to the island and experiments by trying one version in which Ulrich is there with Agathe, and one where he is there with Clarisse, resulting, of course, in very different outcomes. In early notes for the novel, Ulrich has Bonadea and Leona as lovers at the same time, and thus the pattern of these affairs overlaps as each superimposes itself upon the other, highlighting their differences and similarities. What previously had been narrated as simultaneous has been transformed, in the published version, into a description where one event occurs after the other. We can almost envision the plates of patterns shifting, sliding apart and back together and apart again. Ideas expressed by Ulrich and Agathe are uttered by the most unlikely characters, providing the reader with an object lesson of how similar patterns can take on entirely different connotations in different contexts. The madness of Moosbrugger and Clarisse serve as analogies for the desires of society as a whole; if Moosbrugger is *unzurechnungsfähig* (unable to be held responsible for his actions), is Agathe when she forges the will? Or Ulrich when, in an unpublished draft, he tries to free Moosbrugger from prison? Or any citizen when he or she, as Clarisse frantically decries, reads about disasters in the newspaper and does nothing to stop them? In a disturbing sketch called "The Redeemer," Ulrich (who is Anders at this point) dreams that he bites off the tongue of a woman (reminiscent of Bonadea) whom he perceives as sexually aggressive, echoing Moosbrugger's disgust at the "little prostitute" whom he brutally murders. Dream is here a repeating pattern, analogy, another version of reality, and Anders is man in general, is the reader, is society. Elsewhere Musil writes:

> Das Gleichnis . . . ist die Verbindung der Vorstellungen, die im Traum herrscht, es ist die gleitende Logik der Seele, der die Verwandtschaft der Dinge in den Ahnungen der Kunst und Religion entspricht; aber auch was es an gewöhnlicher Neigung und Abneigung, Übereinstimmung und Ablehnung, Bewunderung, Unterordnung, Führerschaft, Nachahmung und ihren Gegenerscheinungen im Leben gibt, diese vielfältigen Beziehungen des Menschen zu sich und der Natur, die noch nicht rein sachlich sind und es vielleicht auch nie sein werden, lassen sich nicht anders begreifen als in Gleichnissen. Ohne Zweifel ist das, was man die höhere Humanität nennt, nichts als ein Versuch, diese beiden grossen Lebenshälften des Gleichnisses und der Wahrheit miteinander zu verschmelzen, indem man sie zuvor vorsichtig trennt. Hat man aber an einem Gleichnis alles, was vielleicht wahr sein könnte, von dem getrennt, was nur Schaum ist, so hat man gewöhnlich ein wenig Wahrheit gewonnen und den ganzen Wert des Gleichnisses zerstört. . . . (*MoE*, 593)

[Metaphor . . . is like the image that fuses several meanings in a dream; it is the gliding logic of the soul, corresponding to the way things relate to each other in the intuitions of art and religion. But even what there is in life of common likes and dislikes, accord and rejection, admiration, subordination, leadership, imitation, and their opposites, the many ways man relates to himself and to nature, which are not yet and perhaps never will be purely objective, cannot be understood other than in metaphorical or figurative terms. No doubt what is called the higher humanism is only the effort to fuse together these two great halves of life, metaphor and truth, once they have been carefully distinguished from each other. But once one has distinguished everything in a metaphor that might be true from what is mere froth, one usually has gained a little truth, but at the cost of destroying the whole value of the metaphor. (*MwQ*, 647)]

Implicit in this analysis is that there is something beyond even "a little truth" that is valuable and that, paradoxically, can be used to approach, through metaphor, a more comprehensive sort of truth. Everything, in other words, cannot be reduced down to definitions and percentages; anything, rather, that brings "Schönheit und Erregung in die Welt" (*MoE*, 573; beauty and excitement into the world, *MwQ*, 625) probably is the product of some sort of imprecision. If this imprecision provides us with the illusion of a repeated pattern, where a strict observation of slight differences might not allow for the justification of groupings or correspondences, it also may remind us that other groupings and correspondences are equally provisional, thereby providing us with a glimpse of the larger truth of the ultimate irreducibility of the constantly shifting nature of reality. In the note on Anders quoted above, Musil comments: "A[nders] glaubte einstweilen an den Wert der Unordnung; es gibt eine Unordnung, welche höher steht als die ihr vorangegangene Ordnung. Er liebte es, zu sehen, wie sie täglich reicher wuchs" (*MoE*, 1996; sometimes A[nders] believed in the value of disorder; there is a disorder that stands higher than the previous order. He loved to watch how it grew richer every day). This disrespect for the necessity of any given order seems to acknowledge nothing more than newness or, perhaps, an order that is made of the dis-ordering of established essence. And yet there are echoes and echoes, as disturbing similarities between people who consider themselves safely contained within categories take on contagious taints and discolor; as "qualities" bleed through the boundaries, reflecting distorted images of our own most repressed desires. Referring to the way in which Moosbrugger, the sex-murderer in his novel, seems to infect the healthier body (and mind) of society, Musil writes: "Ja, es mochte sich ereignen, dass beim Zubettgehn der korrekte Herr Sektionschef Tuzzi oder der zweite Obmann des Naturheilsvereins . . . seiner schläfrigen Gattin sagte:

was würdest du anfangen wenn ich jetzt ein Moosbrugger wäre?" (*MoE*, 1984; Indeed it might happen that on going to bed the very correct Section Chief Tuzzi, or the second in command of the Nature Cure Association, said to his sleepy wife: What would you do if I were a Moosbrugger now? *MwQ*, 1708). Ulrich asks himself, and others ask as well, does he fit more into the pattern of Gerda and her Germanic-anti-Semitic boyfriend Hans Sepp, or that of her Jewish bourgeois father? Is he more like that "big rooster" Diotima when he speaks of mysticism than the practical General Stumm von Bordwehr, who also speaks like him on occasion? Is Arnheim his friend or his fiend? From moment to moment the man without qualities has the ability to slip in and out of repeating patterns, thereby calling their solidity into question and perhaps pointing to something behind all these analogies and metaphors.

Although this proliferation of shifting metaphors, analogies, and likenesses might seem to suggest meaninglessness, Musil's theory of metaphor points to something else, something surprising: the possibility that there may be something constant that the many possible variations play upon. In a list of seventeen essential points about the novel, the fifth describes the relationship of metaphor to a perception of the world as something that easily dissolves into breath. Implicit in these notes is that there is something behind this floating, absurd world, something Musil calls in these notes "inner necessity" or "the feeling of a deep life." He writes:

Man könnte tagelang in Gleichnissen fortfahren. Was heißt das? . . .

Gleichnisse gehen mehr an als Wirklichkeit.
Es kommt nicht auf das an, was ich tue, es konnte ebensogut etwas anderes sein, aber es muss den gleichen *Gleichniswert* haben.
Obgleich Gleichnis, Gefühl der inneren Notwendigkeit[.]
Nichts ist fest. Jede Ordnung führt ins Absurde. Nur hier ist das Gefühl des tiefen Lebens[.]
Die Kategorien der Welt erscheinen als erstarrte Gleichnisse . . .
Die Welt nur ein möglicher Versuch[.]
Zugleich mit den Gleichnissen fühlt man, das Leben löst sich in einem Hauch auf.
Es ist da u[nd] nur bis zu einem gewissen Grad da. (*MoE*, 1834)

[One could continue all day with metaphors. What does that mean? . . .
Metaphors are more meaningful than reality.
It doesn't depend on what I do, it could just as easily be something else, but it must have the same *metaphoric value.*
Despite metaphor, feeling of inner necessity[.]
Nothing is certain. Every order leads to absurdity. Yet the feeling of deep life is found here[.]

The categories of the world appear as frozen metaphors . . .
The world is only one possible attempt[.]
Along with the metaphors one feels life dissolve in a breath.
It is there and only there to a certain degree. (emphasis mine)]

The idea of "metaphoric value," a little like the concept of "value"
of colors, emphasizes the idea that beneath these metaphors there is
something essential — an "inner necessity" or idea that can be illustrated or approached in an infinite number of ways, corresponding
via many different hues. The core of this idea may be, fundamentally,
that the world of concepts and forms dissolves itself into "breath" as
soon as we try to approach it too directly or to pin it down to an
absolute and enduring value. "Metaphor is more important than reality" because whatever is essential can be approached only obliquely
and contingently; only temporarily or extratemporally. It has to be
expressed through many possible images, through an image of multiplicity itself, through the realization that the world itself is constantly
created and re-created by the formation and dissolution of these varied images. The coincidence of individual experiences and entities
approximates what cannot be approached directly through the analysis of singularities; the coincidence reaches instead toward an essential
something beyond particular examples.

For Proust an experience of essence comes as the result of the formal transubstantiation from individualized exceptional experience to general and repeated pattern or theme. This abstracted essence functions as
a transcendence and release from the specific experience of suffering or
indifference into an aesthetic pleasure and sense of eternal significance.
Any given experience, person, or place becomes meaningful only in relationship, correspondence, or affinity with a memory of some other place,
person, or experience; only by elevating a particularity through a non-
rational, non-intellectual experience of metaphoric involuntary memory.
This experience, moreover, is mediated by the all-important element of
time. In his chapter "Series and Groups," Gilles Deleuze explicates the
process by which Proust's narrator finds the recurring theme within the
variations of his series of loves, and, "disengages from them something
general, which is also a source of joy."[37] "The work of art," he continues,
quoting from *Remembrance*,

"is a sign of happiness, because it teaches us that in any love the
general borders on the particular, and to pass from the second to the
first by a gymnastics that fortifies us against despair (by helping us
neglect the cause in order to intensify its essence" (III, 904). What
we repeat is each time a particular suffering; but the repetition itself
is always joyous. . . .[38]

Toward the end of his novel, Proust himself further clarifies his tendency toward the essence in a statement about the limitations of artistic creation: "Thus I had already come to the conclusion that we are not at all free in the presence of the work of art to be created, that we do not do it as we ourselves please, but that it existed prior to us and we should seek to discover it as we would a natural law because it is both necessary and hidden."[39]

Musil would probably disagree with this last statement and uphold the artist's infinite capacity to invent, and would probably disagree that the work, particularly his own novel, which was developing in an emphatically organic and unpredictable manner, was already somehow predetermined. Yet Proust's celebration and explanation of the transcendence and eternal essence of aesthetic form does help us to understand Musil, who was also searching for bridges to and from extraordinary aesthetic and mystical experiences. Both experimental novelists found these bridges through metaphoric correspondences and through interaction with seemingly eternal recurring patterns, mediated and qualified by the element of time. Proust's allegiance to predetermined essence is, indeed, reminiscent of Musil's description of Ulrich as someone who believes that morality is to be discovered, not invented, that morality must itself have a morality behind it. Yet Musil's aesthetic and ethical explanation of the world included an explicit discussion of the human need to break off from what he calls the "fürchterliche Gewalt der Wiederholung" (*MoE*, 1672; fearful violence of repetition, *MwQ*, 1471) demonstrated both by the oscillation of the novel's form and by Ulrich and Agathe's boredom in the face of the eternity of paradise or the ocean, which is one metaphor for this eternity: "Und was ist geschehen? Es hat sich in eine seelisch-optische Täuschung aufgelöst und in einen wiederholbaren physiologischen Mechanismus. Wie bei allen Menschen!" (*MoE*, 1674; And what happened? It [Ulrich and Agathe's longing] dissolved into a spiritual and optical illusion and into a physiological mechanism that is repeatable . . . As with all people!: *MwQ*, 1473). Thus, while experiences seem at first to gain meaning for Proust's narrator when they align themselves into pattern, and, conversely, lose significance for Musil's characters when they cease to be exceptional, this might be too literal a reading on both counts. For both novelists operate in an oscillation between two sorts of meaning, that is, the meaning of the individual human with his or her specific momentary sufferings, and the larger sort of general meaning culled by the individual over time, a collection of probabilities and themes that make of random events and experiences a work of art, a philosophy, or an attitude toward life. Proust's form, as much as Musil's, pays tribute to the need for interruption and variation, to the *frisson* of difference created by the oblique shifts from repeating series to groups to individual deviating instances and back. Surely Proust's narrator admits repeatedly that actually possessing Albertine becomes tedious, a chore over time, as all the imagined, desired experiences, places, and people are disappointing when actually attained, consummated, and reduced to repetition, and only "regain" their magical significance when they metaphorically and abstractly collide with other experiences in memory. What he desires, more than anything else, is *the knowledge* of the formal process or cycle of, in this case, desire, jealousy, betrayal and loss; the distillation of the individual experience into a general and aesthetically satisfying law. This realm of integrated memory functions, of course, only within an exceptional extratemporal metaphoric realm like the Other Condition, a realm of abstracted universalizing. Both Proust and Musil characterize themselves as writers who see the general, the typology, instead of the specifics, Proust even surprisingly confessing that he doesn't notice details (if he does not, who does?). Musil, in a conversation with Oskar Maurus Fontane, likewise admits: "Die reale Erklärung des realen Geschehens interessiert mich nicht . . . Die Tatsachen sind überdies immer vertauschbar. Mich interessiert das geistige Typische, ich möchte sagen: das Gespenstische des Geschehens"[40] (The real explanations of the real occurrences do not interest me . . . The facts are always interchangeable anyway. What interests me is the spiritually typical, I mean to say: the ghostly sense of that which happens). In a *Diary* note, he also comments that he notices "selten Einzelheiten, sondern immer nur irgend einen Sinn der Sache" (*T*, 314; details rarely, but, instead, simply some general sense of the matter in question, *D*, 186). Speaking of himself, Musil uses the metaphor of polyamorous love affairs to describe his working relationship with themes and metaphors:

> Es gibt Schriftsteller, die von einem Stoff gepackt werden. Sie fühlen: mit diesem oder keinem; es ist wie die Liebe auf den ersten Blick. Das Verhältnis des Robert Musil zu seinen Stoffen ist ein zögerndes. Er hat mehrere gleichzeitig und behält sie bei sich, nachdem die Stunden der ersten Liebe vorbei sind oder auch ohne dass sie dagewesen sind. Er tauscht Teile von ihnen willkürlich aus. Manche Teilthemen wandern und kommen in keinem Buch zum Ausdruck.[41]

> [There are writers who are obsessed with one theme. They feel: this one or none at all; it's like love at first sight. The relationship of R[obert] M[usil] to his themes is a hesitant one. He has many at once and keeps them after the hours of first love are over, or even if there never were any. He exchanges parts of them arbitrarily. Many half-developed themes wander and never surface in any book.]

In exploring the difference between what he calls specific and non-specific emotion, and touching on this theme of individual love and love patterns,

Ulrich reflects that while a non-specific emotion is enduring and repeatable, the specific, individualized emotion is "ein-malig" (coming only once) and fleeting, but both can reasonably be considered part of human perception of reality:

> Natürlich ist es vornehmlich die Entwicklung zum bestimmten Gefühl, was die Unbeständigkeit und Hinfälligkeit des seelischen Lebens nach sich zieht. Dass man niemals den Augenblick des Fühlens festhalten kann, dass die Gefühle rascher verwelken als Blumen oder dass sie sich in Papierblumen verwandeln, wenn sie erhalten bleiben wollen, dass das Glück und der Wille, die Kunst und Gesinnung vorbeigehen, alles dies hängt von der Bestimmtheit des Gefühls ab, die ihm auch eine Bestimmung unterschiebt und es in den Gang des Lebens zwingt, von dem es aufgelöst oder verändert wird. Dagegen ist das in seiner Unbestimmtheit und Unbegrenztheit verharrende Gefühl verhältnismässig unveränderlich . . . "Das eine stirbt wie ein Einzelwesen, das andere dauert an wie eine Art oder Gattung." (*MoE*, 1198)

> [It is chiefly the development toward a specific emotion that brings with it the fragility and instability of the life of the soul. That the moment of feeling can never be sustained, that emotions wilt more quickly than flowers if one tries to preserve them, that happiness and will, art and conviction, pass away; all this depends on the specificity of emotion, which always imposes upon it a purposiveness and forces it into the pace of life that dissolves or changes it. On the other hand, the emotion that persists in its non-specificity and boundlessness is relatively impervious to change . . . "The one dies like an individual, the other lasts like a kind or a species." (*MwQ*, 1306)

The nonspecific is comparable to the abstract repeatable pattern (flowers may be perennial); the specific, to the individual difference (the particular pansy lasts a month). But of course, even this is far too black and white for Musil and Ulrich, who qualify this categorization into a more realistic blend, stating that

> Und wirklich geschieht es auch fast immer, dass sich die beiden Möglichkeiten des Gefühls zu einer gemeinsamen Wirklichkeit verbinden, worin die Eigenart des einen oder des anderen bloss vorherrscht. Es gibt keine "Stimmung", die nicht auch bestimmte Gefühle enthielte, die sich in ihr bilden und wieder auflösen; und es gibt kein bestimmtes Gefühl, [das] . . . die Eigenart des unbestimmten durchblicken ließe. (*MoE*, 1199)

> [In truth it almost always happens that both possibilities combine in a common reality, in which merely the characteristics of one or the other predominate. There is no "mood" that does not also include

specific emotions that form and dissolve again; and there is no specific emotion that . . . does not allow for the characteristics of the
nonspecific emotion to peer through. (*MwQ* 1307)]

"Es wird also nur noch auszumachen sein" (So all that remains is to settle), continues Ulrich, "warum die Eigenart des unbestimmten Gefühls,
und die ganze Entwicklung zu ihr, für weniger wirklich gilt als ihr Gegen-
spiel" (why the particularities of the nonspecific emotion, and the whole
development leading up to it, is taken to be less real than its counterpart),
despite the fact, as he adds, that "in der Natur liegt beides" (*MoE*, 1199;
Nature contains both, *MwQ*, 1307). While, as Ulrich continues, the inner
world of abstraction related to the nonspecific emotions "für das Schön-
ste und Tiefste erklärt wird, was das Leben birgt" (is proclaimed the best
and most profound thing life has to offer), this world is treated merely as
an "Anbau der äusseren" (annex of the outer world), that is, the world
of experience and specific, fleeting emotions (*MoE*, 1200; *MwQ*, 1307),
as something less real. Here we see Ulrich championing the abstract
and lasting as something that is hypocritically neglected by an all-too-
materialistic and empiricist world view. He favors here the world of the
aesthetic, of art, of imagination, of metaphor as more meaningful than
reality. Elsewhere, however, he calls upon empiricism — and its tendency
toward observing the specific and non-repeatable — as the solution to
the problem of petrified values, even proposing a Utopia of Empiricism
or of what he calls the "Inductive Attitude." But there is perhaps less of
a contradiction in this than appears at first glance. For all experienced
knowledge must, like the metaphors used to describe or imagine it, be
reactualized, kept fresh. He muses:

> Die "merkwürdige Erscheinung des nicht frischbleibens des Gefühls"
> wird durch den Hinweis zu erklären versucht, dass alle Vorstellungen
> verdorren, deren Erlebnis nicht reaktualisiert wird. (zb. Worte) Die
> Folgerung wäre: *Gott als Empirismus*. Ausserdem wird beschuldigt
> die Umwandlung des Ahnens, das man erlebt, in einen Glauben, den
> man nicht erlebt. (*MoE*, 1869)

> [We can attempt to explain the "remarkable phenomenon of emo-
> tions not remaining fresh" by pointing out that all impressions
> wither whose experiences are not reactualized. (e.g. words) The
> conclusion would be: *God as empiricism*. Further, the intimation that
> can be experienced deteriorates into faith that is not experienced.]

"*Ahnen*" (intimation) is a *Stichwort* that appears repeatedly in Musil's notes,
contraposed by "*Glauben*" (belief), a differentiation that can be explained as
that between empirical observation and acceptance of an abstract concept.
While Ulrich can accept and condone *Ahnen*, because it is a product of

individual experience, *Glauben* is a sort of suspicious reification of something that may not even exist at all, an abstraction for which we have no sensory evidence. Any knowledge that bypasses experience altogether is somewhat suspect, but even knowledge acquired through the senses can wither, or become stale (*verdorren*) if it is not *reactualized* by new experience. Relating its origin and development, Ulrich muses that empiricism had

> das immerhin erstaunliche Vorhandensein und unveränderliche Walten von Gesetzen in der Natur und in den Regeln des Geistes kurzerhand für eine täuschende Ansicht erklärt . . . die aus der Gewöhnung an die häufige Wiederholung der gleichen Erfahrungen entstehe. Was sich oft genug wiederhole, scheine so sein zu müssen, ist ungefähr die klassische Formel dafür gewesen; und in dieser übertriebenen Gestalt, die ihr das 18. und 19. Jahrhundert gegeben hat, war sie eine Rückwirkung der langen vorhergegangenen theologischen Spekulation, das heißt des in Gott gesetzten Glaubens, seine Werke mit Hilfe dessen erklären zu können, was man sich in den Kopf setzt. (*MoE*, 1270)

> [declared the really astonishing presence and unchangeable sway of laws of nature and in the rules of the intellect to be a deceptive view that originated in habituation to the frequent repetition of the same experiences. The approximate classical formula for this was: whatever repeats itself often enough seems to have to be so; and in this exaggerated form, which the eighteenth and nineteenth centuries bestowed upon it, this formula was a repercussion of the long antecedent theological speculation: that is, of the faith placed in God, of being able to explain His works with the aid of whatever one takes into one's head. (*MwQ*, 1351–52)]

Up until now, we see empiricism mostly as a liberation from the rule of Essence, carried over from the period before the death of God into its eighteenth and nineteenth century mode as idealism. As Sartre writes in his *Existentialism is a Humanism*, "Eighteenth-century atheistic philosophers suppressed the idea of God, but not, for all that, the idea that essence precedes existence."[42] Clearly, remnants of belief in a preexistent essence still remain throughout the nineteenth, twentieth, and even into the twenty-first century. Too much empiricism, however, despite the work it may have done to dispel superstition and the acceptance of untested beliefs, may also, as Ulrich continues to point out, have a tendency toward foolishness, discouraging respect for science and "natural laws" by an all-too-radical dependence on individual non-repeatable experience. For all knowledge, he writes elsewhere, is created by the repetition of experience: "Und wir könnten uns überhaupt von nichts einen Begriff oder ein Urteil machen, wenn alles nur einmal vorüberhuschte. Was etwas gelten soll und einen Namen tragen, das muss sich wiederholen lassen, muss in vielen

Exemplaren vorhanden sein, und wenn du noch nie den Mond gesehen hättest, würdest du ihn für eine Taschenlampe halten" (*MoE*, 377; We'd have no way of understanding or judging anything if things flitted past us just once. Anything that has to be valid and have a name must be repeatable, it must be represented by many specimens, and if you have never seen the moon before, you'd think it was a flashlight, *MwQ*, 409). Continuing with his genealogy of empiricism, Ulrich questions the attempt to base all knowledge on experience, relating its impulse to youth's "Neigung, alles selbst erfahren zu wollen" (*MoE*, 1271; inclination to want to experience everything itself, *MwQ*, 1352).[43] Ulrich

> lächelte, als er an ein Beispiel dachte, und sagte nicht weshalb. Denn man warf nicht ungern dem allzu schlichten, auf seine Regel beschränkten Empiricismus vor, es geschähe nach ihm, dass die Sonne im Osten auf- und im Westen untergehe, aus keiner anderen Notwendigkeit, als dass die Sonne es bisher immer getan habe. Und wenn er das nun seiner Schwester verraten und sie gefragt hätte, was sie davon halte, so würde sie wohl, ohne sich für die Gründe und Gegengründe zu erhitzen, kurzerhand zur Antwort gegeben haben, dass die Sonne es ja einmal auch anders tun könnte. (*MoE*, 1271)

> [smiled when he thought of an example, but did not say why. For it was not reluctantly that one reproached empiricism, which was all too simple-minded and confined to its rules, that according to it the sun rises in the east and sets in the west for no other reason than that up till now it always has. And were he to betray this to his sister and ask her what she thought of it, she would probably answer arbitrarily, without bothering about the arguments or counterarguments, that the sun might one day do it differently. (*MwQ*, 1352)]

Empiricism also may err on the other side of the spectrum as well, as newly experienced sensations are often all too quickly congealed into an all-too-limited circle of established beliefs. Thus the empiricist, in a few small steps, becomes an idealist of sorts, or, paradoxically, a materialist with a profit motive:

> Wahrscheinlich sollte man dazu sagen, dass eben eine neue Eigenart des Menschen ungefähr seit der Urgroßväterzeit zum Vorschein gekommen ist; und es wäre die des empirischen Menschen oder Empirikers, des sattsam zur offenen Frage gewordenen Erfahrungsmenschen, der aus hundert gemachten Erfahrungen tausend neue zu machen weiß, die doch immer nur im gleichen Erfahrungskreis verbleiben, und der damit das gewinnreich erscheinende riesenhafte Einerlei des technischen Zeitalters erzeugt hat. Der Empirismus als Philosophie könnte als die philosophische Kinderkrankheit dieser Art des Menschen gelten. (*MoE*, 1271)

[Apparently we should also add that approximately since the days of our great-grandfathers, a new kind of individuality has made its appearance: this is the type of the empirical man or empiricist who has become such a familiar open question, the person who knows how to make from a hundred of his own experiences a thousand new ones, which, however, always remain within the same circle of experience, and who has by this means created the gigantic, profitable-in-appearance monotony of the technical age. Empiricism as a philosophy might be taken as the philosophical children's disease of this type of person. (*MwQ*, 1351)]

How soon does an individual experience turn into a law, a prejudice, an *idée reçue*? And how, without comparison, context, or some categorization or provisional arrangement, can humans make sense of reality at all (provided sense is to be made in order to function pragmatically, or even artificially)? According to Nietzsche's breakdown of the evolution and devolution of metaphor as ontology, nature — or natural law — is "nothing other than a highly subjective formation." Were someone to depend too much on the laws of nature, he writes,

he will conclude that everything, as far as we can penetrate, whether to the heights of the telescopic world or the depths of the microscopic world, is so sure, so elaborated, so endless, so much in conformity to laws, and so free of lacunae, that science will be able to mine these shafts successfully for ever, and that everything found there will be in agreement and without contradiction.[44]

Any conception of the world as well ordered and under control is a hopeful fiction, in other words, created by man out of his own wishes and insecurities. That we repeatedly see the same things is, according to Nietzsche, only a result of our socialized expectations. "If," he writes, "we are forced to comprehend all things under these forms alone, then it is no longer wonderful that what we comprehend in all these things is actually nothing other than these very forms" (880–81); and even more vividly imaged earlier in the same essay: "If someone hides something behind a bush, looks for it in the same place and then finds it there, his seeking and finding is nothing much to boast about" (879).

An attack on Natural Law was waged by Dostoevsky in his *Notes from Underground* as well, in an attempt to assert the irrepressible human urge for what he called "that most advantageous of all advantages" — whim, freedom, opposition — overlooked by the smug rationalists and 2x2=4 utilitarians, whose gospel was spreading in the mid 1800s. The order and harmony Nietzsche derides as a fiction was mocked by the underground man as all that is "lofty and beautiful," the ideal of the "Crystal Palace," which, were it ever to be actually realized, would presumably be like Agathe's dreary conception of heaven. The underground man predicts, like Agathe, that attainment of such an ideal would be "frightfully dull," and that it would call upon it man's natural oppositional urge to exercise his "fatal fantastic element,"[45] to "smash things" (78), to "kick over the whole show and scatter rationalism to the winds, simply to send these logarithms to the devil, and to enable us to live once more at our own sweet foolish will!" The underground man admits that the people he addresses will probably counter-argue that "all this, too, can be calculated and tabulated — chaos and darkness and curses" (71). Indeed, Musil may be one of the scientific-minded who would contend that the battle between order and chaos is a natural predictable cycle, which allows for the calculated probability that in a society of "will forgers" Agathe would be "glühend gerecht" (*MoE*, 959; flamingly just, *MwQ*, 1041) out of opposition. But he would not presumably take it to the next level of the underground man's imagined conversational partners, who believe that this pre-calculation of chaos could "stop it all [whim, individual creativity, will], and reason would reassert itself . . ." (76). Musil did not want to do away with reason altogether, as the underground man sometimes seems to have wanted (contradicting himself from section to section: "Gentlemen," Dostoevsky writes, "I am joking . . . jesting against the grain . . ." [76]). But he probably would have agreed with the underground man's qualification that "reason is nothing but reason and satisfies only the rational side of man's nature, while will is a manifestation of the whole of life, that is, of the whole of human life including reason and all the impulses. And although our life, in this manifestation of it, is often worthless, yet it is life, and not simply extracting square roots . . ." (73). The implication is that reason sets a limit on possibility and that to go beyond what has already been explained and pigeon-holed we must engage with other parts of human experience which, paradoxically, Musil the modernist scientist would rationally maintain are as valid and real as the measurable, dead, consistent, and repeatable variables.

What concerns Dostoevsky's underground man and Nietzsche (as proto-existentialists) is not that humans create their realities, but that they forget that they have done so, thereby abdicating responsibility. As the underground man deftly points out, the "superfluous luxury" of science will teach man that he has no creative agency:

> That he has never really had any caprice or will of his own, and that he himself is something of the nature of a piano-key or the stop of an organ, and that there are, besides, things called the laws of nature; so that everything he does is not done by his willing it, but is done of itself, by the laws of nature. Consequently, we have only to discover these laws of nature, and man will no longer have to answer for his actions and life will become exceedingly easy for him. (70)

And Nietzsche:

> Only by forgetting this primitive world of metaphor . . . only
> because man forgets himself as a subject, and indeed, as an artisti-
> cally creative subject, does he live with some degree of peace, secu-
> rity, and consistency.[46]

Such peace, security, and consistency are, of course, characteristics of what
Nietzsche would call "wretched contentment," a bourgeois and ethically
lazy embrace of comfort in direct opposition to the struggle and complexity required of meaningful life. And here we might return to the conflu-
ence of ethics and aesthetics, for the ability to understand man's role as
"artistically creative subject" and the metaphoric nature of perception is the
prerequisite for a belief in human agency or the possibility or responsibility to create reality. As already noted, Musil makes the distinction between
morals and ethics within the context of the aesthetic quesion of dead and
living words: "Ich unterschied damals zwischen Moral und Ethik, wobei
ich der Moral die toten Vorschriften überließ, während mir die Ethik als ein
bewegtes Strahlen erschien" (I differentiated in those days between morality and ethics, whereby I relegated the dead prescripts to morality, while
ethics appeared to me as a living radiance).[47] Musil's sense of morality, in
its positive sense as something more like a personal *metastable* ethics than
a socially limiting system, depends on this consciousness of existential creative responsibility. As such, Kant's influential discussion of abstraction and
free play in his *Critique of Aesthetic Judgment*, which has come to be seen as
the seed of (a frivolous) "art for art's sake," must also be seen as an ethical
(categorical) imperative. When Kant favors an art that does not conform
to a preconceived "concept," he is arguably describing not an escapist or
frivolous activity but a fundamental activity of critical "possibilitarianism."
Autonomous art would require in this respect the ability to imagine other
shapes, other ideas, other worlds — unbound by constraints of use or ideology, unlimited by previously repeated and habitual concepts, powered by
Nietzsche's "multiform, irregular, inconsequential, incoherent, charming,
and ever-new"[48] metaphors. Musil writes:

> Zieh den Sinn aus allen Dichtungen, und du wirst eine zwar nicht
> vollständige, aber erfahrungsmäßige und endlose Leugnung in
> Einzelbeispielen aller gültigen Regeln, Grundsätze und Vorschriften
> erhalten, auf denen die Gesellschaft ruht, die diese Dichtungen
> liebt! Vollends ein Gedicht mit seinem Geheimnis schneidet ja den
> Sinn der Welt, wie er an tausenden alltäglichen Worten hängt, mit-
> ten durch und macht ihn zu einem davonfliegenden Ballon. Wenn
> man das, wie es üblich ist, Schönheit nennt, so sollte Schönheit ein
> unsagbar rücksichtsloser und grausamerer Umsturz sein, als es je
> eine politische Revolution gewesen ist! (*MoE*, 367)

[Extract the meaning out of all literature, and what you will get is a denial, however incomplete, but nonetheless an endless series of individual examples all based on experience, which refute all the accepted rules, principles, and prescriptions underpinning the very society that loves these works of art! In the end, a poem, with its mystery, cuts through to the point where the meaning of the world is tied to thousands of words in constant use, severs all of these strings, and turns into a balloon floating off into space. If this is what we call beauty, as we usually do, then beauty is an indescribably more ruthless and cruel upheaval than any political revolution ever was. (*MwQ*, 399)]

Notes

[1] Modernist primitivism was also connected to the modernist revival of mystical studies and models, as Wagner-Egelhaaf points out in her book *Mystik der Moderne*. Abstraction in the visual arts, she writes, went hand in hand with a mysticism that revealed "an inner necessity . . . something unfalsified from out of man's interior [something that] eludes the grasp of the rational" (57–58).

[2] Wilson, *God's Funeral*, 20.

[3] Nietzsche, *Untimely Meditations*, 141.

[4] See Harrison, "Two questions immediately arise: Does this functional process of impersonal structures afford any opportunity at all for individual expression? Or is the personal, subjective domain structured just as mechanically as the setting in which it operates?" And further, in response to Ulrich's famous statements that he would abolish reality and that God does not mean the world literally, Harrison maintains, "In fact, only when taken literally does the figurative process of life degenerate into a petrified mass of formulas, correlates of an inflexible reality principle. And that is precisely when one should think of abolishing it. One must abolish the real and 'regain possession of unreality.' 'To regain possession of reality would mean to erase all the congealed metaphors . . . It would mean recalculating the sum of unreal and unspirited reality principles in accordance with the selective principle of artist and reader, who leave out of the story everything they have no use for." "All of these are metaphors for metaphor itself, for experience as a figurative process, in which repossessing oneself of unreality means nothing less than restoring the 'primal condition of life' . . . It is easy to see that this restoration envisions art as the real task of life, art 'as life's metaphysical activity' [Nietzsche]. One should stress, however, that this vision implies neither an aestheticist negation of nor subjective flight from the objective order of things. For it is the objective order itself that contains this 'nonsensical yearning for unreality [Unwirklichkeit] as the motivating principle of its constitution." Harrison, "Suspension of the World," 35–36; 41, 42.

[5] Porchia, *Voices*, 9.

[6] Thomas Sebastian notes that Musil does not "distinguish precisely between metaphor and synecdoche. Both fall under the general title of analogy. To 'leave things out' by taking a 'part for the whole' is the way the 'pseudo reality' (seinesgleichen) comes about in which, according to Ulrich's observations, people pass their lives. The figurative assimilation is, in fact, a necessary condition for having something to hold onto at all, for holding the chaos at bay . . . However . . . any wholeness is an oscillating figure . . . to be utterly precise, it would ultimately seem to make any order or figuration impossible. It would make impossible any meaningful action. . . ." Sebastian, *Intersection of Science and Literature*, 46.

[7] Friedrich Nietzsche, "On Truth and Lying," 874–84; here 878.

[8] Nietzsche, "On Truth and Lying," 878, emphasis mine.

[9] See, for example, Walter Sokel's discussion of Musil and Sartre and the atrophying role of language, which "blocks," he writes, "the path to varied perspectives" (Der Weg zur Perspektivenvielfalt). Sokel, "Musil und die Existenzphilosophie Jean-Paul Sartres," 674. "For Musil as for Sartre, language fosters that cliché-like

seeing, a thinking in narrowly fixed, stable mono-meanings, with which we create the illusion that we are 'at home' in the world. The signifiers are orientation signs that make the signified objects seem familiar. As soon as we become aware, from whatever cause, that that which is signified is not at all identical with the 'true' things outside, the world begins to become alienating." Sokel, "Musil und die Existenzphilosophie Jean-Paul Sartres," 674. What Sokel does not, however, mention in this essay, is that language has another role as well, a role that determines Musil's and Sartre's chosen life-work as writers.

[10] Marcel Proust, *Remembrance*, 1:628.

[11] Emerson, *Journals and Miscellaneous Notebooks*, 23.

[12] Robert Musil, "Vinzenz and the Mistress of Important Men," act 1.

[13] Proust, *Remembrance* 1:628: "The names which denote things correspond invariably to an intellectual notion, alien to our true impressions, and compelling us to eliminate from them everything that is not in keeping with itself."

[14] Nietzsche, "On Truth and Lying," 880.

[15] Proust, *Remembrance*, 2:993.

[16] Ricoeur, *Rule of Metaphor*, 22.

[17] Ricoeur, *Time and Narrative*, vol. 3, 128.

[18] *KA*: Lesetexte. Band 19: Wiener und Berliner Korrespondenz 1919–1938. 1931. Robert Musil an Bernard Guillemin, 26. Januar 1931.

[19] Proust, *Remembrance*, 2:1013.

[20] *KA*: Lesetexte. Band 16: Frühe Tagebuchhefte 1899–1926. I. Brünn/Stuttgart/Berlin (1899–1908). 4: Altes schwarzes Heft (1900–1904). Tagebuch und literarische Projekte.

[21] Dostoevsky, *Notes from Underground*, 61.

[22] "'Was mögen jetzt die Uhren machen?' fiel Agathe mit einemmal ein und erinnerte sie an den kleinen, idiotischen Sekundenzeiger von Ulrichs Uhr mit seinem genauen Vorrücken den engen Kreis entlang: die Uhr stack in in der Tasche unter dem letzten Rippenbogen, als wäre dort die letzte Rettungsstelle der Vernunft, und Agathe sehnte sich danach, sie hervorzuziehen" (*MoE*, 1434; What might the clocks be doing now?" suddenly occurred to Agathe, and reminded her of the small, idiotic second hand of Ulrich's watch, with its precise forward motions along its narrow circle; the watch was in the pocket under the bottommost rib, as if that were where reason's last place of salvation lay, and Agathe yearned to draw it out, *MwQ*, 1517–18).

[23] Tadie, *Marcel Proust*, 443.

[24] Proust, *Remembrance*, 1:33.

[25] Nietzsche, "On Truth," 882.

[26] Nietzsche, "On Truth," 879, 882.

[27] Steiner, *Grammars of Creation*, 123.

[28] Steiner, *Grammars of Creation*, 124–25.

[29] *KA*: Transkriptionen und Faksimiles. Nachlass Mappen. Mappen Gruppe II. Mappe 11/8: "II R Fr". Fragen zur Reinschrift von Band II. 11/8/252 2 R Fr 29 2.

[30] Proust, *Remembrance*, 2:374–75.

[31] Sartre, *Nausea*, 54.

[32] Woolf, *Mrs. Dalloway*, 142.

[33] Woolf, *Mrs. Dalloway*, 143.

[34] Woolf, *Mrs. Dalloway*, 143.

[35] Observation itself, or the process of seeing new ("Ich lerne Sehen"), as described by Musil's favorite poet Rilke in his novel *The Notebooks of Malte Laurids Brigge*, may be the primary ethical and aesthetic imperative since, as Sokel points out, "'Seeing' in this context amounts to 'seeing through' the perspectives which have come to be routine, fixed and 'obvious' . . . 'To learn to see' means the progressive unsettling and shattering of this way of seeing, whose destruction clears the way for the possibility of a new seeing that moves far beyond the borders of the previous one." Sokel, "Robert Musil und die Existenzphilosophie Jean-Paul Sartres," 660.

[36] Ryan, *Vanishing Subject*, 223.

[37] Deleuze, *Proust and Signs*, 2000.

[38] Deleuze, *Proust and Signs*, 74.

[39] Proust, *Remembrance*, II:1002.

[40] Fontane,"Was Arbeiten Sie?,"1.

[41] *KA*: Lesetexte. Band 14: Gedichte, Aphorismen, Selbstkommentare. Selbstkommentare aus dem Nachlass. Zum Roman Parerga und Paralipomena 1921–1937. Vermächtnis.

[42] Sartre, *Existentialism is a Humanism*, 21.

[43] See for comparison Thoreau, *Walden and Resistance*, especially Thoreau's radical affirmation in *Walden* that he had not learned a bit of useful knowledge from an elder, et cetera, and his injunction to youth to try everything themselves: "What old people say you cannot do you try and find out you can. Old deeds for old people, and new deeds for new . . . I have lived some thirty years on this planet, and have yet to hear the first syllable of valuable, or even earnest advice from my seniors" (5). Like Musil (and Emerson), Thoreau oscillates between this extreme empiricism and a devotion to reading the classics (see his chapter, "Reading") and communing with the eternal ancient reverberating Truths of the cosmos.

[44] Nietzsche, "On Truth," 880–81. References from this essay will be given in parentheses from here on.

[45] Dostoevsky, *Notes*, 75. References from this source will be provided in parentheses from here on.

[46] Nietzsche, "On Truth," 880.

[47] *KA*: Ulrichs Tagebuch. Die Utopie der Höflichkeit.

[48] Nietzsche, "On Truth," 882.

3: Word Magic

IN THE VIENNESE *Kunsthistorisches Museum*, where Robert Musil surely must have wandered during his years in the Austrian capital, the Egyptian rooms are dominated by the figures of the sibling lovers Isis and Osiris, and, as one would expect, by artifacts representing the Egyptian fascination with the themes of death and resurrection. One of the many depictions of the corn god Osiris[1] is accompanied by a tiny hunting arrow in the shape of a back bone, which, the inscription reads, was, in larger size, often affixed to the backs of mummies. This amulet is, on its own, the hieroglyph for "duration." When upright, however, the caption explains, the hieroglyph changes its meaning to "resurrection." Duration, in other words, within the context of an agricultural mythos of death and regeneration, comes to mean resurrection. A vitrine labeled simply "Magic," contains statuettes of enemies with bound arms, tiny male figurines with gigantic phalli, women figurines exposing their genitals, examples of metaphoric ritual magic ensuring the continuation and maintenance of the agricultural cycle. A prostrate Osiris figure is described as a "mummy resurrected to life with aroused penis." Just around the corner we find a Death-papyrus that reads: "There are three kinds of eternity, the kind that constantly renews itself, the kind that is always changing, and the kind that constantly *is*," reminding us of Musil's *Isis and Osiris* poem, which, he wrote, contained the novel "in nucleo" (*T*, 847). The lovers in the poem renew each other (and presumably the world) over and over again, as the last stanza says, "wenn Mond und Sonne wechseln" (*KA*;[2] when the moon and sun change places). This suggests a much more positive reading of Ulrich and Agathe's experimental ritual activity than is usually granted — and of the novel's eternally unfinished state.[3] Where duration equals resurrection, Musil's novel remakes the world over and over again with its experimental discourse, returning unashamedly to the suspect realms of the eternal and endless. "The face of Modernity," as Benjamin writes, "blasts us with its immemorial gaze."[4]

The Vienna collection, compiled in large part during the "Egyptomania" of the late eighteenth century, reflects a Romantic interest in the exotic and mysterious, which had evolved by Musil's time into a modernist interest in varied forms of the so-called primitive, ranging from African masks and Oceanic totems, to the literature, artifacts, and rites of the ancient pagans, to indigenous European folk art, Japanese woodcuts, or the art of children and the insane. The artifacts of ancient cultures were transferred, over a number of decades around the turn of the century, from ethnographic collections such as the one in the *Kunsthistorisches Museum* into art museums, galleries, and artists' ateliers. These artifacts, in turn, became direct inspiration and justification for the development of abstraction, expressionism, and other new modes of interpreting and re-creating the world — modes that served to heighten the status of art and art-making to ritual — a reality-relevant activity. The post-First World War generation, disillusioned by the insufficient and all-too-often hypo-critical reach of didactic language and reason to describe the inner realms and subjectivity that were becoming increasingly important, turned away from a mimesis that seemed merely to validate status quo reality instead of questioning it. Primitivism fulfilled these needs by providing a model of art-making and art experience whereby creation was thought to actu-ally affect or transform physical reality. The conception of word or image magic, whether taken literally or "merely" as a metaphoric description of existential action, presupposes that an individual's actions (art, crime, everyday activity, even not-doing) and ways of looking at the world (thoughts, perceptions, subjective experience) determine the nature of a changing, *metastable* reality.

The modernist fascination with the artifacts of primitive culture and its ideas about both art/ritual-making and the aesthetic, magical expe-rience of art/ritual reception simultaneously participates, however, in a fundamentally opposing assumption about reality. In seeming contra-diction to the idea of art as activating force, primitivism simultaneously accepts some species of *a priori* essence, originary phenomenon, Ur-Idea or archetype to which, or through which, the creative individual returns in his or her process of eternal re-creation of the world. Primitivism seemed to provide the modernists with evidence for universal archetypes, or at least to be another example of what Goethe had earlier called, while looking at the repeating patterns in plants, "originary phenomena" or what the Bloomsbury critic Clive Bell, in an essay on abstract art, would call "significant form." This harking back to *a priori* Platonic forms seems at first glance to be anathema to the various tendencies of modernism, whether conceptualized as magical thinking — the existential idea of changing reality through thoughts, actions, words, and formal arrange-ments — or embodied in the revolutionary political movements of mod-ernism. Essence, like "outmoded concepts such as creativity and genius, eternal value and mystery," was increasingly suspect to the modernists, as Benjamin writes in his famous essay celebrating the death of the aura. Such ideas were considered to be "concepts whose uncontrolled (and at present almost uncontrollable) application would lead to a processing of data in the Fascist sense."[5] And yet despite such understandable reserva-tions, primitivism may have afforded modernists an opportunity to inves-tigate the possibility of universals in a realm explicitly not associated with

Nationalism or the increasingly discredited ethos of the Western militaristic heritage of glory, patriotism, and progress. In terms of art, the question of universality was central to abstraction, as the abstract modernist often seemed to assume that powerful abstract shapes, unintelligible sound poems, or irrational dream images were connected to a subconscious arousal of some ancient primal truth, accessible across cultures and times, provided the artist or viewer free herself from the artificial trappings of civilization, science, and rationality.

While the creative subject thus was enjoined to affect reality by his or her arrangements of words, sounds, images, or actions, it was often assumed that these gestures were related to some ancient core or primeval store of possibilities. The tension between a modernist experimental imperative to participate in the creation of a changing reality (existence precedes essence) and an almost irresistible attraction to some ancient forms or necessary core combines in a study of modernist/primitivist ideas in an inquiry into what it is that is always present, lasting, eternal in the process of ever-changing, regenerative fruitfulness. In a diary entry, Musil writes: "die Dinge, die an die Ursubstanz rühren, haben Kontinuität. Unter diesem Sein ein andres. Ich ist Täuschung. Darunter ein Allgemeines, Beharrendes. Substanz" (KA;[6] The things that touch the primeval substance possess continuity. Under this level of being is another. "I" is an illusion. Beneath it something general, something that lasts. Substance, D, 280).

On the "Island of Health," in one of Musil's unfinished drafts for *The Man without Qualities*, Clarisse constructs a genesis story that mixes primal elements and eternally fertile re-creation, volcanic origins, and a "heroische Respektlosigkeit gegenüber allem, was vor ihr geschaffen worden war" (heroic lack of respect for everything that had been created before):

Feuerflocken aus dem Vulkan des Wahnsinns wurden von den Dichtern geraubt; irgendwann in Urzeiten und später, so oft ein Genie wiederkehrte; diese lodernden, noch nicht zu bestimmten Bedeutungen eingeengten Wortverbindungen wurden in die Erde der gewöhnlichen Sprache gepflanzt und bilden deren Fruchtbarkeit. "Die ja bekanntlich von ihrem vulkanischen Ursprung kommt." — "Aber" so schloss Clarisse "daraus folgt, dass der Geist immer wieder zu Urelementen zerfallen muss, damit das Leben fruchtbar bleibt." (KA)[7]

[Flakes of fire were stolen by poets from the volcano of madness: at some point in primeval times and later, every time a genius revisited earth; these glowing connections of words, not yet constricted to specific meanings, were planted in the soil of ordinary language to form its fertility, "which as we know comes from its volcanic origins." "But" — so Clarisse concluded — "it follows from this that

the mind must decay to primal elements again and again in order for
life to remain fruitful." (*MwQ,* 1565)]

And Ulrich, who is both seduced and concerned by Clarisse's visions on
the island, makes connections between her theory and the art movements
of the early twentieth century, thinking of "die neuen Gebilde . . ., die sich
daraus formen ließen" (these new structures that could be formed) . . .
"um 1900 als man das Andeutende und Skizzenhafte liebte, wie nach
1910 wo man in der Kunst dem Reiz der einfachsten konstruktiven Elemente unterlag und die Geheimnisse der sichtbaren Welt anklingen hieß,
indem man eine Art optisches Alphabet aufsagte" (*MoE,* 1754,around
1900, when people loved the suggestive and sketchy, as after 1910, where
in painting people succumbed to the charm of the simplest constructive
elements and bid the secrets of the visible world echo by reciting a kind
of optical alphabet" (*MwQ,* 1565). Although elsewhere in Musil's philosophical speculations one finds skepticism about whether or not *a priori*
reality, as such, even exists without the subjective perception and imagination of the individual within a welter of relativity (see chapter 2, above:
Ulrich's discussions of empiricism), here we have Ulrich referencing the
"secrets of the visible world," as if there were, indeed, embedded truths
or forms that the individual might discover and make echo through the
right arrangement of words, images, or optical alphabets.

Musil's studies of occult Kabbalistic forms of mysticism, or letter
and number mysticism, including an interest in anagrams, palindromes,
and other secret codes of formal magic, relate to the early twentieth-
century interest in art as ritual and the intensely spiritual exploration of
formal experimentation (abstraction, cubism, Dada, surrealism) as sacred
work. A representative sampling of titles on this topic listed in Musil's
notes includes: *Rosenkreuz u[nd] Bafomet, Versuch der Lösung zweier alter
magischer Quadrate* (1932), *Das Alphabet in Mystik* (1922), *Die Kabbala*
(1910), *Entwicklung u[nd] Untergang des Tempelherrordens* (1887), and
Preisendanz's classic *Papyri Graecae Magicae* (1928), many of which he
mined, along with ethnographic studies of primitive cultures, for models
for the depiction of the many magical rituals and motifs in his novel.[8] In
his essay "Ansätze zu neuer Ästhetik" he alludes to some of these models with an obscure aside reference to "Tiermenschen und multiple Tiere
der primitiven Kulturen, Traum- und Halluzinationsbilder" (Animal people
and multiple animals of primitive cultures, dreams, and hallucinations) and
the "Magische Rolle von Haaren, Fingernägel, Schatten, Spiegelbild und
dergleichen" (*KA;*[9] magical role of hair, fingernails, shadows, reflections
in the mirror, and the like, *P,* 194–95). Not only did Musil depict magical
rituals within his novel, but the act of novel-writing itself, including, I sub-
mit, the formal fact of the unfinished/unfinishable state of *The Man without Qualities,* participates in a magical process of interacting with the world

and recreating it through discourse. To finish the novel, according to some magical beliefs, might be like adding the last letter in a magical palindrome square, or like Alexander Scriabin finishing and performing his masterpiece, *The Mysterium* — both acts that were purported by some to be capable of making the world come to an end. If not quite so physically cataclysmic, finishing would entail at least a loss of interest in the creation itself; for what good is a world that will continue to turn even without us?

At the end of Musil's essay "Literat und Literatur" (Literati and literature) he invokes a modernist reading of primitive poetics, writing that ancient dance songs were "Anweisungen, um das Naturgeschehen in Gang zu halten und die Götter zu bewegen" (usages designed to keep natural occurrences within bounds and to move the gods). "Was die Dichtung zu machen hat" (what poetry has to do), he continues, is, "doch für die seit den Tagen des Orpheus verlorene Überzeugung, dass sie die Welt auf zauberhafte Weise beeinflusse, eine zeitgemäße Umwandlung erst zu suchen" (*KA*;[10] is to seek a contemporary metamorphosis for its conviction, lost since the days of Orpheus, that it influences the world in a magical way, *P*, 89). And in an essay on *Döblins Epos*, Musil writes that "es gibt nicht viele Fragen, welche für die Dichtung so wichtig sind, wie diese, auf welche Weise man ihr den Rausch, die Götter, den Vers, das Überlebensgroße wiedergeben könnte" (*KA*;[11] there are not many questions that are as important for creative writing as the question of how we might bring back the ecstasy, the gods, the verse, its larger-than-life quality). In a notebook entry entitled "Rückblick" (retrospective glance) Musil writes:

> Ethnologen sagen, dass die paläolithischen Felszeichnungen magische Zwecke hatten, dass heute noch Neger am Abend vor der Jagd ähnliche anfertigen. Die Kunst wäre also religiös-zauberischen Ursprungs. Das gleiche, was mein verstorbener Gefährte auf kurzem Wegstück, v. H. [von Hornbostel], von der Dichtung nachgewiesen hat und was ich schon in dem Aufsatz . . . benutzt habe. Diese Auffassung passt zu meinen Gefühlen und Erfahrungen. Aber der (schwache) religiöse Ausbruch, den meine Kindheit einschließt, fällt ins zehnte oder elfte Jahr und weder vorher noch nachher . . . bis . . .? Also Kunst und Religion sind verwandt. (Darum auch Konkurrenten.) Mehr weiß ich nicht . . . Die Kunst ist natürlich selbständig geworden, man könnte aus der Kunst Anhaltspunkte dafür gewinnen, wie Religion heute aussehen müsste, würde sie nicht historisch gelebt, sondern neuzeitlich behandelt: Ich glaube, auch das gehört zu den Piloten, auf denen mein Haus steht.[12]

> [Ethnologists say that Paleolithic rock drawings — and today negroes still make similar ones before they go hunting — were intended to make magic. According to them, art originates in religion and magic. This is the same as my now deceased companion on a short stretch

of the way, v. H. [Hornbostel] once proved about creative writing, which I have already made use of in the essay. This view matches my experiences and feelings. But the (weak) outbreak of religion that is locked away in my childhood happened in my 10th or 12th year, and neither before nor after . . . until . . .? Art and religion, then, are related (for this reason they also compete with each other.) {I don't know more than this.} . . . Art, of course, has become independent; one might come across, in the field of art, some clues about how religion would have to look today if it were not lived out historically, but treated in a contemporary way. I believe this, too, is one of the supports on which my house stands. (D, 428)]

This need for a metamorphosis, or contemporary treatment, of magical processes, he continues in the essay "Literat und Literatur," would have something to do with paying more attention to the "how" of creation than the "what," and would correspond with the modernist movement away from mimesis and toward abstraction and symbolism — and in Musil in particular, toward the subjunctive presentation of alternate versions, possibilities, and a general ethos of the "als ob" (as if).

Modern art was a means of questioning the absolute necessity of the already ordered systems and of bringing about new orders that, ideally, do not turn into fixed ideas. In his 1914 book *Art*, Clive Bell wrote: "The representative element in a work of art may or may not be harmful; always it is irrelevant . . . Art transports us from the world of man's activity to a world of aesthetic exaltation. For a moment we are shut off from human interests; our anticipations and memories are arrested; we are lifted above the stream of life . . ."[13] Wilhelm Worringer, whose 1906 *Abstraction and Empathy* was reprinted for more than forty years and provided another important theoretical basis for the link between primitivism and modernism, combated what he called the "European-classical prejudice of our customary historical conception and valuation of art." The urge to abstraction," he continued, "stands at the beginning of every art" and is a result of "an immense spiritual dread of space."[14] Abstraction for early man — and, he suggests, for the modernist — provided a comfort in a world of confusion. He continues:

> Abstraction provided the possibility of taking the individual thing of the external world out of its arbitrariness and seeming fortuitousness, of externalizing by the approximation to abstract forms, and, in this manner, finding a point of tranquility and a refuge from appearances . . . to wrest the object of the external world out of its natural context, i.e., of everything that is arbitrary.[15]

And, finally, Worringer, quoting Arthur Schopenhauer, tells us that modern man is, indeed, in the same place as primitive man had been:

Having slipped down from the pride of knowledge, man is now just as lost and helpless vis-a-vis the world picture as primitive man, once he has recognized that this "visible world in which we are is the work of Maya, brought forth by magic, a transitory and in itself unsubstantial semblance, comparable to the optical illusion and the dream, of which it is equally false and equally true to say that it is, as that it is not."[16]

Mimesis, in contrast, presupposes the absolute authority of the real and the desirability of maintaining it through continual reinforcement and acceptance. Abstract elements, however, like rhythm, metaphor-making, and repetition, according to Musil, had "their origins"

> in sehr alten Kulturzuständen und insgesamt bedeuten sie eine ausserbegriffliche Korrespondenz des Menschen mit der Welt und abnormale Mitbewegung, deren man übrigens in jedem Augenblick inne werden kann, wenn man, vertieft in ein Kunstwerk, plötzlich kontrollierend Normalbewusstsein einschaltet. Liest man die genialen Beschreibungen, welche Lévy Bruhl in seinem Buch . . . vom Denken der Naturvölker gegeben hat . . . so wird der Zusammenhang mit dem Kunsterlebnis an vielen Stellen derart fühlbar, dass man glauben kann, in diesem eine späte Entwicklungsform jener Frühwelt vor sich zu haben.[17]

> [in quite ancient cultural conditions, and taken together they signify an extraconceptual correspondence of the human being with the world along with abnormal or correlative movements. We can see this at any moment when we find ourselves lost in a work of art and the normal controlling consciousness suddenly switches on. If one reads the brilliant descriptions of the thinking of primitive people that Lévy-Bruhl has given in his book, *Les fonctions mentales des sociétés* primitives, in particular his characterization of that special [metaphoric] attitude toward things that he calls participation, the connection with the experience of art becomes at many points so palpable that one could believe that art was a late form of development of that early world. (*P*, 196–97)]

It is a question of "die Sprengung des normalen Totalerlebnisses" (*KA*;[18] exploding the normal totality of experience), he writes later in the essay, which constitutes, "ein Grundvermögen jeder Kunst" (the basic capacity of every form of art; *P*, 200). "Art's tendency to deny life" suggests that art is "eine Störung bei der Elemente der Wirklichkeit zu einem unwirklichen Ganzen ergänzt werden, das Wirklichkeitswert usurpiert" (*KA*;[19] a "disturbance" in which elements of reality are reconstituted as an unreal whole that usurps the value of reality, *P*, 196). Art — or more specifically, abstraction — usurps the authority of the stasis of the already established real, actually negating it, by bursting its temporary structure and creating new possible structures. Abstraction — a form of selecting and ignoring differences to create metaphors or commonalities — makes palpable and transparent the process by which we perceive, understand, and continually re-create our shared reality.

In *Totem and Taboo* Freud discusses this power struggle with reality, explicating a symptom he calls a belief in "omnipotence of thought" found in the neurotic and the "savage," a belief that thoughts can alter physical reality: "Only in one field," he writes, "has the omnipotence of thought been retained in our own civilization, namely in art."[20] Picasso summed this idea up after viewing the African masks in the Trocadero in Paris in 1907 (the same year he painted *Les demoiselles d'Avignon*), exclaiming: "Men had made these masks and other objects for a sacred purpose, a magic purpose. I realized that this was what painting was all about. Painting isn't an aesthetic operation; it's a form of magic designed as a mediation between this strange hostile world and us, a way of seizing power by giving form to our terrors as well as our desires."[21] Musil, whose readings in Lévy-Bruhl and others would have instructed him about the magical power of naming, invokes this process of taking hold of a strange hostile world by the giving of names or ordering of forms in the scene wherein Ulrich tries to remember the names of flowers as salvation from the abyss of infinity (as I mentioned in chapter 2). Yet at the same time there exists in Musil (and in modernism on the whole) an opposing characteristic desire to expose this hostile world and to unleash the demons of chaos by dis-ordering, un-naming, leaving open. The two impulses, to order and disorder, or, put another way, to discover and construct and to deconstruct and derange, work together as the modernist artist or existential subject grapples with the sibling rivals of necessity and possibility, law and law-breaking.

Wittgenstein wrote that the central question that exercised his entire life's work was: "Is there, *a priori*, an order in the world, and if so, of what does it consist?"[22] What, in other words, is the nature of the order of the world and what is the role of the human subject in maintaining, producing, destroying, or rebuilding our shared reality? And while the easy answer is that Wittgenstein negated the possibility of an *a priori* reality, declaring instead that humans construct their shared reality out of language and perception, the fact remains that in many pronouncements he suggests that there might actually be such an "essence of the world," one that we simply cannot access or express. "What belongs to the essence of the world," he writes, for example, "cannot be expressed by language" (31). Making meaning of the world, whether through discovery of, or invention of, patterns and recurring forms, seems to be a requirement for survival, an aesthetic operation conducted upon possible random chaos to make life bearable. Gunter Gebauer explains, quoting Wittgenstein:

"Only if we see the world in the proper perspective are we filled with 'enthusiasm . . . (But without art, the object is a piece of nature like any other)'; this occurs through a particular method of description. With the help of the art of description, the wonderful side of the world can be grasped" (35). Conversely, Gebauer continues, "Wittgenstein also knows the moments in which he loses this vision of the world," when he has, "'done with the world,' he has created an amorphous (transparent) mass, and the world in all its variety is abandoned like an uninteresting junk closet" (34–35).

This description is eerily reminiscent of many of Musil's descriptions of a world miraculously flooded with, and just as suddenly drained of, meaning. In keeping with Musil's constant allegorical comparison of world and word, this process of meaning and meaninglessness is most often described by him as the difference between living and dead words. The living word, like the living world, does not mean anything definite or fixed, but is imbued with meaning by the creative subject. The dead word, or "concept," like the petrified world of received ideas and unexamined "facts," is always the same word/world, no matter what one brings to it. Musil writes: "'Das Wort bezeichnet nichts Fixiertes[.] Lebendiges Wort voll Bedeutung und Beziehung im Augenblick, von Wille u[nd] Gefühl umflossen. Eine Stunde später nichtssagend, obgleich es alles sagt, was ein Begriff enthält'" (*KA*;[23] The word does not signify anything fixed[.] Living word full of meaning and correspondence in the moment, bathed in will and feeling. An hour later it says nothing although it says everything that a concept contains).

Art then, becomes a method for both ordering the random elements of a chaotic unformed reality and, at the same time, giving glimpses of the "true state" of unformed meaninglessness, through the balancing Apollonian salvation of form. The "moments of being" celebrated by Virginia Woolf, or the extraordinary moments described by Roquentin in Sartre's *Nausea*, like Musil's "exceptional moments" of the Other Condition, are species of this aesthetic/ethical extra-temporal experience of meaning by which artistic arrangement suddenly and miraculously brings everything into place, turning what was moments before a horror of alienation and meaninglessness into glowing significance — but only for a moment. Nietzsche suggests that the great horror and terror of existence is, in fact, its lack of meaning, its utter chaos, ending in death. Pierre Hadot, in his book *The Veil of Isis*, explains:

> The Greeks were superficial out of profundity, says Nietzsche . . . The Greeks knew the truth, they knew the terrors and horrors of existence. Yet it was precisely for this that they knew how to live. To know how to live means knowing how to construct or create for oneself a universe in which one can live, a universe of forms, sounds,

and illusions as well, and dreams, and myths. [Nietzsche writes] "To create, for us, is to veil the truth of nature."[24]

Without this superimposed meaning, without the artistic (possibly artificial) creation of order through metaphor, we may be left with an unbearable situation. As Nietzsche writes in *Der Wille zur Macht*, "Let us think this thought in its most terrible form: existence as it is, without meaning or aim, yet recurring inevitably without any finale of nothingness: 'the eternal recurrence'" (35).[25] And, if there is nothing, it remains for the artist to create something, anything, everything — out of words and images.

Speaking of Ulrich and Agathe's holy discourse, Musil notes:

Das Sprechen besaß für sie einen großen Grad von Wirklichkeit. Die Dinge werden erst in den Worten fertig.[. . .]
Ag. hatte noch den ursprünglichen Glauben an die Zaubermacht (belebende Macht) des Worts.[. . .]
Im Anfang war das Wort — Die Welt sollte aus dem Wort entstanden sein, aber sie entsteht immer noch aus ihm [. . .] — Logos; Besprechen; Wer das Wort hat, hat die Sache.[26]

[Speech possessed for them a high level of reality. Things became real in words first [only in words] . . . Ag. still believed in the original magical power (enlivening power) of the Word — In the beginning was the Word — The world was said to have been created from the Word, but it continued to be created by it [. . .] Logos; discuss; he who possesses the Word possesses the thing.]

The world was said to be created by the Word. Although, as Dharman Rice points out, this notion of Logos may be seen "as a Greek, intellectualist prejudice," actually, he continues, "in the beginning of John's Gospel ('In the beginning was the Word, and the Word was with God, and the Word was God,' and so on), the Word being discussed is not just an idea. It is the burning bush that is not consumed. It is Yahweh, who really refuses to take a name (which would freeze what is above all Dynamism itself)."[27] This more mystical understanding of the Word, a modernist or even postmodernist reading of our Western rational heritage, sees the Word as multivalent, metaphoric, an open sesame to the realms of the subjective, ineffable, the dream state, or other more unaccountably fruitful seed beds of utopian or imaginary zones; this is the Word that Emerson, in his essay *The Poet,* declares is nailed by the (dogmatic) mystic "to one sense, which was a true sense for a moment, but soon becomes old and false," while the (mystical) poet is one who explores, "the double meaning, or, shall I say, the quadruple, or the centruple, or much more manifold meaning, of every sensuous fact." Such words, as Clarisse stresses, are "not yet constricted to specific meanings," are words that Musil would characterize as "living" as opposed to "dead." The world, further, not only *was* created at some time in the ancient past by this multivalent Word but continues to be created by it — a classic mystical notion whereby God gives birth to his son over and over again; or, in more secular terms, man participates in the continual maintenance and co-creation of the world/word. In Musil's consciously aesthetic pronouncement, the ongoing, infinite holy discourse of the siblings, and of his unfinished novel, opens the door to an infinity of possible interpretations or even an infinity of worlds/words, and an infinity of possible creators. The primitive model of "omnipotence of thought," combined with ancient and medieval ideas about eternal co-creation, serve Musil as models for his theory and practice of writing as an on-going, circular, infinite process of rearrangement and re-creation of the world through discourse. As Burton Pike recently said in an interview about *The Man without Qualities:* "and [the novel] is still not finished," inadvertently suggesting — perhaps by a slip of the tongue — that despite its author's death over half a century ago, the novel continues to write itself. This process of continual re-creation with reference to eternal or ancient energies (traced by Musil in his studies of such differing realms as primitivism, mysticism, and psychology) runs through Musil's fictional and essayistic work. The process becomes a cipher for philosophical and aesthetic questions about the role of art and of the artist, or the creative subject, in constructing our shared reality and is related to the differentiation between representation, interpretation, and creative imagination repeatedly stressed in Musil's essays and notes on the novel.

In "Ansätze zu neuer Ästhetik" (toward a new aesthetic) Musil explores again the tension between the two conceptions of knowledge as something already embedded, as Reason or Form, in the mind, and an ever-changing empiricist observation of phenomena:

> Bekanntlich sehen wir was wir wissen: Chiffren, Sigel, Abkürzungen . . . Dies geht so weit, dass ohne präformierte stabile Vorstellungen, und das sind Begriffe, eigentlich nur Chaos bleibt, und da anderseits die Begriffe wieder von der Erfahrung abhängen, entsteht ein Zustand des gegenseitigen Sichformens wie zwischen Flüssigkeit und elastischem Gefäss. (*KA*)[28]

> [It is common knowledge that we see what we know: ciphers, signs, abbreviations . . . This goes so far that without pre-formed stable representations — and these are concepts — really only chaos remains; and since on the other hand concepts are dependent on experience, there arises a condition of mutual formation, like that between a fluid and an elastic container. (*P*, 201)]

This arrangement of reality according to pre-formed conceptions may be nothing but a pragmatic necessity, yet it is sobering to consider that to this day scientists still do not understand why matter clusters together in particular forms in the universe. Is it because of a process akin to what Clarisse calls "the chemistry of words"? And what happens when we consciously try to keep words and forms from adhering together into their habitual combinations?

Frank Kermode, in his essay, "Modernism, Postmodernism, and Explanation," characterizes modernism and its avant-garde as movements that eschewed explanation and its logical strategies in favor of the inexplicit. According to this theory, the modernists saw in the primitive

> a model of that which is not discursive, explanatory, that which baffles us by its isolation, its manifest inexplicitness, its apparent indifference to our concerns, its masks — in short, by its possession of an indistinct power that seems alien but that calls on us — with an urgency . . . to interpret it in such a way that we may discover the significance that we sense it must have, namely, the unutterable contained in it, which it does not attempt to utter.[29]

Ulrich, commenting on Clarisse's mystical theory of language and, by extension, the problem with didactic and cliché language and literature, notes: "in unsren Gedichten ist zuviel starre Vernunft; die Worte sind ausgebrannte Begriffe, die Syntax reicht Stock und Seil wie für Blinde" (*MoE*, 1753; In our poems there is too much of rigid reason; the words are burned-out notions, the syntax holds out sticks and ropes as if for the blind, *MwQ*, 1564). While Clarisse cannot find "Worte . . . welche keine Begriffe sind" (*MoE*, 1753; Words that are not ideas, *MwQ*, 1564), she plays her serious game with word pairs, such as "Ichrot" (*MoE*, 1753; I-red, *MwQ*, 1564), which are "noch von nichts festgehalten und flog empor" (*MoE*, 1753; not yet imprisoned by anything, and flew upward, *MwQ*, 1564). When Ulrich tried to work with the word pairs, or groups of words,

> Sein Gehirn griff sie gleich als Satz auf oder trennte sie durch Beistriche, um zu betonen, dass es dies nicht tue. Cl[arisse] nannte es die Chemie der Worte, dass sie sich immer zu Gruppen zusammenschließen, und gab Gegenmaßregeln an . . . Gott!!rot!!!fährt! . . . Gott fährt grün grün grün. (*MoE*, 1753)
>
> [his brain immediately either understood them as a sentence or separated them by commas in order to underline that it was not making them into a sentence. Clarisse called this the chemistry of words, that they always cohere in groups, and showed how to counter this . . . God!! red!!! goes! . . . God goes green green green. (*MwQ*, 1564)]

In the review of Alfred Döblin mentioned above, Musil writes about what modern prose writers could learn from early prose, referring to

Wiederholung. Assonanzen und Alliterationen—wie "Rieselrassel-rausch," "gurrendes Zackelzucken," oder . . . "Wolken gewallt . . ., wallende Wolken gerollt" — wechseln mit direkten, das psycholo-gische Gewicht mehrmals hintereinander auflegenden Wiederhol-ungen, wie "Du wirst dein Blut und Blut fühlen," oder "Nie und nimmer, nimmer und niemals." (*KA*)[30]

[Repetitions, assonances and alliterations — like "ripple-rattle-rush," "cooing zigzagging," or "clouds coruscating . . . coruscating clouds rolling" — take turns with repetitions that pile the psychological weight directly upon each other, like, "You will feel your blood and blood," or "never and no-time, no-time and nevermore."]

Sounding as if he were explaining Clarisse's word magic, Musil continues, writing that

manchmal werden vier zu ersteigende Berge durch viermal hintere-inander dastehendes "Berg" ausgedrückt, unverarbeitet, genau so, wie sie in Wirklichkeit dastehen für einen verzweifelnden Blick . . . manchmal wiederholt sich die gleiche Zeile in den verschiedensten Verkettungen, unerwartet, widerspenstig . . . oft kein europäisches Kunstmittel mehr zu sein scheint, sondern der Gesang eines Wahn-sinnigen, der sich seine Worte auf den Schädel trommelt, oder die religiöse Verzückung eines Kannibalen . . . Und da kann man, glaube ich wohl, daran erinnern, dass diese geheime Übereinstimmung zwischen Lautbild und bezeichnetem Gegenstand zum Urzauber der Sprache gehört, ebenso wie die Beeinflussung der Atemkurve und das Geheimnis der ungleichen Wiederholung zu Rhythmus und Reim gehören. (*KA*)[31]

[sometimes four mountains that are to be climbed are depicted by [the word] "mountain" repeated four times, each one standing behind the other, unaltered, exactly as they stand in reality for a despairing moment . . . sometimes the same line repeats itself in the most var-ied connections, unexpectedly, refractorily . . . [until] it often doesn't seem like a European artistic method at all, but rather like the song of a madman, drumming on a skull, or the religious ecstasy of a can-nibal . . . And then one is well reminded, I believe, that this secret harmony between sound-picture and designated object belongs to the original magic of language, just as the influence of the curve of breath and the secret of irregular repetition belong to rhythm and rhyme.]

Clarisse's attempts to free words from their ideas and liberate the immemorial energies of language, reminiscent of Gertrude Stein's *Ten-der Buttons* and other modernist experiments with reinvigorating dead words, demonstrate the difficulty of the problem of making and seeing anew in a world already so named, categorized, and arranged — but stress the importance of rediscovering the "Urzauber" (original magic) necessary for such new seeing. Hugh Kenner, in his portrait of modernism, *The Pound Era*, marks the discovery and gradual decipherment of fragments of the Greek poetess Sappho's verses, from 1896–1909, as one point (along with the discovery of the artifacts of Troy and of the cave paintings of Lascaux) when modernists began to look for new forms in primitive cultural artifacts. The Sappho fragments, he argues, provided the modernists with a powerful model of concision, spareness of words, and fragmentary beauty; since the papyrii were miserably crumbled, all that existed were phrases and, in some instances, single words, and these small gems were wondered over for decades by translators, scholars and modernist poets who imitated the unintentional unintelligibility of the poetess of Lesbos. Kenner also points to advances in the field of etymology, to extensive scholarship in Sanskrit, Anglo Saxon, Provençal, Arabic, and Chinese by modernist poets and scholars, to Skeats's Etymological Dictionary, famously pored over by James Joyce. Ezra Pound's *Cantos*, he tells us, contain archaic words,

> Borrowing from the Greek, Latin, Chinese, Italian, French, Proven-çal, Spanish, Arabic, and Egyptian Hieroglyphic language; this list is not complete. And as for *The Waste Land* . . .; and as for *Ulysses* . . .; and one shrinks from a linguistic inventory for *Finnegan's Wake*, where even Swahili components have been identified. The province of these works, as never before in history, is the entire human race speaking, and in time as well as space.[32] (ellipses in original)

There was, Kenner continues, an attempt to return old words to usage because they were thought to contain more force and latent magic than modern watered-down words. Eliot studied Sanskrit circa 1910; Kenner explains:

> It was with the example of a scholarship committed in this way to finding the immemorial energies of language that he [Eliot] perceived how the most individual parts of a poet's work "may be those in which dead poets, his ancestors, assert their immortality most vigorously." And also how in language used with the right attention "a network of tentacular roots" may reach "down to the deepest terrors and desires."[33]

The seeming paradox, then, of reaching down or back to ancient, immemorial energies in order to reinvigorate or release new, modern forces is somehow a key to the tension between existential co-creation of reality and the more mystical, or "essential" attempt to uncover the source of foundational archetypes or possibilities (and, by association, potential limitations) of an already determined system.

Despite Musil's frequent discussions of possible Ur-phenomena or original energies, despite Ulrich's consideration of an *a priori* morality, Musil's conception of ritual magic is described in one passage as emphatically not imitation of or even uncovering of pre-existent reality, but creation of it, that is, *Vorbildzauber* (modeling magic; reality imitates art). One might, however, raise the question of whether or not it is possible to create anything that is not already somehow waiting to be created, like a seed or a pre-existent possibility. Perhaps we create only "what must be made." In another note on the work of his friend the ethnologist and musicologist von Hornbostel, Musil paraphrases:

> Die Formstrengen alter Gedichte sind Ritualgesänge. Die Bedeutung des Rituals: Erneuerung, Inganghaltung des Naturgeschehens[.] Ritual ist eine Verfahrungsweise dazu. Inhalt: *was gemacht werden muss.* Es ist "Vorbildzauber." "Das Ritual ist nicht Darstellung, sondern Herstellung des Geschehens . . ." Geschaffen wird durch die Tat und durch das Wort"[.] Die Form des Ritualtextes ist die der Ritualhandlung. (*KA*)[34]

> [The formal strictures of ancient poetry are ritual songs. The meaning of the ritual: renewal, maintenance of natural occurrences [.] Ritual is a procedure with this end. Content: *what must be made.* It is "imitative magic." "The ritual is not depiction, but creation of the occurrence . . ." "Creation occurs through the act and through the word." The form of the ritual text is the same as the ritual act.] (emphasis mine)

And Musil continues with an unexplained list of a repeated word pair somehow related by virtue of "correspondences":

> Fülle, Milch, Fülle, Fülle, Milch: d[ass].i[st]. Bild - u[nd] Wortzauber . . . Irgendwo gebraucht H[ornbostel] als übergeordneten Begriff zu Parallelstellen udgl. "Entsprechungen." Schrift ist nicht Mitteilung, noch Gedächtnishilfe, sondern Bildzauber. (*KA*)[35]

> [Fullness, milk, fullness, milk, fullness, fullness, milk: that is picture and word magic . . . Hornbostel uses "correspondences" somewhere as a general term for parallels and the like. Writing is not communication or memory aid, but picture magic.]

This reference to "correspondences" brings us back to metaphor and to its wide-reaching importance for Musil's aesthetic and ethical theory of experience and creation. Word and picture magic, as a process of correspondences, parallels, likenesses, sympathies, and metaphors, is an aesthetic concern, a question of formal importance. While Musil once wrote to a disapproving uncle that he ought to consider that a man who likes incest is really sometimes just a man who loves metaphors, one could take this saying a step further: for those who are made uncomfortable by the taboo realms of the irrational, consider: a man who loves magic or mysticism is also just a man who loves metaphors. Musil's fascination with magic and mysticism is itself a metaphor for his process of art-making.

Writing of Proust and Baudelaire, Benjamin makes a connection between ritual magic, metaphors, and time that is fitting for Musil's aesthetic and mystical metaphysics as well. The forging or seeing of correspondences (metaphor-making) was for Proust a central method in the "lifelong exercises in which he strove to bring to light past things saturated with all the reminiscences that had worked their way into his pores during his sojourn in the unconscious."[36] Proust saw kindred elements in Baudelaire's *Fleurs du mal*, writes Benjamin, — elements kindred to Musil's experiments as well. Benjamin quotes Proust on Baudelaire: "Time is peculiarly chopped up in Baudelaire, only a very few days open up, they are significant ones. Thus it is understandable why turns of phrases like 'One evening' occur frequently in his works." And then Benjamin makes some of his own connections:

> These significant days are days of completing time, to paraphrase Joubert . . . They are not connected with the other days, but stand out from time. As for their substance, Baudelaire has defined it in the notion of the *correspondances*. . . . The important thing is that the *correspondances* record a concept of experience which includes ritual elements. Only by appropriating these elements was Baudelaire able to fathom the full meaning of the breakdown which he, a modern man, was witnessing . . . What B[audelaire] meant by *correspondances* may be described as an experience which seeks to establish itself in crisis-proof form. This is only possible within the realm of the ritual.[37]

The methodology of *Wortzauber* and *Vorbildzauber* combined with the idea of symbolic universalism and significant form are illuminated by an understanding of the concept of essential time, duration, eternity, and fleetingness in Musil (and in the kindred experiments of Proust, Baudelaire, and Benjamin as well). The concept of "crisis-proof form" seems to point to the inviolate world of the extra-temporal aesthetic, that is, the only place where these metaphoric moments can last, and to the Other Condition as ritual space. In his essay "Lessons from Likenesses," Benjamin writes that "an understanding of the realm of 'likenesses' is of fundamental importance for illumination of large areas of occult knowledge," adding that modern man uses "considerably less of these magical correspondences" than ancient cultures or the primitives.[38] What is left of the mimetic ability to see likenesses, according to Benjamin, may be the onomatopoetic quality of language itself, that quality that he further qualifies as a "nonsensual [i.e. non-physical] likeness," which not only creates tension between the spoken and the intended, but also between the written and the intended and similarly between the spoken and the written. And every time in a fully new, original, un-plumbable way.[39]

The mimetic ability to see likenesses, writes Benjamin, which was "earlier the foundation of prophetic seeing," now is to be found in language and writing, which explains the double sense of the word "reading" in its "profane and also magical meaning," comprising both the student's reading of an ABC primer and the astrologer's reading of the future in the stars.[40] In the same essay he writes that the perception of likenesses "is in every case, bound to a [momentary] flaring up" and that it "appears, thus, to be bound to a temporal moment."[41] Reading and writing in the magical sense enact a temporal disturbance or interruption to the flow of normalcy, "the gift of allowing the spirit to participate in that tempo in which likenesses fleetingly flare up from out of the river of things, only to sink away again."[42] Rolf Tiedemann further explicates Benjamin's "theory of mimetic ability":

The theory holds that experience rests on the ability to produce and perceive similarities, which Benjamin identified as the achievements of language and writing. . . . Vis-a-vis abstracting cognition, his concept of experience wanted to maintain immediate contact with mimetic behavior. He was concerned about "palpable knowledge" (gefühltes Wissen), which "not only feeds on the sensory data, taking shape before his eyes, but can very well possess itself of abstract knowledge — indeed, of dead facts — as something experienced and lived through" . . . Images take the place of concepts — the enigmatic and vexing dream images which hide all that falls through the coarse mesh of semiotics.[43]

While modernist thinkers like Musil and Benjamin are always grappling with the seeming contradiction between abstract concepts and palpable, experienced knowledge, the temporal tension between *a priori* forms and continual recreation of reality does not seem to have constituted a philosophical problem for Plato. In his *Timaeus* Plato posited a "likely fable" describing the genesis of the world, which, he wrote, reenacted the divine creation, consequently giving birth to the world once again through his discourse. Pierre Hadot, in his *Veil of Isis*, writes that discourse for Plato was a means for mankind to attempt to understand the secrets of the construction of the world, and that Plato meant to suggest that we "should try to imitate the generation of the universe — that is, by a divine being — through the generation of discourse; in other words, we should try to rediscover the genetic movement of things in the motion of discourse."[44] "This is why," Hadot continues, "the

Timaeus is presented as a *poiēsis*, that is, both a discourse and a poem, or an artistic game that imitates the artistic game of the poet of the universe, the divinity. Thus, Plato believes that the god World is born in his discourse ('this god who once was truly born one day, and who has just been born in our discourse')." The space of discourse, of the generation of words and images, becomes a ritual, metaphoric realm for magically enacting and reenacting reality.

While for Plato this fictional world of discourse is a more or less true copy of one perfect ideal world, for Musil — who wrote that "God doesn't mean the world at all literally" — every fictive world is only one possible metaphoric world of numberless possible "intentions of God" — or the author. Musil and other modernists, suspicious of any established norms or values, either struggled to reconcile the coexistence of an ethos of creative existential world-making and a belief in a pre-existent (and limited) form or model of the world, or they chose to ignore the inherent contradiction. Plato's *Timaeus* clearly rejects the idea of there being more than one world, thus implying that the likely fable of his discourse is a copy of one perfect ideal world, more or less correct, rather than one of many possible versions. He writes, "Are we right in saying that there is one world, or that there are many and infinite? There must be only one, if the created copy is to accord with the original."[45] Musil's cosmology, in contrast, seems to *require* a multiverse of possible drafts, the "not-yet-actualized experiments of God," in Musil's phrase, more in line, perhaps, with Hadot's description of Augustine's idea of natural magic, which

> consisted of extracting from the hidden bosom of nature the beings contained within it. All the effects of divine creation, he [Augustine] wrote, all the beings or phenomena that might appear over the course of the ages, potentially exist in the texture of the elements: "As females are great with their litter, the world too is great with the causes of the beings that are to be born." Since the Stoics, these hidden causes had been called "seminal reasons" . . . It is God, says Augustine, who brings it about that "seeds develop . . ." . . . Yet there can also be external interventions that unleash these forces and their program. The magical operation is just such an external intervention: "To use external causes — which, although they are not natural [writes Augustine] are nevertheless used in conformity with nature — so that the things that are contained in a hidden way in the secret bosom of nature may burst free and are, as it were, produced outside, deploying the measures, numbers, and weights that they have received, in secret, from Him . . ."[46]

Albrecht Schöne, in his inspiring essay "Zum Gebrauch des Konjunktivs bei Robert Musil" (On the use of the subjunctive mood in Robert Musil) describes the history of the idea of the artist as "continuing creation" within the context of Musil's use of the subjunctive and the tension between utopian thinking and frozen utopia.[47] This artistic creation, he writes, in a parallel to the Augustinian cooperation between what was already given (God's creation) and what external causes might intervene, "would only be conceivable as a mere execution of divine intention through mankind . . . the creative writer becomes empowered by this same subjunctive mood, he appears to be no longer executor, but a participant in the divine experimental potential for 'continual creation.' Thus," Schöne continues, "do we find in [Musil's] notes, corresponding to this man of possibility, 'the not yet awakened intentions of God.'"[48] Schöne proceeds to categorize ideas about the artist as "second maker," enumerating tensions between mimesis and imagination and explaining that Gottsched's requirement for the imitation of nature included Aristotle's proviso that one ought to imitate nature not only as she is but as she could or should be.[49] And Schöne notes that in 1740, echoing again Augustine's seed possibilities and prefiguring Musil's infinite alternate worlds, Breitinger declared that "there have to be besides the real world, also countless possible worlds, in which there is another relationship and connection of things, other laws of nature and movement."[50] Musil, in keeping with his primary allegiance to the interests of the creative writer, was not interested in finished, closed, perfected states (of being, of thought, of art, of politics), but dwelt in the world of subjunctive possibilities, correspondences, and transformation.

Thus the essential difference between a Platonic utopia of perfected forms and a Musil utopia of, alternately the Other Condition, the Next Step or the Inductive Sensibility, lies in the two elements of time and metaphoric transparency, that is, a concept of time that is flexible, relative, and subjective, and a concept of reality that is based on the eternal construction of new metaphoric descriptions and visions. While neither Musil nor Nietzsche could ever be considered idealists or utopians in the Platonic sense, yet they both are continually on the lookout for new possibilities, trans-valuations of values, and new perspectives on material "reality" that are bound to overturn any outworn status quos. Musil was a trained scientist and mathematician, and Nietzsche was at all times a defender of life and nature against the "enemies of life" who look to other worlds for consolation. Yet at the same time their relationship with the so-called real (that is, physically real world) is almost as tentative as Plato's. While Nietzsche sees the real world as something constructed by a process of competing human perceptions and inventions, filtered through the metaphors that we mistakenly or lazily take to be faithful descriptions of reality, Musil, the sometime empiricist scientist, repeatedly raises the world of imagination above the supposedly real world of "facts." "Metaphor," again, proves "more meaningful than reality." In a kindred tone, in *Der Wille zur Macht* (*The Will to Power*), Nietzsche prefigures Musil's tendency:

A "thing-in-itself" just as perverse as a "sense-in-itself," a "meaning-in-itself." There are no "facts-in-themselves," for a sense must always be projected into them before there can be "facts." The question "what is that?" is an imposition of meaning from some other view point.

"Essence," the "essential nature," is something perspectival and already presupposes a multiplicity. At the bottom of it there always lies, "what is that for *me*?" (For us, for all that lives, etc.). A thing would be defined once all creatures had asked "what is that?" and had answered their question. Supposing one single creature, with its own relationships and perspectives for all things were missing, then the thing would not yet be "defined." In short: the essence of a thing is only an *opinion* about the "thing." Or rather: "it is considered" is the real "it is," the sole "this is". . . . The origin of "things" is wholly the work of that which imagines, thinks, will, feels. The concept "thing" itself just as much as all its qualities. — Even the "subject" is such a created entity. A "thing" like all others: a simplification with the object of defining the force which posits, invents, thinks, as distinct from all individual positing, inventing, thinking as such. Thus a capacity as distinct from all that is individual — fundamentally, action collectively considered with respect to all anticipated action (action and the probability of similar actions).[51]

And Musil writes, paraphrasing Ludwig Klages:

Das Schauen verwandelt den Schauenden; der Wahrnehmungsakt hebt den Wahrnehmenden vom Wahrnehmungsding ab. Die Wachheit des Menschen von ehedem ähnlich unsren Träumen ohne Schlaf zu sein. Hauptkriterium: die ständige Verwandelbarkeit des Gegebenen. Die Strasse wird Kanal usw. So auch im Märchen. (*T*, 623)

[Observation transforms that which is observed; the act of perception separates the perceiver from the thing that is perceived. The wakefulness of mankind is thus similar to our dreams without sleep. Main criterion: the constant changeability of the given. The streets become canals, etc. Also in fairy tales.]

Thus, despite their well-founded and important suspicion of "Schleudermystik" (Musil's coined term for wishy-washy mysticism and the sloppy thinking associated with it) and of faith in the otherworldly, both Musil and Nietzsche are related to Emerson, as transcendentalist — and therefore also to the often maligned idealist Plato — by their privileging of the human imagination, its creative power and responsibility, over the status quo of the material world: "Main criterion: the constant changeability of what is given."

Furthermore, Nietzsche, again in *Der Wille zur Macht*, reframes the debate as a tension between *being* (finite, *a priori*, static) and *becoming* (creative, subjective, engaged), concluding: "That everything recurs is the closest approximation of a world of becoming to a world of being— high point of the meditation."[52] The important distinction between what is given and what might come, between being and becoming, crystalizes in the concept of time. Duration, as the Osiris arrow in the Egyptian wing tells us, equals resurrection.

While a fixed physical reality is not privileged by any of these thinkers, Plato seems to have believed in a secondary reality that was eternally the same, ideal, *a priori*, perfected (*being*). The revolutionary thinkers Emerson, Nietzsche, and Musil see the world as continually reinventing itself (*becoming*) — albeit with reference and eternal recurrence to some abstracted Ur-ideas — into infinite, always changing, never enduring alternate worlds, perspectives, values, and possibilities. While for Plato the physical world is a poor and deceiving copy of the "really real" ideal world,[53] for Nietzsche and Musil it is more like an unfinished and unfinishable collaborative work-in-progress that more faithfully reflects the imaginings and dreams of artists, writers, and creative subjects.

As Schöne writes: "How could the grasped *potentialis* in the experimental 'other condition' of incest, its momentary illumination and clarification, be carried over into the enduring reality mode of a new indicative? The carrying over of the *potentialis* into a new, better indicative is held back on its side by the subjunctive case: is preserved in the mode of promise."[54] Musil's intention, then, despite the siblings' occasional attempt to make the "other condition" into a "lasting condition," cannot be to freeze the subjunctive into an indicative. The subjunctive, as potential, is always necessarily a futuristic tense; something that may come in the future, but which is never completed and done with. Schöne concludes: "This futuristic tendency of the *potentialis*, however, possesses a necessary durative character. As a mode of possibility thinking, wherein every goal can only be a temporary result, only a 'partial solution,' the experimental, utopian subjunctive throws itself likewise into the future and never catches up with itself — except if it itself dissolves."[55] And Burton Pike, in his essay "Unfinished or without End," concludes similarly:

> The universe, viewed as a limbo of pure potentiality, is a place of perfect harmony. But the delicate balance is constantly being upset, giving rise to the specifics of the real world. Musil's new form of fiction is future-oriented, and the future can be neither fragment nor torso because, like the characters in the novel, we do not know what form it will take. To counterbalance this cosmic uncertainty, Musil engages in the novel in an obsessive search for a mystic condition that might offer a potential synthesis of human time and essential time, modern precision and ancient soul, science and human experience.[56]

Musil's future-looking subjunctive sense of limitless possibilities plays with the mercury of what is and what could be interminably, stopping time in moments of likeness, seeing patterns in moments of imprecision, finding meaning in intermittent eternal correspondence. And conclusion, completion, duration, are not the categories that carry creative valance. We cannot see anything at all without preconceptions and concepts, but seeing anew (experience) changes them. And in Musil's aesthetic theory, abstraction — a form of metaphor whereby things that are in actuality not the same as each other are stripped of their differences to create likenesses, patterns, formal arrangements — is the dynamic process by which one sees anew. In "Ansätze zu neuer Ästhetik" (Toward a new aesthetic), Musil writes:

> Je eindrucksärmer ein der Wahrnehmung dargebotenenes Material ist, desto deutlicher die darin enthaltenen Beziehungen hervortreten werden. Der Rhythmus wird am skandierten Vokal deutlicher als am Wort und am deutlichsten am Klopfgeräusch, das zwar akustisch kompliziert, aber sozusagen seelisch einfach ist; ebenso treten an einer Statue die linearen und flächigen Zusammenhänge deutlicher hervor als am lebendem Körper. (*KA*)[57]

> [We know that in general the weaker the impression made on us by material offered to our perception, the more clearly the relations contained within it become apparent. Rhythm is clearer in a scanned vowel than in a word, and clearest in the sound of a beat, which is, to be sure, acoustically complex but, as it were, physically simple; similarly, relations in line and surface stand out more clearly in a statue than in a living body. (*P*, 195)]

This passage is reminiscent of Baudelaire's defense of maquillage in his programmatic essay "The Painter of Modern Life." "Who," Baudelaire asks, "would dare to assign to art the sterile function of imitating nature?" Cosmetics, he argues, when used not to imitate nature but rather to abstract into art, strives "to rid the complexion of those blemishes that Nature has outrageously strewn there, and thus to create an abstract unity in the colour and texture of the skin, a unity which, like that produced by the tights of a dancer, immediately approximates the human being to the statue, that is to something superior and divine. . . ."[58] The painter of modern life, like Monsieur G., Baudelaire's exemplary flaneur/artist, has the task of, first of all, observing the details of life, and then distilling from modern dress, modern types, modern reality, that which transcends time. "By 'modernity'," Baudelaire explains, "I mean the ephemeral, the fugitive, the contingent, the half of art whose other half is the eternal and the immutable."[59]

As Musil writes in a short prose piece entitled "Schwarze Magie" (Black magic), "Das Denken hat neben anderen Zwecken den, geistige

Ordnungen darin zu schaffen. Auch zu zerstören. Aus vielen Erschei-
nungen des Lebens macht der Begriff und eben so oft macht eine Erscheinung des Lebens aus einem Begriff viele Neue . . ." (*KA*;[60] Thinking
has, among other goals, the task of creating spiritual arrangements. Also
destroying them. The concept is made out of many appearances of life,
and just as often an appearance of life makes of one concept many new
ones). This discourse, in other words, gives birth (again and again) to a
(multitude of) world(s), none of them more real than any others, none of
them finished, all of them possible, all always changing, always becoming,
always being. Duration is only possible through a creative process of eternal metaphoric resurrection and recreation.

Notes

[1] Since a number of scholars have taken umbrage with my designation of Osiris
as a corn God on several occasions, I refer anyone with similar scruples to Sir
James Frazer's chapter 40, "The Nature of Osiris: Osiris a Corn God" in *The
Golden Bough*. Despite quite reasonable doubts as to whether there was even corn
in Egypt, Tacitus refers to Egypt as "the great corn country" in *Annals*, Book 2
in *The Works of Tacitus*, Oxford translation, revised (New York: Harpers, 1881),
92; and, of course, in Genesis 42:1 we find a description of Egypt as corn-filled. It
seems quite probable that what has been translated as "corn" or "Maize"in modern English and German was actually another plant, possibly a general designation
for "grain," but the fact remains that mythically and metaphorically the image
and symbolism of a corn stalk surrounds our reception of the Osiris myth. This
controversy is not of great importance to Musil studies, and the factual historical
reality of whether or not what we now consider corn existed in Egypt or whether
or not Osiris *was really* a corn god (or was *really* cut up into pieces and then reas-
sembled by his sister/wife), is mostly irrelevant to the question of whether Musil
may have *understood* Osiris in relationship to the idea or image of corn. The metaphoric association suggested by the fertile corn and Osiris's lost penis (eaten by
the fishes when he is cut up into pieces) which is then recreated out of wax by Isis,
is, however, indeed relevant to our subject, as an ancient mythologem of metaphoric transubstantiation of created object becoming body, becoming symbol for
food and regeneration.

[2] *KA*: Lesetexte: Band 14: Gedichte, Aphorismen, Selbstkommentare. Gedichte.
Isis und Osiris.

[3] Lowell Bangerter reads "Isis and Osiris" as an example of the longing to merge
the "fundamental antithetical tendencies of morality" and, by association, the irrationality of Isis with the rationality and materiality of Osiris, through the power
of love." "As ultimately developed within the novel," he continues, "the longing
for completion of the self, which is the focus of 'Isis and Osiris,' is Musil's most
extreme projection of the sense of possibility. It is the motivation for Ulrich's
attempt to join Agathe in the Utopia of the 'Other Condition' through actualiza-
tion of what Marie-Louise Roth has called 'the felt inkling of unity between spirit
and nature, subject and object, the dream of termination of the duality between

'I' and 'you.'" Bangerter, "Experimental Utopias," 18. This summary neglects the essential point that the union of Isis and Osiris in the poem, as sun and moon in a cycle, is explicitly a temporary one, one that recurs but involves meeting and parting, meeting and parting, one in which a duration of union could only mean a cancelling out of both light and dark, an eclipse.

4 Benjamin, *Arcades Project*, 23.

5 Benjamin, *Illuminations*, 218.

6 *KA*: Lesetexte. Band 16: Frühe Tagebuchhefte 1899–1926 IV. Wien (1918–1926) 21: Die Zwanzig Werke III (1920–1926). Wien/Berlin/Mödling, Herbst 1920–Anfang 1921.

7 *KA*: Lesetexte. Band 4: Der Mann ohne Eigenschaften. Die Vorstufen. Aus dem Nachlass Ediertes. Die Romanprojekte 1918–1926. Die Zwillingsschwester. S6 Clarisses Reisen.

8 See my essays "Versuche ein Scheusal zu lieben" and "Musil and Mysticism."

9 *KA*: Lesetexte. Band 12: Essays. Ansätze zu neuer Ästhetik, 490.

10 *KA*: Lesetexte. Band 12: Essays. 1936–1921. Literat und Literatur 412.

11 *KA*: Lesetexte. Band 13: Kritiken. Buchrezensionen. Literatur. Alfred Döblins Epos.

12 *KA*: Lesetexte. Band 17: Späte Tagebuchhefte 1928–1942. I. Wien/Berlin (1927–1939) 34: Schwarzes Heft weich (1930–1938)/

13 Clive Bell, *Art*, 27.

14 William Worringer, "Abstraction and Empathy," 69.

15 Worringer, "Abstraction and Empathy," 68.

16 Worringer, "Abstraction and Empathy," 69.

17 *KA*: Lesetexte. Band 12: Essays. 1918–1926. Ansätze zu neuer Ästhetik 492.

18 *KA*: Lesetexte. Band 12: Essays. 1918–1926. Ansätze zu neuer Ästhetik 496.

19 *KA*: Lesetexte. Band 12: Essays. 1918–1926. Ansätze zu neuer Ästhetik 491.

20 Freud, *Totem and Taboo*, 149.

21 Pablo Picasso quoted in Enrique Mallen, "Stealing Beauty," 1.

22 Gebauer, *Wittgensteins anthropologisches Denken*, 12: "Ist, *a priori*, eine Ordnung in der Welt, und wenn ja, worin besteht sie?" Quotes from this source will henceforth be cited in the text in parentheses.

23 *KA*: Nachlass: Mappe VII/11 E und E VII/11/130 E 16 2.

24 Hadot, *Veil of Isis*, 292.

25 Nietzsche, *Will to Power*.

26 *KA*: Transkriptionen und Faksimiles. Nachlass Mappen. Mappen Gruppe II. Mappe II/4. "AE" Anders- Einzelblätter. II/4/88 AE 20 9.

27 Correspondence with author, 24 Aug. 2009.

28 *KA*: Lesetexte. Band 12: Essays 1918–1926. Ansätze zu neuer Ästhetik 497.

29 Kermode, "Modernism, Postmodernism, and Explanation," 365.

[30] *KA*: Lesetexte. Band 13 Kritiken. Buchrezensionen. Literatur. Alfred Döblins Epos.

[31] *KA*: Lesetexte. Band 13: Kritiken. Buchrezensionen. Literatur. Alfred Döblins Epos.

[32] Kenner, *Pound Era*, 95.

[33] Kenner, *Pound Era*, 110. Kenner is quoting Eliot in "Tradition and the Individual Talent" and in "Ben Johnson" here.

[34] *KA*: Transkriptionen & Faksimiles. Nachlass: Mappen. Mappengruppe VI. Mappe VII/3. "Aufsätze." Literat und Literatur. VI/3/6. Hornbostel-Vortrag.

[35] *KA*: Transkriptionen & Faksimiles. Nachlass: Mappen. Mappengruppe VI. Mappe VI/3. "Aufsätze." Literat und Literatur. VII/3/9. Hornbostel-Vortrag 4.

[36] Benjamin, *Illuminations*, 180.

[37] Benjamin, *Illuminations*, 181.

[38] Benjamin, *Aura und Reflexion: Schriften zur Ästhetik und Kunstphilosophie*, 124–25.

[39] Benjamin, *Aura und Reflexion*, 127.

[40] Benjamin, *Aura und Reflexion*, 127.

[41] Benjamin, *Aura und Reflexion*, 126.

[42] Benjamin, *Aura und Reflexion*, 128–29.

[43] Tiedemann, "Dialectics at a Standstill," 929–45, qtd. 934.

[44] Hadot, *Veil of Isis*, 156.

[45] Plato, *Timaeus*, 136.

[46] Hadot, *Veil of Isis*, 107–8.

[47] Schöne, "Gebrauch des Konjunktivs," 207, 217, 220.

[48] Schöne, "Gebrauch des Konjunktivs," 212.

[49] Schöne, "Gebrauch des Konjunktivs," 214.

[50] Schöne, "Gebrauch des Konjunktivs," 215.

[51] Nietzsche, *Will to Power*, 301–2.

[52] Nietzsche, *Will to Power*, 330.

[53] Plato referred to the world of ideal forms as the "ontos on," or "the really real." See, for example: Kroner, "What Is Really Real," 1.

[54] Schöne, "Gebrauch des Konjunktivs," 206.

[55] Schöne, "Gebrauch des Konjunktivs," 208.

[56] Pike, "Unfinished or without End," 367.

[57] *KA*: Lesetexte. Band 12: Essays. 1918–1926. Ansätze zu neuer Ästhetik. 490.

[58] Baudelaire, "Painter of Modern Life," 792–802, qtd. 802.

[59] Baudelaire, "Painter of Modern Life," 796.

[60] *KA*: Lesetexte. Band 8: Nachlass zu Lebzeiten [Posthumous Papers of a Living Author]. Einzelveröffentlichungen. Schwarze Magie.

4: Still Life: (Not) Doing What Isn't Done

M USIL BEGAN WRITING the different versions of the chapter "Atemzüge
eines Sommertags" (Breaths of a summer's day) as early as 1937
or even 1934; and, in an almost perfect circling, he was still working on
the chapter on 15 April 1942, the day he died.[1] In these chapter drafts,
which feature what appears to be a profusion of more metaphors per
paragraph than in any other section of the novel, Ulrich and Agathe
continue their "holy conversations." These conversations are part of
an epic deferral of physical consummation in their gated garden, which
comes to represent an island excepted from normal time and space, a
sort of shimmering framed still life. All still lives, Ulrich explains, in one
of the many "Umschreibungen" (circuitous rewritings) that he essays
in order to both approach and avoid their significance, paint "die Welt
vom sechsten Schöpfungstag; wo Gott und die Welt noch unter sich
waren, ohne den Menschen!" (*MoE*, 1230; the world of the sixth day
of creation, when God and the world were still by themselves, with no
people!, *MwQ*, 1325). This is practically the image of their garden, cut
off from society, its requirements, its morals, its temporal and spatial
laws. And yet there *are* two people in the picture, in their garden. These
two people, although separated from the world by their garden fence, by
the special mission that they have assigned themselves, and their exceptional state of shimmering stillness, are both alive — circling, fountaining — moving within an enclosed area. And Musil's novel, despite its
resistance to action, is still a sort of a narrative existing in a sort of time,
or many different sorts of time (progressive, essential, subjective, objectively measurable, non-linear) — a novel made up of seemingly infinite
small enclosed areas of infinitude — and decidedly not a painting of a
bowl of fruit. The two people walk around within the confines of their
garden, in circumnavigations, like Rilke's caged "panther," who "moves
in the smallest possible circle," and whose stride "is like a dance of force
around the center/ Of a great numbed will."[2]

   Although the will is numbed, or deferred, it may still, at any moment,
break out of its cage into violence and action; no wonder the need for
bars. Ulrich and Agathe's cage is self-created (or created by their author)
out of more than the garden fence; it is made of their infinitely expanding and contracting discourse, by the almost obsessive accumulation of

metaphors and likenesses, by words themselves, words that play games
with time and its "fließende Band, die rollende Treppe, mit ihrer unheimlichen Nebenbeziehung zum Tod" (*MoE*, 1094; flowing ribbon, the rolling staircase with its uncanny incidental association with death, *MwQ*,
1190), a discourse that repeatedly, always, once again, once again, once
again, "wie ein Wirtel das Gespräch nochmals spannte und von neuem
abrollen ließ" (*MoE*, 1231; recharged the conversation once more like a
flywheel . . . giving it more energy: *MwQ*, 1325). If the appetitive way of
life leads to war, action, grasping, destruction, and the inevitable dulling
of passion, infinite (or almost infinite) deferral via a thousand-and-one-
night's strategy of words is a natural strategy. The association with Adam
and Eve before the Fall — before the act — is also unavoidable. To take
a bite of the apple (even if fictional, painted, safe, deferred) in the bowl
on the table would thus have the most extreme consequences. Appetite,
muses Ulrich, is always a bit ridiculous — and how much more so, he
continues, when it is appetite for a painted lobster. Yet, as often is the
case with Ulrich, his irony hardly masks the serious stakes and the terror involved in setting the wheel of time spinning, of starting the roll of
the inevitably downhill-bound roll of life. Were the fruit not painted but
real, it would, like Shakespeare's medlar pear, be "rotten before it was
ripe" — for "Bleiben," as Rilke reminds us again, "ist Nirgends" (There
is no stopping place),[3] except perhaps in the work of art.

Deferral of action here is a reflection on considerations about the
relationship between forms of art (painting, still life, novel writing)
and the relationship between art in general — as eternalization — and
life, with its active, grasping, devouring movement. Faust's rewriting
or retranslation of the beginning of *Genesis* may serve as a distant chorus. Goethe's protagonist reads aloud from the book: In the beginning
was *the word*. Then he tries another translation: In the beginning was
meaning. And then he comes to the mystic third: In the beginning was
the act! And his alchemical incantations transform thought into word
into deed, indifference into passion, possibility into tragedy or possible
redemption. Goethe's eighteenth-century metaphysical struggle begins
with the transformation of a word and the work of the ultimate author,
thereby circling back to the Ur-moment, never quite coming to absolute resolution, remaining still engagingly inconclusive. The tension
between the triad of word, meaning, and act is never quite resolved, not
even in Musil's modernist text that consciously grapples with the quick-
silver conflict. Faust, rather like Ulrich, is a jaded man crying out against
a world gone hollow, a world that has lost its significance and value, a
world of books and learning, yes, but also a world of flesh and love and
the supposed rewards of social success. Goethe's play, like Musil's novel,
is an existential essay; it poses serious questions about time, meaning,

and the relationship between art and life, questions about word-magic, desire, and indifference — questions with which Musil would still be grappling over a century later. The unresolved and unresolvable struggle, the Faustian striving itself, in its insistence upon maintaining a fruitful space between knowledge and mystery, self and other, art and life, time and death, still and moving, may actually constitute the energetic frisson of all great works of art. And this frisson is created and maintained by Musil's experiments with the endless possibilities and necessities of metaphor-making.

If one thinks that the narrator of *The Man without Qualities* and his characters take a long time to come to no conclusions and consummations, one need only look at Musil's notes to see how much longer the author ruminates before we get to a more or less clean draft. For example:

> U[lrich] verstand auch sie u[nd] machte wieder eine theol[ogische] Paraphrase/ Beschreibung /Auslegung/Übertragung/umschrieb es wieder . . . gibt jedes — wieder/ u[nd] übertrug es /aber wieder . . . Er ergänzte es . . . Still[eben] malen die Dinge vom 6ten . . . Nun umschrieb es U[lrich] wieder: . . . es ließe sich . . . sagte er . . .[4]

> [U[lrich] understood her also a[nd] made another theol[ogical] paraphrase/description/presentation/transposition/circled around it again . . . offered it again/ a[nd] translated it again . . . He added . . . Still [lives] paint things on the 6th . . . now he redescribed it again . . . one could . . . he said . . .]

Sometimes variations on a single word are tried out in a whole page filled with different possibilities. Is this diversion, digression, or is it an attempt to hit the mark directly, a consummate artistry? Or, rather, is Musil's particular consummate artistry a sort of metaphysical juggling act with metaphors, a death-defying ability to keep the slight differences between words, images, possibilities flying, combining, changing places, and hovering in the air eternally? A legerdemain which consistently reminds us of the ultimate provisional character of all descriptions of "reality"? Musil's preoccupation with the metaphor of still life reveals his particular vision of correspondences and deviations and their particular metaphysical, aesthetic, and ethical significance.

Still life, the narrator insists, "plays a major role," presumably in the whole complex of ideas, questions, and activities (or lack thereof) embarked upon by the sibling experimenters and by the author of this novel. Even their very relationship with the topic itself (engagement, deferral, touch, touch not) has metaphoric valence for their experiments and the import of these experiments for the novel as a whole. While the actual discussion of the genre of painting takes up no more than two or three paragraphs in the novel, Musil's notes reveal that it was one of a number of central concepts to which he returned repeatedly in the elaborate cross-referencing of ideas, images, and scenarios for the novel. A few more examples of excerpts from his notes demonstrate a little bit the concentration of associations:

Oder: Das - Genre des Still[ebens] od[er] N[atur] m[orte]
Kunst
Dämonie
der seltsam gesteigerte Ausdruck
die - - u[nd] reglose Gefühlswirkung
(Denn) (Es) bedurfte bloß der Erwähnung. Ag[athe] u[nd] U[lrich] . . .
erinnerten sich . . .
Das Nichtantworten, u[nd] Nichtkenntnisnehmen
Denn eigentlich: (war das Stilleben . .)
Beziehungen, (Sie hatten oft die Natur so gesehn)
(wie Nichthandelnkönnen)   Auch Beziehungen
Zirkus. - Nekrophilie
Berührte: was sie selbst für einander waren
seltsame Verwandtschaft mit ihren früheren Erlebnissen . . . darunter
wenn man sich eines früheren Gesprächs über gemalte Zirkustiere gedenkt,
Auch mit ihren Kindheitserinnerungen. Und alle die weit einander
zugebeugten Erlebnisse, Augenblicke u[nd] Zustände
Die persönl[iche] Bedeutung des Stillebens, gesteigerten
Ausdrucks, des Nichtantwortens. Mit Gotterwähnung verwandt. (*KA*)[5]

[Or: The - genre of Still[lives] or N[atur] M[orte]
Art
Demonism
The strangely heightened expression . . .
The motionless effect on the feelings
(Because) (it) needed to only just be mentioned. Ag[athe] a[nd]
U[lrich] . . .
Remembered . . .
Not answering, and not noticing
because really (still life was . .)
Correspondences (they had seen nature like this often)
(Like not being able to act)
Circus necrophilia
touched on what they were to each other
strange relationship with their earlier experiences . . . including
remembering an earlier discussion about painted circus animals
And with their childhood memories and all of the vastly deflected
experiences, moments and states of being

The personal meaning of still [life], heightened expression,
not answering, related to saying God's name.]

. . .

Auch: Der schöne Schatten des Wie es wäre. Das Verbot. Die Schranke.
Seinesgleichen . . . Zwei Gefühlszustände . . . Die Unwirklichkeit
der Welt u[nd] des Menschen . . . Myst[ische] Anteilnahme . . .
Arten der weltl[ichen] Wirkl[ichkeit].[6]

[Also: the beautiful shadow of how it would be, the prohibition, the
limitation, the same thing again . . . two states of feeling . . . Unreality of the world a[nd] of people. . . . myst[ical] sympathies . . . Kinds
of world[ly] real[ity]]]

. . .

Es ist nicht einfach[7]
Versuch: Schluß u[nd]
Abrundung
(Es ist nicht einfach)

nature morte <– Handlung.
Pferdchen
Hund, Abstrakta.
Übergeordnet. Genialität.
Moral Gn[Genialität?].
Allegorisch usw.
Gegenstand = Affekt
Etymologie

Zusammenhang mit
Leidenschaft, mit Gewohnheit:
bringt zusammen: ein Kapitel wo
von ihrem subjektiven Zustand
die Rede ist, Erkennen; u[nd]
Spiegel gehört zu den beiden,
Pferdchenkapitel.

Gibt das Gespräch über die
Puppe, die Illusion in der Liebe
wieder. Man liebt das Ganze,
hieße es. Also die Handlung, was
man erlebt, produziert usw. Sich
daran erinnernd, kommen sie
jetzt vom Gegenstand springen
auf Handlung, was nun nicht
theoretisch ist, sondern wieder
persönlich berührt. Dahin gehört
Zirkustiere, nicht handeln können
u[nd] Analogie mit dem nicht
antwortenden Gott. (KA)[8]

It is not easy
Attempt: completion a[nd]
rounding off
(It is not easy)

[Connection with
passion, with habit:
pull together: A chapter that
talks about their subjective state,
realization a[nd] mirror belongs
with the pony chapter

nature morte <– action
pony
dog, abstractions
higher-placed genius
Morality g[enius?]
allegorical, etc.
Object = emotion
Etymology

Have the discussion about the
dolls, about illusion in love once
more, one loves the whole,
they say. Thus action, what one
experiences, produces, etc.,
remembering that, they begin
to discuss the subject, jump to
action, which again isn't purely
theoretical but touches on the
personal. Circus animals, not
being able to act, a[nd] the god
that doesn't answer belong here.]

One could decode these passages, phrase by phrase, but let us just look at one concept — the two states of feelings mentioned in the second line of the second notation. As discussed earlier, in Ulrich's notebooks on feeling, he differentiates between two kinds of feelings: specific and non-specific. The specific, related to the concepts "appetitive" and "living for" rather than "in" life, is, the narrator explains elsewhere, active and focused, like "a being with grasping arms," and it is by its nature fleeting, temporary, doomed to change. It

> spitzt [. . .] sich gewissermaßen zu, es verengt seine Bestimmung und endet schließlich außen und innen wie in einer Sackgasse; es führt zu einer Handlung oder zu einem Beschluss, und wenn es darin auch nicht aufhört zu sein, so geht es doch später so verändert weiter wie Wasser hinter der Mühle. Entwickelt es sich hingegen zur Unbestimmtheit, so hat es anscheinend gar keine Tatkraft. (*MoE*, 1198).

> [focuses itself, so to speak, it constricts its purposiveness, and it finally ends up both internally and externally in something of a blind alley; it leads to an action or a resolve, and even if it should not cease to exist in one or the other, it continues on, as changed as water leaving a mill. If, on the other hand, it develops toward non-specificity, it apparently has no energy at all. (*MwQ*, 1305)]

This is the same, according to Musil, as the fetishistic act of concentrating the all in the one. The non-specific feeling, related to the concepts of "non-appetitive" and "living in" life, however, transforms the world

> auf die gleiche wunschlose und selbstlose Weise, wie der Himmel seine Farben, und es verändern sich in ihm die Dinge und Geschehnisse wie die Wolken am Himmel; das Verhalten des unbestimmten Gefühls zur Welt hat etwas Magisches an sich . . . (*MoE*, 1198).

[in the same way the sky changes its colors, without desire or self, and in this form objects and actions change like the clouds. The attitude of the nonspecific emotion to the world has in it something magical . . . (*MwQ,* 1305–6)]

This is then the opposite action: instead of concentrating the all into the one, the non-specific feeling expands the one into the all. Both actions are actions of metaphor-making. Ulrich continues, illuminating the difference further by adding the all-important fourth dimension of time:

Dass man niemals den Augenblick des Fühlens festhalten kann, dass die Gefühle rascher verwelken als Blumen oder dass sie sich in Papierblumen verwandeln, wenn sie erhalten bleiben wollen, dass das Glück und der Wille, die Kunst und Gesinnung vorbeigehn, alles dieses hängt von der Bestimmtheit des Gefühls ab, die ihm auch eine Bestimmung unterschiebt und es in den Gang des Lebens zwingt, von dem es aufgelöst oder verändert wird. Dagegen ist das in seiner Unbestimmtheit und Unbegrenztheit verharrende Gefühl verhältnismäßig unveränderlich. Ein Vergleich fiel ihm ein: "Das eine stirbt wie ein Einzelwesen, das andere dauert an wie eine Art oder Gattung." (*MoE,* 1198)

[That the moment of feeling can never be sustained, that emotions wilt more quickly than flowers if one tries to preserve them, that happiness and will, art and conviction, pass away; all this depends on the specificity of emotion, which always imposes upon it a purposiveness and forces it into the pace of life that dissolves or changes it. On the other hand, the emotion that persists in its non-specificity and boundlessness is relatively impervious to change . . . the one dies like an individual, the other like a species. (*MwQ,* 1306)]

"Species" or genre ("Gattung") — a form of abstraction, allows for duration, while specific flowers wilt or transform themselves into *art*-ificial paper versions of themselves in order to "live" on: the idea of flower remains. The work of art, because of its abstraction and universalization, its symbolic essence, endures, while the specific feeling, thing, or person, as long as it is not compared, connected, corresponded, or related to another person, thing, or feeling, is necessarily fleeting. And yet we can also see that for Musil, the choice of any one specific word, action, or direction in his novel threatened to obviate the universe of infinite possibilities, thus impelling him to remain open to alternative arrangements and descriptions, to allo-centrism. Metaphor, in other words, is a means to recover lost time, in the Proustian sense, by raising the specific singularity into a universal union; and, also, a means to keep the possibilities open, to try to compete, catch up with, celebrate the force of speeding time. To definitively choose one metaphor out of the infinity of possible combinations might seem to be a surrender to death; yet any one choice is potentially synecdochally connected to eternity.

All art presents us with the problem of eternalization and an artificial experience of time and reality. But the still life brings the tension into focus and calls into question, by association, the sense of time in all forms of art, including ones that are usually more associated with forward successive movement, that is, novel narrative, in spite of the fact — or perhaps because of it —that still life is "the genre at the furthest remove from narrative."[9] The still-life painting, as extreme case of stopping time midmoment in art, a vision of grapes on the verge of rotting, of flies buzzing about a just unwrapped fish, of the death's head grimacing "memento mori," illuminates the horror of being left behind by time and narrative, but also a resistance to its inevitable triumph. Musil wants us to see the way the genre of still-life painting is related to a much larger complex of ideas within and outside the novel.

This synecdochic relationship of part to whole, that is, one word suggesting a vast map of complexities, parallels, correspondences, and vice versa, provides an example of the way in which Musil creates multiple centers, nuclei of attention and importance. The concept of still life seems, when one concentrates on it, infinitely connected, infinitely important; while yet another would presumably bring equally fruitful associations and relevance. It is in itself an image of the microcosmic-macrocosmic dimension of Musil's thinking: the one image of still life is specifically associated with other images (incest, sister, pony, circus animals, necrophilia, fetish, et cetera) in Musil's notes, and this complex of images and terms is related to larger themes of the novel, such as action and inaction, life and art, participation and indifference, possibility and finality. It is daunting even to begin unraveling one of these tightly wound balls of idea-strands to try to disentangle the significance of the distinct terminologies. But while there may be hundreds (at least) of them in Musil's notes and novel, a closer examination of just one, the still life, proves illuminating both for what this particular thematic tells us about Musil's ideas about life, narrative, and time, and as an object lesson in how astonishingly complex Musil's many metaphorical micro-systems were. This thematic, moreover, dramatically projects an image of the role of the temporal in metaphor and the fruitful tension Musil negotiates between duration and movement.

One of the essential characteristics of the still life, like so many of the other idea nuclei, is that it contains an antithesis within itself, that it attempts a coincidence of opposites, an enactment of temporary metaphoric significance. For, above all, a still life is a work of art, a metaphor for "reality" — one that simply in its designation (also called *nature morte*) reflects an essential paradox of art objects, that they are at once both frozen in time and fluid, eternal — dead and alive at once. Abstraction itself, and its accompanying symbolization, are a necessary function of transforming life or imagination into art; they are preservatives. What is abstracted, what is made into a symbol is lifted into the realm of the timeless and spaceless, into the universal and archetypal or non-specific, thereby escaping the ravages of air, sun, boredom, fickleness, and death. The designation of *still* life contains, as well, in its first word — even more strongly in the German — the double meaning of not moving and silent, another paradox when used as a conceptual catalyst driving the endless proliferation of words.

In the unfinished chapter versions of "Atemzüge eines Sommertags," the siblings find that their descriptions and definitions of the nature of the still life are veering too closely toward a description of their own state of being ("Denn sich auskömmlich über die unheimliche Kunst des Stillebens oder der Nature morte zu äußern, war ihnen beiden deren seltsame Ähnlichkeit mit ihrem eigenen Leben hinderlich" (*MoE*, 1230) [For the strange resemblance to their own life was an obstacle that kept both of them from adequately expressing themselves about the uncanny art of the still life or *nature morte, MwQ*, 1325]); so they circle around again, in a fraught labyrinth of contradictions. Still life, Ulrich says, is "das erregende undeutliche, unendliche Echo" (*MoE*, 1230; the exciting, vague, infinite echo, *MwQ*, 1324), a definition itself an echo of Musil's description of Rilke's use of metaphor in his Rilke eulogy as "diese edelsteinklare Stille in der niemals anhaltenden Bewegung" (this jewellike stillness within a movement that never pauses); Rilke's poem, continues Musil in the funeral address, has an expansive openness: "Sein Zustand dauert wie ein gehobenes Anhalten" (*KA*;[10] its condition endures like an elevated pause, *P*, 243). This elevated pause is echoed, in turn, by a stunning passage in Musil's *Nachlass*, wherein Ulrich and Agathe stand at the high point of their passion, perhaps before or just at the moment of their consummation:

> Die Stille nagelte sie ans Kreuz. Sie fühlten, dass sie ihr bald nicht mehr standhalten konnten, schreien mussten, wahnsinnig wie Vögel. Deshalb standen sie mit einem Mal nebeneinander mit den Armen umschlungen. Haut klebte sich an Haut; schüchtern drang durch die große Einöde dieses kleine Gefühl wie eine winzige saftige Blüte, die ganz allein zwischen den Steinen wächst, und beruhigte sie. Sie bogen das Rund des Horizonts wie ein Kranz um ihre Hüften und sahen in den Himmel. Standen jetzt wie auf einem hohen Balkon, ineinander und in das Unsagbare verflochten gleich zwei Liebenden, die sich im nächsten Augenblick in die Leere stürzen werden. Stürzten. Und die Leere trug sie. Der Augenblick hielt an; sank nicht und stieg nicht. (*KA*)[11]

[The silence nailed them to the cross.
    They felt that soon they would not be able to stand it anymore, would have to shout, insane as birds.

This was why they were suddenly standing beside each other, with their arms around each other. Skin stuck to skin; timidly this small feeling penetrated the great desert like a tiny succulent flower growing all alone among the stones, and calmed them. They wove the circle of the horizon like a wreath around their hips, and looked at the sky. Stood as on a high balcony, interwoven into each other and with the unutterable like two lovers who, the next instant, will plunge into the emptiness. Plunged. And the emptiness supported them. The instant lasted; did not sink and did not rise. (*MwQ*, 1455)]

This miraculous elevated pause, this jewellike stillness is effected by the magic of multiplying metaphors. In case we missed the point, the formal act of metaphoric association, analogy and correspondence is carried on to an almost excessive degree: here a small feeling is *like* a tiny blossom growing between the rocks, the horizon is *like* a wreath around their hips, they stand *as if* on a high balcony, *woven* into each other and into the Unsayable, *like* two lovers; they crash down, they float. And this weaving of arms, of horizon, of words, is so total that one loses track of which words are tenor and which vehicle. In the Rilke eulogy, Musil explains why: "Niemals wird etwas mit einem anderen verglichen — als zwei andere und Getrennte, die sie dabei bleiben —; denn selbst wenn das irgendwo geschieht und gesagt wird, irgendeines sei wie das andere, so scheint es schon im gleichen Augenblick seit Urzeiten das andere gewesen zu sein . . . das Metaphorische wird hier in hohem Grade Ernst." (*KA*;[12] Something is never compared with something else — as two different and separate things, which they remain in the comparison — For, even if this sometimes does happen, and one thing is said to be like another, it seems at that very moment to have already *been* the other since primordial times . . . The metaphorical here becomes serious to a high degree, *P*, 245). For as he wrote to Walther Petry on 25 April 1930, as he was just about to publish the first volume of his novel: "Ich muss warnend sagen, dass in seinen Adern einige Tropfen des Bluts der Rilkerede rollen"[13] (I have to warn you that there are a few drops of blood from the Rilke eulogy rolling around in it).

The still life is a prototypical example of blending, weaving, melding — an experience like the merging of love, reminding us of the man Musil proposes who loves incest because he loves metaphor. In a still life, the textures and colors and shapes of each distinct object echo those of the others around it, take on their shadows, their forms, their skins. It is an aesthetic experience, an experience that may help the siblings to understand the Other Condition wherein they are dwelling. Above all, regardless of subject matter, the essential thing is the act, process, *frisson* of making connections, finding likenesses, creating metaphors:

Ohne dass es nötig wäre, in den Einzelheiten zu wiederholen, was bis zu den gemeinsamen Kindheitserinnerungen zurückreichte, beim

Wiedersehen wieder erwacht war, und seither allen Erlebnissen und den meisten Gesprächen etwas Seltsames gab, läßt sich nicht verschweigen, dass der markbetäubte Anhauch des Stillebens darin immer zu spüren war. Unwillkürlich, und ohne etwas Bestimmtes anzunehmen, das sie hätte leiten können, wandten sie darum ihre Neugierde allem zu, was mit dem Wesen des Stillebens *Verwandtschaft* haben könnte; und es ergab sich mehr oder minder der folgende Wortwechsel, der wie ein Wirtel das Gespräch nochmals spannte und von neuem abrollen ließ. (*MoE*, 1230–31, emphasis mine)

[Without it being necessary to repeat in detail something reaching back to the shared memories of childhood that had been reawakened at their reunion and since then had given a strange cast to all their experiences and most of their conversations, it cannot be passed over in silence that the anesthetized trance of the still life was always to be felt in it. Spontaneously, therefore, and without accepting anything specific that might have guided them, they were led to turn their curiosity toward everything that might *be akin* to the nature of the still life; and something like the following exchange of words resulted, charging the conversation once more like a flywheel and giving it new energy. (*MwQ*, 1325, emphasis mine)]

Even in this short introduction to a listing of all that might *be akin*, or have a *relationship* (*Verwandtschaft*) with the still life, or with the siblings' *relationship* (note that the word is even the same: relationship connotes both familial connection and any other connection), the narrator provides us with an explanation of the workings of metaphor, that is, the necessary neglect of the specific in favor of the common factors, traits, or characteristics of the experiences. This action is brought on by a "Wortwechsel," literally an exchange of words — figuratively the act of metaphoric transference — that has the effect of suspending and continually renewing the conversation like a whirling vortex. And now that the narrator has told us what the words will do, he shows us, too:

Vor einem unerschütterlichen Antlitz, das keine Antwort erteilt, um etwas flehen zu müssen, treibt den Menschen in einen Rausch der Verzweiflung, des Angriffs oder der Würdelosigkeit. Ebenso erschütternd, aber unsagbar schön, ist es dagegen, vor einem reglosen Antlitz zu knien, auf dem das Leben vor wenigen Stunden erloschen ist und einen Schein zurückgelassen hat wie ein Sonnenuntergang . . . Von dieser poetischen Knabenhaftigkeit führt eine kurze Linie zu den Schauern der Geister- und Totenbeschwörung; eine zweite zum Greuel der wirklichen Nekrophilie; vielleicht eine dritte zu den krankhaften zwei Gegensätzen des Exhibitionismus und der gewaltsamen Nötigung. (*MoE*, 1231)

[Having to beg for something before an imperturbable countenance that grants no response drives a person into a frenzy of despair, attack, or worthlessness. On the other hand, it is equally unnerving, but unspeakable beautiful, to kneel before an immovable countenance from which life was extinguished a few hours before, leaving behind an aura like a sunset . . . A short line leads from this poetic immaturity to the horrors of conjuring up spirits and the dead; a second leads to the abominations of actual necrophilia; perhaps a third to the pathological opposites of exhibitionism and coercion by violence. (*MwQ*, 1325–26)]

The narrator is a seemingly inexhaustible source of metaphors for still life. They grow out of each other until we no longer remember what is being described, until they become grotesque; and then we are reminded of what they all have in common, and what even the most disturbing perversity may have in common with our normal daily life:

Das mögen befremdliche Vergleichungen sein, und zum Teil sind es höchst unappetitliche. Aber wenn man sich davon nicht abhalten läßt und sie sozusagen medizinisch-psychologisch betrachtet, zeigt sich, dass eins allen gemeinsam ist: eine Unmöglichkeit, ein Unvermögen, ein Mangel an natürlichem Mut oder Mut zum natürlichen Leben. (*MoE*, 1231)

[These comparisons may be strange, and in part they are extremely. But if one does not allow oneself to be deterred but considers them from, as it were, a medical-psychological viewpoint, there is one element that they all have in common: an impossibility, an inability, an absence of natural courage or the courage for a natural life. (*MwQ*, 1326)]

In another passage the narrator says something quite similar, which might be explained by the fact that these pages are drafts that have not yet been purged of their repetitions — yet the repetitions, variations, versions, seem in this context to be more deliberate than not — we may read them all as circling approaches and digressions around the act, around finality and death. All the metaphors for still life, the narrator explains, have in common that

ihnen die zur Welt und von der Welt zurückführende Brücke des Handelns fehlte; und schließlich, dass sie auf einer schwindelnd schmalen Grenze zwischen größtem Glück und krankhaftem Benehmen endeten. *Unheilig betrachtet*, erinnerten sie alle ein wenig an ein Porzellan-Stilleben, und an ein blindes Fenster, und an eine

Sackgasse, und an das unendliche Lächeln von Wachspuppen unter
Glas und Licht, die auf dem Weg zwischen Tod und Auferstehung
steckengeblieben zu sein scheinen und weder einen Schritt vor noch
zurück tun können. (*MoE*, 1311, emphasis mine)

[They were missing the bridge to action leading to and from the
world; and finally, they ended on a vanishingly narrow borderline
between the greatest happiness and pathological behavior. *Looked at
in an unholy way*, they were all somewhat reminiscent of a porcelain
still life, and of a blind window, and of a dead-end street, and of
the unending smile of wax dolls under glass and light; things that
appear to have got stuck on the road between death and resurrection, unable to take a step forward or backward. . . . (*MwQ*, 1386,
emphasis mine)]

This raises the question of how they would seem if looked at in a
holy — instead of an unholy — way. Each sentence, in effect, opens up
onto another possible bifurcation. But then, as all music requires temporal dynamics, Musil syncopates the text with a pause, bringing the siblings
back to themselves, stopping, temporarily, the discourse, in a timeless
moment of silence:

Das Stilleben aber, ist sein seltsamer Reiz nicht auch Spiegelfechterei? Ja, fast eine ätherische Nekrophilie?
   Und doch ist eine ähnliche Spiegelfechterei auch in den Blicken
von glücklich Liebenden als Ausdruck ihres Höchsten. Sie sehen einander ins Auge, können sich nicht losreißen und vergehen in einem
wie Gummi dehnbaren unendlichen Gefühl!
   Ungefähr so hatte der Wortwechsel also begonnen, aber an dieser
Stelle war sein Faden recht eigentlich hängen geblieben; und zwar
eine ganze Weile ehe er wieder weiterlief. Die beiden hatten einander wirklich angesehen und waren dadurch nämlich ins Schweigen
verfallen. (*MoE*, 1231–32)

[But isn't the strange charm of the still life shadowboxing too?
Indeed, almost an ethereal necrophilia?
   And yet there is also a similar shadowboxing in the glances of
happy lovers as an expression of their highest feelings. They look
into each other's eyes, can't tear themselves away, and pine in an
infinite emotion that stretches like rubber!
   This was more or less how the exchange of words had begun, but
at this point its thread was pretty much left hanging, and for quite a
while before it was picked up again. For they had both really looked
at each other, and this had caused them to lapse into silence. (*MwQ*,
1326)]

While discourse, then, is a method of proliferation that defers action, silence, too serves an important role as an island of pause amid the movement of conversation. "Island" is another of Musil's metaphors for still life, which, as Walter Fanta points out, is paradoxically a *Stichwort* in Musil for "journey," itself a cipher for incest, and its ultimate transformation from word to meaning to act and back again. As their garden is a sort of island, it supersedes, at least for a momentary eternity of transcendental discourse, the actual journey to actual islands; it makes the physical enactment recede into insignificance amid the palpable magic of the possible. While lying in their garden on their recliners, Fanta glosses, the siblings are also in two boats, floating on the water. Their landed discourse metaphorically transports them to the island where the act of incest is bound to take place. The siblings finally leave their garden enclosure in a number of drafts, only to visit another small body of land surrounded on all sides. It is only one of many islands — just as there are many drafts entitled "Island," and in one draft wherein Ulrich is on the island with Clarisse instead of Agathe, the island is broken up into three separate ones, further variations, options, diversions. While in early versions of the novel the act of incest was planned to occur at the beginning, Fanta explains that over the decades of writing the act was pushed further and further into the future. Although it is clear that Musil did mean us to understand that the siblings do indeed commit the "act," the actual moment of consummation is never literally described, not even in notes. The *act* of incest, as Fanta suggests, transforms over time into a proliferation of metaphors, into the discourse that it originally was intended to represent. And this proliferation of words is paradoxically symbolized by, among other things, the silence and suspended space of the "island." The silence and staying, the stillness of any one moment, choice, landing is a sort of suspension — for the length of one breath — of the inevitable cycling vortex of time. Fanta writes, referring to the chapter, "Atemzüge eines Sommertags," "In any case, the last draft of the 'journey of the journey' ends in the 'magic of life and death' in a still life and a condition of hovering, as Musil puts aside his pen for a good reason."[14] This "ending" in hovering and still life, in between the magic of life and the magic of death, or, as Musil puts it, "stuck on the road between death and resurrection," or "on a vanishingly narrow borderline between the greatest happiness and pathological behavior," of the novel itself, and the siblings' mystical experience, is, then, not a random result of Musil's sudden tragic death in the middle of a sentence, but the necessary, inherently requisite, and only "ending" possible. Since, as we know, incest equals metaphor in Musil's idiolect, we might venture that the novel "ends" in the openness of the extratemporal metaphorical moment, in the Other Condition, that is, by necessity does not end but infinitely casts its playful net of possibilities out into the ever-moving fractal sea.

But before the author's last lead-in word there are more essential likenesses, as the expanse forward or outward in time and space curls back in upon itself to begin once more: still life, Musil's notes tell us directly, equals "sister," the separate but connected, the untouchable, the other version of one's self. Still life is also related in Musil's notes directly to a scene wherein Ulrich recalls his childhood fascination with cardboard circus animals, which he loves with an undying thirst that he never could have felt for real animals, or for people for that matter, who might have returned his love or interrupted his timeless, spaceless imaginary rapture with their reality. The narrator presents some more corresponding concepts and parallel images, culminating in a description of these cardboard circus animals, which he compares to the essence of art, to sister, to a stage set, to an unresponsive porcelain figurine — we hardly know what is being compared to what to illuminate what. Tenor and vehicle are, once again, completely melded together. The proliferation of images is once again excessive, as image displaces image, as they all become metaphors for the metaphoric process and for the impact of the unreachable that this process signals:

Wahrscheinlich gehört *auch* zum Wesen der Kunst, und namentlich dort, wo es dem des Künstlichen *verwandt* ist, eine solche scheinbar erhöhte: er hatte von dem *isoliert-verbundenen* Dastehn seiner Schwester einen Eindruck empfangen, der in manchem den Beleuchtungskünsten einer Bühne *ähnlich* war *oder* der sich selbst genügenden albisch anlockenden Abgeschlossenheit einer Porzellanfigur in einem Ausstellungsschrank, Erlebnissen, die eine eigenartige Beklemmung enthalten, eine unbeschreibliche Ansammlung unbeschreiblichen Gefühls an der Oberfläche eines künstlich vereinzelten Gegenstands. *Es erinnerte ihn auch* an die Tiere, die Ulrich einst als Knabe aus dem Papier der Zirkusankündigungen herausgeschnitten hatte, um ihnen Selbständigkeit zu geben, *und* an den Durst des verlangenden Auges, den ihr Anblick nicht löschte, sondern ins unendliche verlängerte. Diese atemraubende Fesselung der sonst immer verteilten Geisteskräfte an den Raum einer Einzelheit gemahnte *aber auch* an das größte, nur noch von seiner eigenen Unstillbarkeit übertroffene Glück, an etwas aus ungeteiltem Wesen zu erleben.[15]

[Probably this sort of seeming elevation was *also a part* of the essence of art, and especially where *it was related* to the artificial: he had gotten an impression from the *isolated-connected* presence of his sister, *which was in many respects like* the artistry of stage lighting *or* the nightmarishly self-contained and seductive insularity of a porcelain figurine in a showcase, experiences that produce a strange anxiety, an indescribable collection of indescribable feelings on the surface of an artificially isolated object. It *also reminded him* of the animals that Ulrich had once cut out from the paper of a circus poster, in order to give each of them their own independence, *and* of the thirst of the longing eye, which was not satisfied by looking at them, but which, rather, extended into infinity. This breathtaking confinement, of the powers of the intellect into the space of one individual entity, powers that were otherwise always spread out, however, *also* brought to mind the greatest happiness, still only surpassed by its own inability to satisfy, of experiencing something in its whole essence. (Emphasis mine)]

Once again the narrator has provided us with an example *and* an explanation of the metaphoric process in the same passage, telling *and* showing. The essence of art is being compared with the experience of still life, and especially where it is most "related" to the artificial; then this is compared to the oxymoronic "isolated-connected" presence of his sister, which is compared to the lighting of a stage: *also a part of, in many respects like, or . . .* a porcelain figurine in a show case. All of these examples are now brought together again under the heading of "experiences that produce a strange anxiety." As if this weren't enough, he continues with: *it also reminded him of. . .* and then we finally arrive at the circus animals, which themselves remind him of the thirst of the longing eye, which is described in another figure as the breathtaking confinement of the usually fragmented concentration in the space of a singularity . . . *but also* as that happiness of experiencing something within its unseparated whole connection to infinitude (specific and non-specific emotions). Then he continues to pile on necrophilia and fetishism, until he circles back to the concept of abstraction, concluding that every idea, and every ideal, every attempt to reduce everything down to one single thing or person (like directing love for only one woman or only to her shoe, like any act of synecdoche) participates in this sort of potentially perverse process. This next passage, riddled with comparative adjectives, contains no less than thirteen metaphors—in Musil's all-inclusive sense of the word—for the one experience:

In alle Seelenkräfte kommt der Rausch des Bienenschwarms[1], der sich an die Königin hängt: Ulrich wußte, dass er und Agathe *nahe daran sein mussten, so zu handeln* [2]. Aber es war ihm in seiner vielseitigen Offenheit viel klarer als ihr, wie gefährlich das sein konnte. Ließen sich diese Heimlichkeiten denn nicht "verkrüppelt" *auch* mit der unheimlichen Liebe zu einer Toten[3] *vergleichen*, die keinen Blick verscheucht, der sich auf ihr niederläßt? Verriet der holde Beziehungswahn, wodurch alle Strahlen der Welt auf dem Umriß eines Geliebten [4] Einzelnen verdichtet werden, nicht auch *Ähnlichkeit* mit dem unholden [5], wo ein Fingernagel [6], ein Schuh [7], irgendein Fetisch[8] alle Winkel des Leibs sich zukehrt, dass ihnen unstillbare Ströme des Begehrens entfließen? War nicht überhaupt jede Idee, [9] die andere verdrängt, und sogar jede Manie [10] *schon eine solche* "erhöhte Zurechnung" des Alls auf das Einzelne? Ulrich gestand sich ein, dass es sich wahrscheinlich so zutrage; aber er sagte sich, dass auch jedes Ideal [11], das man sich *im Verhalten zur* Wirklichkeit mache, *nichts anderes sei* als eine zauberisch beleuchtete Wachspuppe [12]. Es gibt nichts, was nicht kranke Geschwister hatte [13], denn die gesunde Welt ist *aus dem gleichen Stoff* gemacht wie die kranke, nur die Verhältnismaße sind andere. (*KA*; emphases mine)[16]

[In all of the soul's powers there is the intoxication of the swarm of bees [1] that surrounds the queen: Ulrich knew that he and Agathe must be close to acting *like that* [2]. But how dangerous that could be was clearer to him, in his many-sided openness, than it was to her. Didn't these secrecies *also* lend themselves *to comparison* with the uncanny love toward a dead person [3], which isn't frightened off by the appearance of any vision? Does not this lovely delusion ["Beziehungswahn" — literally madness of association, or even a correspondence madness, that is, metaphoric madness!], whereby all the rays of the world are concentrated upon the form of one beloved individual [4] *also have commonalities with* the demonic [5], where a fingernail [6], a shoe [7], any fetish or other [8], draws all recesses of the body toward it, so that insatiable streams of desire flow toward them? Wasn't any idea at all, [9] that pushed out the others, and even any mania [10] already *this sort of* "elevated imputation" of the All into an individual entity? Ulrich admitted to himself that this was probably the way it went; but he also said to himself that every ideal [11] that one creates for oneself *in relationship* to reality *was nothing but* a magically illuminated wax doll [12]. Nothing existed that didn't have sick siblings [13], since the healthy world is made out of *the same* material as the sick one; only the relational measurements are different. (emphases mine).]

In a typical metaphorical tour de force, Musil has gradually followed association upon association until he comes to compare the healthy world and the sick world, abstracting what they have in common — which paradoxically is that they both partake of this questionable, but necessary, act of abstraction and reduction that makes a wax puppet out of reality. A reduction that is illuminated with magic — a still life, a metaphor of many metaphors for the act of metaphor-making.

But what is this sort of writing doing to move a narrative forward or to contribute toward the completion of a novel? What is a "still life" like this doing in a novel at all? The answer lies in the importance of the moment and its relationship to the process of metaphoric abstraction. Any work of art is a sort of selective microcosm of places, events, persons, experiences, and details of all kinds, an attempt to symbolically contain all of time within the boundaries of its form; a still life of sorts, which arranges representative abstracted objects upon a table that will sit and move within a frame, just as the situations, characters, and descriptions in a novel are and are not contained within the bounds of a book's covers. Looking back a few hundred years to Lessing's *Laokoon oder Über die Grenzen der Malerei und Poesie* (Laocoon: An Essay Upon the Limits of Painting and Poetry, 1767), we may begin to appreciate just how significant Musil's preoccupation with still life — as comment on moment, on movement, on art and its relationship to time — was and still is for its implied suggestion about the need for a new kind of novel, an experimental novel that resists and questions progression and action. Lessing's theoretical differentiation between visual art and poetry maintained that "succession in time is the province of the poet, coexistence in space that of the artist."[17] The *Dichter* (writer) narrates an action that is "a visible progressive action, the various parts of which follow one another in time," while the visual artist depicts a "visible stationary action, the development of whose various parts takes place in space" (90). Poetry is a depiction of successive moments and "actions" are its particular subjects. Visual art, therefore, is best suited to depict something *dauernd* (lasting, enduring), while "poetry" best depicts the *transitorisch* (transitory). What would Lessing have said to Musil's novel, which includes chapter 28, "a chapter that may be skipped by anyone not particularly impressed by thinking as an occupation," or countless pages of essayistic reflection, deflection, and regression? It is a commonplace that modernist art turned from the outside to the interior realms, to thought, feeling, impressions, dreams, and psychology for subject matter and focus; naturally, artists would thus be faced with the challenge that Musil speaks of in the above-mentioned chapter, of describing a man thinking. The challenge constituted by the paradox of "narrating" a resistance to or lack of action in the novel, can only be answered by correspondingly new perceptions and valuations of time, duration, and the experience of reality and art. While the strange attraction to an object or person who does not respond is conflated by Musil with a perverse rejection of or revolt against life, will, desire, and action (apraxia), it is simultaneously presented as the only possible (provisionally) ethical, intelligent, meaningful relation to the world. Therefore a novel wherein "not doing" is as "glühend" (flaming) as "doing" is built upon the formal paradoxical structure of still life.

A novel — as "poetry" — should, according to Lessing, depict a progression of action over time, and a work of visual art should depict a moment in space. Further, and most importantly for Lessing's analysis of the *Laocoon* sculpture, the work of visual art must depict a moment that is by its nature durative. The portrayal of something transitory in durative art, "at last wearies or disgusts us."[18] Lessing asks the question already raised by Winckelmann: Why isn't Laocoon screaming, when he screams so regularly in poetry? While Winckelmann had argued that he isn't depicted as screaming because the Greeks valued physical beauty above all things, and the depiction of screaming would be ugly, Lessing brings the discussion into the context of his own time, and argues instead that the depiction of a transitory action, a scream, would be "anti-natural," thereby becoming grotesque and losing its original meaning. No one screams forever; no one cries out in ecstasy forever; a fury that lasts for five days, as Ulrich muses in a notebook entry, transforms into a mental illness. Ulrich sounds surprisingly like Lessing here, albeit with no direct mention of the subject of artistic genres:

> Denn ein Gefühl verändert sich in dem Augenblick, wo es dauert; es hat keine Dauer und Identität; es muss neu vollzogen werden. Gefühle sind nicht nur veränderlich und unbeständig — wofür sie wohl gelten —, sondern sie würden das erst recht in dem Augenblick, wo sie es nicht wären. Sie werden unecht, wenn sie dauern. Sie müssen immer von neuem entstehen, wenn sie anhalten sollen, und auch dabei werden sie andere. Ein Zorn, der fünf Tage anhielte, wäre kein Zorn mehr, sondern eine Geistesstörung; er verwandelt sich entweder in Verzeihen oder in Rachebereitschaft. (*KA*)[19]

> [For a feeling changes in the instant of its existence [of its lasting, literally]; it has no duration or identity; it must be consummated anew. Emotions are not only changeable and inconstant — as they are well taken to be — but the instant they weren't, they would become so. They are not genuine when they last. They must always arise anew if they are to endure, and even in doing this they become different emotions. An anger that lasted five days would no longer be anger but be a mental disorder; it transforms itself into either forgiveness or preparations for revenge. (*MwQ*, 1229)]

In a reflection on what Musil would call the difference between dead and living words, images, or forms, Sartre's Roquentin likewise comments on what happens when he looks too long at a particular portrait, raising the question of the role of the viewer or reader in this genre differentiation. Perhaps paintings and sculptures are not even meant to be gazed at for indefinite periods? Sartre writes:

> I know . . . that when one is confronted with a face sparkling with righteousness, after a moment this sparkle dies away, and only an ashy residue remains: this residue interested me. Parottin [the subject of the painting] put up a good fight. But suddenly his look burned out, the picture grew dim, what was left? Blind eyes, the thin mouth of a dead snake, and cheeks.[20]

Sartre may be suggesting a skepticism about the possibility that any images, ideas, or forms might last beyond a moment. A few pages later he writes: "The true nature of the present revealed itself: it was what exists, and all that was not present did not exist."[21] Yet where does that leave the work of art? Can it be alive? Present? Eternally significant?

According to Lessing, an attention to genre and its limitations and tendencies can expand the durative possibilities of the work of art. The visual artist should choose the moment that is the most pregnant with possibilities, the moment that allows the mind of the viewer the broadest range of ethical and aesthetic consideration of what might come, of the choices and their potential consequences (for example, the moment *before* Medea kills her children). Visual depiction, then, despite Lessing's assertion that visual art is concerned with space, and "poetry" with time, is actually very much concerned with time, and with its utmost expansion in the imagination. Goethe, who wrote on the Laocoon theme thirty-three years after Lessing, stressed this oxymoronic potential for movement within the frozen depiction of the moment and the aesthetic experience of the viewer. The nature of the *Augenblick* (moment, blink of the eye) is always actually a comment upon the movement and passing of time:

> In order to conceive rightly the intention of the Laocoon, let a man place himself before it at a proper distance, with his eyes shut; then let him open his eyes, and shut them again instantly. By this means he will see the whole marble in motion; he will fear lest he finds the whole group changed when he opens his eyes again. It might be said that, as it stands, it is a flash of lightning fixed, a wave petrified in the moment it rushes towards the shore.[22]

Goethe's game of opening and closing the eyes is a proto-filmic experience that emphasizes the tendency of the sculpture to rebel against its genre and to explode the confines of its material. The marble is a wave, petrified the moment it hits the shore; it still seems to move. In another draft chapter, "Mondstrahlen bei Tage" (Moonbeams by day) from the complex of "Garden Chapters," which includes "Atemzüge eines Sommertags," Agathe plays a game with time by closing and opening her eyes in the way Goethe recommends:

> Wenn sie die Augen eine Weile geschlossen hielt und dann wieder öffnete, so dass der Garten unberührt in ihren Blick trat, als wäre er eben erst erschaffen worden, bemerkte sie so deutlich und unkörperlich wie ein Gesicht, dass die Richtung, die sie mit ihrem Bruder verbinde, unter allen anderen ausgezeichnet sei. (*MoE*, 1093–94)
>
> [If she kept her eyes closed for a while and then opened them again, so that the garden met her glance untouched, as if it had just that

moment been created, she noticed clearly and as if disembodied, as in a vision, that the course that bound her to her brother was marked out above the others. (*MwQ*, 1189–90)]

This game reveals the special heightened character of the still life or garden — that everything is sweeter there, that life and death are inextricably woven together, that

alle die umgebenden Gestalten auf das unheimlichste verlassen dastanden, aber auch, auf das unheimlichste entzückend, belebt waren, in dem Anschein eines zarten Todes oder einer leidenschaftlichen Ohnmacht, als wären sie soeben von etwas Unnennbarem verlassen worden, was ihnen eine geradezu menschliche Sinnlichkeit und Empfindlichkeit verlieh. (*MoE*, 1094)

[all the surrounding shapes stood there eerily abandoned but also, in an eerily ravishing way, full of life, so that they were like a gentle death, or a passionate swoon, as if something unnameable had just left them, and this lent them a distinctly human sensuality and openness. (*MwQ*, 1190)]

Time and space have somehow conflated, collapsed, expanded, and contracted — the metaphors are of fluids and solids, of borders and infinity, shores, measurements and immeasurability, of death, swooning, aliveness, of inanimate objects that seem to gain human sensibilities:

Und etwas Ähnliches wie am Eindruck des Raums hatte sich überdies am Gefühl der Zeit ereignet; dieses fließende Band, die rollende Treppe mit ihrer unheimlichen Nebenbeziehung zum Tod schien in manchen Augenblicken stillzustehn, und in manchen floß sie ohne Verbindung dahin. Während eines einzigen äußeren Augenblicks konnte die innen verschwunden sein, ohne eine Spur davon, ob sie eine Stunde oder eine Minute ausgesetzt habe.

Einmal überraschte Ulrich seine Schwester bei diesen Versuchen und erriet wohl etwas von ihnen, denn er sagte leise und lächelnd: "Es gibt eine Weissagung, dass für die Götter ein Jahrtausend nicht mehr als ein Öffnen und Schließen ihres Auges sei!" (*KA*)[23]

[And as with the impression of space, something similar had happened with the feelings of time: that flowing ribbon, the rolling staircase with its uncanny incidental association with death, seemed at many moments to stand still and at many others to flow on without any associations at all. In the space of one single outward instant it might have disappeared into itself, without a trace of whether it had stopped for an hour or a minute.

Once Ulrich surprised his sister during these experiments, and probably had an inkling of them, for he said softly, smiling: "There is a prophecy that a millennium is to the gods no longer than a blink of the eye." (*MwQ,* 1190)]

While this passage doesn't say anything directly about the genre of still life, it is clearly related to the still-life passages in "Atemzüge eines Sommertags," as we can see from its preoccupation with stillness, moving, and death, and its reference to a fresh vision of the world garden as if it had been — indeed, like Goethe's vision of the Laocoon group — just created upon contact. And in another version Musil's description reminds us of Goethe's game once more:

> Die Zeit stand still, ein Jahrtausend wog so leicht wie ein Öffnen und Schließen des Auges, sie war ans Tausendjährige Reich gelangt, Gott gar gab sich vielleicht zu fühlen. Und während sie, obwohl es doch die Zeit nicht mehr geben sollte, eins *nach* dem andern das empfand; und während ihr Bruder, damit sie bei diesem Traum nicht Angst leide, *neben* ihr war, obwohl es auch keinen Raum mehr zu geben schien: schien die Welt, unerachtet dieser Widersprüche, in allen Stücken erfüllt von Verklärung zu sein. (*KA*)[24]

> [Time stood still, a century weighed as lightly as the opening and closing of an eye; she had attained the millennium: perhaps God was even allowing his presence to be felt. And while she felt these things, one *after* the other — although time was not supposed to exist anymore — and while her brother, so that she should not suffer anxiety during this dream, was *beside* her, although space didn't seem to exist any longer either: despite these contradictions, the world seemed filled with transfigurations in all its parts. (*MwQ,* 1328)]

The millennium is to come *after* the fullness of time, after normal human life, and the paradise of the still life presumably *before* the advent of mankind. But in their shared timelessness the before and after may conflate. A still life, then, depicts the moment *before* God made mankind, the paradise *before* we came to desire and ravage and build and destroy; the moment before the fish begins to smell, before the sleeping dog awakens and devours the roast, before the wine spills; the moment of perfect hunger then, rather than the moment of possession, or the dreaded moment of satisfaction, over-fullness, and disgust — but also the millennium, when we will, it is said, also be free of the burden (and particularly tragic pleasure) of time. Faust, who knows all too well the drama of world-weariness, demands of Mephistopheles a "food which never satiates";[25] in other words, something that is not subject to time and disaffection, or to the normal laws of nature. Ulrich and Agathe are as surprised as Goethe's scholar to find themselves in a condition where they would say with Faust: "to the Moment flying/Ah, still delay, thou art so fair"[26] — to find themselves in a condition to which they would want to hold fast. Yet for once in their lives they do find themselves there, as Faust also does, reluctant as he is to be rushed by Mephistopheles away from his Gretchen and on to new thrills. And what do the mystic lovers Ulrich and Agathe find when they try to hold the moment? Of course they discover that to hold a feeling fast, as Lessing argues above, is anti-natural, distorting it into a grotesquery of itself. It ends once more, as Musil writes in a *Nachlass* note, "in Kot und Erbrechen" (in vomiting and excrement). (*KA*)[27]

In answering the question, "But how do you hold a feeling fast" (*MwQ*, 1229) Ulrich, in his notebooks on feeling, concludes:

> Jedes Wort will eindeutig und dauernd sein; aber jedes Gefühl verändert sich in dem Augenblick, wo es dauert. Gefühl hat keine Dauer und Identität; festgehalten, wird es in einem Nu unecht. Gefühle sind nicht nur veränderlich und unbeständig, wofür sie immer gegolten haben, sondern sie wären es mehr denn je auch in dem Augenblick, wo sie sich bemühten, es nicht zu sein. Ein Gefühl, das sich erhalten soll, muss von jedem Augenblick neu erschaffen werden, es muss beständig etwas Neues um dieses Gefühl geschehn, damit man es wieder fühlt. (*KA*)[28]

> [Every word wants to be definitive and enduring; but every feeling changes in the moment that it lasts. Feeling has no duration or identity; held fast, it becomes instantly ungenuine. Feelings are not only changeable and inconstant, as they have always been known to be, but they would be that way all the more at the instant they attempted not to be so. A feeling that means to preserve itself must be recreated out of every moment, something new must constantly happen to this feeling, so that one feels it anew.]

Ulrich distinguishes here between the *word* (as he himself is writing in his diary) and *feeling* (unwritten, changing, alive), harking back, perhaps, to Socrates's suspicion of writing. This part of the novel is a diary entry and thereby suspends the narrative, such as it is, in contemplation. Goethe, of course, used this same technique in *Die Wahlverwandtschaften* (The elective affinities; in Ottilie's rather philosophical aphoristic notebooks), another novel that perhaps has as much to do with the theme of painting, stillness, and artistic genre and its relationship to time, space, and narrative as Musil's. *Die Wahlverwandtschaften* seems to play consciously with Lessing's categories, as Goethe arranges literal *tableaux vivants* in his novel, as well as more subtle vignettes and pictures that stall the flow of the narrative. Photography plays a cameo role as well in this proto-modernist novel of 1809, calling attention to the flexibility of categories. Indeed, the very idea of *Wahlverwandtschaften* itself is a metaphor for shifting affiliations, cross-pollination and alternating correspondences between persons, values, time, space, and significance. The characters go on frequent walks within the confines of their estate (rather like Ulrich and Agathe within their garden world), and self-consciously stop at the points where the best views (still pictures) are to be attained. The stopping, pausing, situating in space is as significant in Goethe's novel as the movement, supposed progress, or plot. Goethe's novel (like Musil's) raises questions about the nature of novels and their relationship with visual art and the human perception of time, space, and values. It ends inconclusively and provides no optimistic answers about the shifting affections and elective affinities (metaphoric or literal) of humans, thus suggesting the probability of further shifts of allegiance, category, identity, and significance. Anything less would be like trying to hold a feeling fast or to pretend that when a narrator concludes with "and they lived happily ever after" that that is really the end of the story. But every word that comes to be written down, not struck through, definitively proofed, printed, and published, may be a sort of prison. And this may be one of the reasons why a modernist novel comes to explore the genre and implications of still life.

Writing, although Lessing maintained that it was better suited to depict progressive time than visual art, also may be deemed an insufficient medium for representing or allowing for the living interchange of ideas — particularly writing that attempts to freeze the moment. That writing, too, could stop time is not strictly a modernist idea. As Anne Carson points out in her fascinating book *Eros the Bittersweet*, Socrates was very wary of the tendency of writing to freeze time and thus inhibit the natural interplay of ideas and of change. Writing, according to Socrates, is like painting (in anachronistic answer to the Lessing theory: just as time-bound as painting). "If you question words on a page it is the same as questioning figures in a painting: 'they keep on giving the one same message eternally'."[29] "Like painting," Carson continues, "the written word fixes living things in time and space . . . *Logos* in its spoken form is a living, changing, unique process of thought . . ." (132). Writing in this sense is a means of murdering time and petrifying what was once alive.

Carson compares this process with the inevitably tragic desire of the lover to keep love alive at its highest peak, which is, she writes, using a metaphor from a poem by Sophocles, like holding on to an icicle to try to keep it from melting (111). She points out that Plato worries in *Phaedrus* about the power of writing to control time and meaning: to "render things 'clear and fixed' for all time" (121). And Socrates asks: What does the lover want from time? Answering: "To remain in the 'now' at any cost, even to the extent of radically damaging and deforming [or] stunt[ing] the growth of his beloved . . . inhibit[ing] the boy from normal physical development" (132). What Carson calls the "fundamental erotic dilemma," that is, to "sustain the present indicative of pleasure" without killing it or deforming it (139), is very much the same problem posed by

Ulrich and Agathe when they ask, "But however does one hold a feeling fast?." And for both it is a question of the nature of metaphor and its resistance to the direct statement of the indicative and its presumption of duration. Damage is done by lovers in the name of desiring, just as damage is done by writing and reading in the name of communication, or by a too-literal metaphor-making. Writing and the attempt of the lover to stop the love and the beloved from changing, like any metaphor-making that is not conscious of its provisional, transitory nature, "violate reality by the same kind of misapprehension." Reader and writer attempt to "fix words permanently outside the stream of time" (130). For Socrates — and for Musil — "wisdom is something alive, a 'living breathing word' . . . that happens between two people when they talk. Change is essential to it, not because wisdom changes but because people do, and must" (132). While Plato paradoxically *writes* about the dangers of writing (and, elsewhere, creates parables and allegories and beautiful prose dialogues about the danger of art), Musil obsesses in thousands of pages of circling, essayistic, digressing text about the dangers of consummation, of grasping, or devouring, of finishing. They both succeed in creating living, open, dialogical texts that resist petrification. The dialogic discourse itself perpetuates the openness of the exploration. Transparency of metaphor and variability of truth(s) and perspective(s) ensure continual fruitfulness.

The implication is that good writing approximates or imitates the aliveness and open-endedness of thought, of love, of "real" life and that it actually vivifies the reader — a modernist imperative — to change his or her life, to read the book as if he or she were walking through fire. And good writing does this in great part by virtue of the displacing creative subterfuge of metaphor, in the suspended time of art. Carson writes, "We love such suspended time for the sake of its difference from ordinary time and real life," or real thinking. "In any act of thinking," she continues,

the mind must reach across this space between known and unknown, linking one to another but also keeping visible their difference. It is an erotic space . . . this "erotic ruse" in novels and poems now appears to constitute the very structure of human thinking. When the mind reaches out to know, the space of desire opens and a necessary fiction transpires. (171)

All knowing is metaphor-making; all knowing happens in the space between one thing and another, a space that is incommensurable, ultimately unbridgeable; it must remain open: "We think," writes Carson, "by projecting sameness upon difference, by drawing things together in a relation or idea while at the same time maintaining the distinctions between them" (171). Socrates was, according to Carson, a "lover of these divisions and collections" (172). Musil, likewise, was simultaneously Monsieur le vivisecteur *and* combiner, collector, metaphorist *par excellence*.

Socrates's wisdom was, as Carson points out, to be found precisely in the space between what he knew and did not know, that is, the unbridgeable space of metaphor, which is created not only in art but every time we think or see — but only if we succeed in maintaining the distinctions.

The still life then, like living self-contradicting metaphor-making, depicts something that one can never really reach, or devour, or possess — something that, furthermore, according to Musil, is itself "teilnahmslos," or non-responsive, non-participatory. This lack of response is part of the charm of the still life; it increases desire by its silence, its lack of movement, its non-participation, its maintenance of distinctions. It ensures its inviolate presence amid the destructive forces of normal time — untouched, unpossessed, unbitten. Proust, another consummate time-expanding metaphorist, describes this particular charm of the silent unreachable still life in his essay on Chardin:

> Into these rooms . . . Chardin enters like the light, giving its colour to everything, conjuring up from the timeless obscurity where they lay entombed all nature's creatures, animate or inanimate, together with the meaning of her design, so brilliant to the eye, so dark to the understanding. As in The Sleeping Beauty, they are all brought back to life, resume their colour, begin to talk to you, put on life and duration. On the sideboard everything, from the stiff creases of the turned-back cloth to the knife lying askew and jutting out by the length of its blade, records of the hurry of servants, witnesses to the gluttony of guests.
>
> The dish of fruit, still as glorious and already as ravaged as an autumnal orchard, is crowned with swelling peaches, rosy as cherubs, smiling and inaccessible as the gods on Olympus. A dog with an outstretched neck cannot reach up to them, and makes them the more desirable for being desired in vain. He eats them by sight, divining their fragrant flesh from the downy skin that it moistens. Wine glasses, clear as daylight, enticing as spring water, are grouped together, those in which a few sips of sweet wine display themselves as though lingering in a gullet standing beside others already almost drained, like emblems of a lively thirst, beside emblems of a thirst allayed. One glass has half tipped over, tilted like the bell of a withered flower.[30]

Proust's description touches on many of the components essential to Musil's analysis of the still life: the animation of the inanimate, the unreachability of the enticing fruits and wine, the sense of timelessness or, rather, of an expansion of time that includes past, present, and future (the glasses already emptied, the ones desired, and the ones not yet sipped). The still painting has the effect of actually bringing what was dead or sleeping back to life, of animating, of imbuing with color, of lending life and duration.

Proust's sensuous description may explain why Schopenhauer did not class still lifes as meeting the criteria of Kantian "disinterestedness" — because they actually excited desire and hunger. Schopenhauer's reading of Kant's "Critique of Aesthetic Judgment" is, however, according to Nietzsche, a misreading that uses Kantian disinterestedness as an argument for the ascetic ideal. Schopenhauer, in other words, hypocritically has his own hidden interest or agenda: to present art as an escape from his torturous libidinal urges (Nietzsche refers to Schopenhauer as "a torture victim who escapes from his torture"). Nietzsche mocks Schopenhauer's asceticism, favoring the aesthetic over the moralistic:

> "That is beautiful," said Kant "which gives us pleasure *without interest.*" Without interest! Compare with this definition one framed by a true "spectator" and artist — Stendhal, who once called the beautiful a promesse de bonheur [a promise of happiness]. At any rate, he *rejected* and repudiated the one point about the aesthetic state which Kant had stressed: désintéressement [disinterestedness]. Who is right, Kant or Stendhal?[31]

Musil writes: "Stillleben = Gefühl ohne Handlung" (Still life = feeling without action). Still life is, according to Musil, "Apraxie der Liebe" (apraxia of love), is "Nichthandeln" (inaction), is non-appetitive. According to Kant, the judgment of beauty has no concern for whether or not the depicted object actually exists (like desire for a painted fish). In other words, the judge of beauty does not want to possess it, eat it, make love to it. It is a transcendental enjoyment, which engages with the object more as an idea or as a possibility than as a graspable physical reality with a practical use. According to Kant,

> What matters is what I do with this presentation within myself, and not [the respect] in which I depend on the object's existence. Everyone has to admit that if a judgment about beauty is mingled with the least interest then it is very partial and not a pure judgment of taste. In order to play the judge in matters of taste, we must not be in the least biased in favor of the thing's existence but must be wholly indifferent to it.[32]

Kant then continues, calling for: "Flowers, free designs, lines aimlessly intertwined and called foliage: these have no significance, depend on no determinate concept, and yet we like them. . . ."[33] When one reads more carefully, one finds that this independence of determinate concept is also essential. Kant writes, "Both the agreeable and the good refer to our power of desire and hence carry a liking with them . . . what we like is not just the object, but its existence as well. A judgment of taste, on the other hand, is merely *contemplative*, i.e., it is a judgment that is indifferent to the existence of the object."[34]

Nietzsche does not come to a conclusion about whether or not Kant's theory is correct, although he clearly repudiates Schopenhauer's interpretation of it because it would be antithetical to life, to the urges, to the pleasures of the body, and therefore seems to favor Stendhal's aesthetic of interpersonal subjectivity. And yet Kant and Nietzsche may not be as much at odds on the question of disinterestedness in art as this passage from *Die Genealogie der Moral* seems to suggest; and Stendhal's statement on beauty, when looked at alongside his theory of "crystallization" from *On Love*, an almost mystical state of perception wherein one sees the beloved in a mist of probably temporary perfection, may be just as much a matter of abstracting and distancing aestheticism as Kant's. The Nietzsche passage is more about the question of ascetic ideals than it is about aesthetics, and Nietzsche makes a point of saying that it is not the place to come to conclusions about whether Kant's pronouncement is correct. As such, it might not even be worth mentioning here, except that the question of disinterestedness is so central to Musil's analysis of the still life, and that this passage is a marker of a continuing intertextual debate on the subject of Kant's theory of disinterestedness, a debate of which Musil was most certainly aware. Musil mentions Schopenhauer's ideas in a long excerpt and paraphrase from Klages's *Vom kosmogonischen Eros* (On cosmogonic Eros),[35] associating the question of disinterestedness with ecstatic experience and its concomitant characteristic of bursting the bonds of individuation and of communing with something Klages calls the Ur-Bild (universal image). Klages's Eros, one of the models for Musil's Other Condition, is distinguished in Musil's notes from drive and from "sexus" in that it does not want to possess, and in that it

> ist überhaupt kein Trieb, sondern "ein völliger Zustand" und zwar kein Zustand der Bedürftigkeit, sondern einer der Erfüllung "'an sich'" . . . Vollkommen frei von Streben; darf daher nicht mit Liebe und Gefühl verwechselt werden, die Streben enthalten. Ist eine Art der Ekstasis und zwar wollüstig-seelige Ekstasis. Keine Glückseligkeit (geistige oder sinnliche) (Wunsches oder Triebes). Jede Befriedigung ist nur Augenblick des Übergangs vom Nochnichtbesitzen ins Besitzen, worauf Leere folgt. (*KA*)[36]

> [is not a drive at all, but rather a "complete condition" and not a condition of neediness at all, but a condition of fulfillment "in itself." Completely free from striving; may not therefore be mistaken for love or feeling, which both contain striving. Is a kind of ecstasis and really a sensuous-soulful ecstasis. No bliss (spiritual or sensual) can have the character of a satisfaction (wish or drive). Every satisfaction is only [a] moment in the transformation from not-yet-possessing to possessing, followed by emptiness.]

Musil's concern with the ecstatic condition of "disinterestedness" thus has little to do with Schopenhauer's ascetic ideal or any moral inhibition against physical pleasure or experience; the narrator clearly states, in fact, that Ulrich and Agathe's hesitancy to consummate their relationship has little to do with such scruples. What, then, is it about? What kind of disinterestedness is Musil really talking about in the complex of the still life? And what does the durative or momentary nature of a work of art have to do with the difference between what Klages calls "Ur-image," what Schopenhauer calls "Motiv" (motif), what Musil might call "Gattung" ("genre" or "species") or abstraction, and the fleeting momentariness of a non-repeatable singular experience? We can glean that disinterestedness has something meaningful to do with the question of metaphor, pattern, and abstraction and that this something is a matter of duration, repeatability, and the difference between general and specific feelings. Musil's notes on Klages are some small help. Another section reads:

> Aus der polaren Berührung von innen und außen gebärt sich unablässig das selber beseelte Bild: unaufhörliche Ausgeburt. (Aber das Äußere ist doch schon Bild?) "Das Äußere ist ein in Geheimniszustand erhobnes Innere," Novalis. (Bei Schopenhauer, sonst sehr ähnlich, kommen noch die Begriffe Interesselosigkeit und Motiv hinzu. Wahrscheinlich ist aber die Polemik richtig, die nachweist, dass Schopenhauer nicht Urbilder sondern allgemeinste Begriffe meint und ihnen unterschiebt.) Welt als Wille und Vorstellung, drittes und viertes Buch?

> [The self-generated image is constantly born of the polarized touching of the inner and the outer: uninterrupted spawn. (But the external is already an image, isn't it?) "The external is the internal in its elevated secret condition," Novalis. (In Schopenhauer, otherwise very similar, the concepts of disinterestedness and motif are added. But probably the polemic is correct that suggests that Schopenhauer meant the most general concepts, not Ur-images . . . World as Will and Idea, third and fourth book?]

In contradistinction to Schopenhauer, Musil's explication of Klages explains further:

> Im Gegensatz zur Allgemeinheit des Begriffs ist das Urbild absolut augenblicklich und darum unwiederholbar einzig. Ding, Geschehnis, Gegenstand hat im Verhältnis zum Bild die Natur der Allgemeinheit oder Begrifflichkeit; dem gegenwärtigen Eindruck wird ein bleibend Selbiges unterschoben, auf das man jederzeit zurückkommen kann. Das Erlebnis des Liebenden gilt nicht der Person des Geliebten, sondern dessen mit dem Zeitstrom strömenden Bild. Man muss vom Begriffsgegenstand absehen, um zum Bild zu kommen. (*KA*)[37]

[In contrast to the generality of the concept, the Ur-image is absolutely momentary and therefore unrepeatably singular. Thing, occurrence, object has, in relationship with the image, the nature of generality or conceptuality; the current impression is substituted by a durative similarity, to which one can return again and again. The experience of the lover is not about the beloved, but about the beloved's image as it flows with the stream of time. One must look away from the conceptual object in order to arrive at the image.]

And in another notebook entry, we read:

Gefühle bin ich.
Vorstellungen habe ich.
Schopenhauer verlangt für den kontemplativen Zustand Freiheit von den "Motiven" des Willens, Dinge ohne Subjektivität betrachten, rein objektiv, ihnen ganz hingegeben, sofern sie bloß Vorstellungen, nicht sofern sie Motive sind. . . . (*KA*)[38]

[I am Feeling.
I have ideas.
Schopenhauer demands freedom from "motives of the will" for the contemplative condition, to observe things without subjectivity, to abandon one's self completely objectively to them, as long as they are merely ideas, not if they are motifs. . . .]

Nietzsche, at least in so far as he is talking about the ascetic ideal and the philosopher's suspicious turning away from fleshly desires, differentiates in this context between different kinds of objectivity:

To see differently in this way for once, to *want* to see differently, is no small discipline and preparation of the intellect for its future "objectivity" — the latter understood not as "contemplation without interest" (which is a nonsensical absurdity), but as ability to *control* one's Pro and Con and to dispose of them, so that one knows how to employ a *variety* of perspectives and affective interpretations in the service of knowledge. Henceforth, my dear philosophers, let us be on guard against the dangerous old conceptual fiction that posited a "pure, will-less, painless, timeless knowing subject"; let us guard against the snares of such contradictory ideas as "pure reason," "absolute spirituality," "knowledge in itself": these always demand that we should think of an eye that is completely unthinkable, an eye turned in no particular direction, in which the active and interpreting forces, through which alone seeing becomes seeing *something*, are supposed to be lacking; these always demand of the eye an absurdity and a nonsense. There is *only* a perspective seeing; *only* a perspective knowing; and the *more* affects we allow to speak about one thing, the *more* eyes, different eyes, we can use to observe one thing, the more complete our "concept" of this thing, our "objectivity," will be. But to eliminate the will altogether, to suspend each and every affect, suppose — what would that mean but to *castrate* the intellect?[39]

This passage brings us back to the imperative of creative metaphoric transparency, the infinite variability of seeing with many and new eyes, and the existential agency of the creative subject. It is impossible to remove the will, but the will need not be utterly blind to its own agency in the creation of realities. Aesthetic objectivity, then, may be an amalgam of what is sometimes (mistakenly, according to Nietzsche) called "disinterestedness" and the aesthetic intellectual state of perspectival openness. Objectivity in this Nietzschean sense would then have more to do with the ability to see non-specific entities instead of merely specific ones, a perspectival shift from the particular to the general and back again. When a work of art (or an idea, a utopia, an ideal) is not an imitation of an already existent concept, object, reality, prejudice, or political system, when it is created without concern for likeness/mimesis or conformity to established laws, the mind is set free to play, invent, and dream, thereby allowing for the truly creative abstract invention of new forms, values, and relationships.

Musil, in other paraphrases from Klages's *Vom kosmogonischen Eros*, describes the difference between a love that is desiring and grasping and a love that does not desire to possess its object. The love that is desiring is written about in much the same way as the specific feeling, while Eros seems to be related to the sensation of the non-specific. The problem with the appetitive, with the fulfillment of desire, hunger, and expectation is that it inevitably leads to satisfaction and emptiness, with the destruction, in other words, of the inviolately desired object, illusion, and possibility. It is a problem of time, of physical and natural laws, not a moral problem.

The image of still life that Ulrich and Agathe explore as a parallel to their non-consummation is thus perhaps valid only insofar as they do not consummate their relationship. In the notes we find the constellation: Sister = still life = incest, and the idea that to desire one's sister is tantamount to desiring something that one cannot possess. Yet the siblings do eventually possess each other, at least temporarily, and Agathe is not, strictly speaking, an object of necrophilic desire, since she is responsive, active, alive, — even more so, one could argue, than her hesitant philosophical brother. Musil, via a necessarily imprecise process, makes a metaphor of incest (whether committed or just imagined) and still life. We might well ask how the siblings' relationship (perhaps only as long as it is not yet consummated?) is like a still life, and how not; we might also ask which (the relationship or the still life?) is a metaphor for which. Is their relationship a metaphor for the frozen-fluid nature of the still-life painting, which is a synecdochal metaphor for art on the whole, or is art a meta-phor for life, for the relationship between people and for our experience of time, fleetingness, and death? Further, if the siblings' relationship (on either side of the tenor/vehicle pair) breaks out of its stillness by consum-mation, what are the corresponding suggestions about an art that dares to explode the frames and categories of eternal shimmering? Stillness, and an almost debilitating inability to act on the one hand; on the other hand, a decisive act that seems to undo stable structures of morality, aesthetics, and possibility. To do what isn't done, in other words, is the imminent thrill, danger, *frisson* of the suspenseful deferral. And the committing of a crime, or "doing wrong" is, of course, a very central theme for Musil's "criminals" — Ulrich and Agathe — as they explore the mystical, philo-sophical, and aesthetic consequences of taboo-breaking.

The heretic, according to Steiner who could well have been describ-ing Musil, is "the discourser without end. His reinterpretations and revi-sions, his novel translations, even when they profess, strategically, a return to the authentic source . . . generate an open-ended, disseminative her-meneutic."[40] A crime may be committed against received order and for-mal harmony where "dogma can be defined as hermeneutic punctuation, as the promulgation of semantic arrest." And yet the ultimate criminal act for Musil and his mystic siblings may occur precisely in the moment of silence, wordlessness, the pause amid the infinite propagation of words, images, and movement — in the action that takes place when the words stop. Still life, then, becomes a fruitful contradiction in terms, a shimmer-ing aliveness within an enclosed form, a symbol of the ever-changing tran-scendent potential of the creative subject caught within the boundaries of linear and measurable time.

Any work of art has this potential not only to stop and fix, but also to explode and expand time, space, and possibility. While art can and has always been capable of being a force for controlling and constructing meaning, and thereby limiting individual perspectives and creative vision, Nietzsche, in his notes for *Der Wille zur Macht*, addresses the tension between art as eternalization and art as engaged critique of reality, sug-gestively calling for "new arts":

> Becoming as invention, willing, self-denial, overcoming oneself: no subject but an action . . . positing, creative . . . [as opposed to] Art as the will to overcome becoming, as "eternalization" . . . [con-versely art as becoming requires] the destruction of ideals, the new desert; new arts . . .[41]

Paul Celan, in his "Meridian" speech of 1960, in which, it is said, he attempted to respond to the question of "what poetry is, can, and must be after the Holocaust,"[42] explores the still-prevailing modernist fear of what he describes as the automaton or the Medusa head of art. This congealing, freezing force threatens to turn living, breathing, changing beings into stone. It is, perhaps, a force easily associated with fear of control and thus possibly related to the concept of hostility toward art explored by Celan in his speech.[43] Celan explicates a passage from Büchner's story "Lenz," in which the lapsed poet aims to raise reality over art by arguing that the beauty of two living girls by a mountain stream is more valuable than any picture or description of them. Yet, as Celan points out, Büchner also writes that seeing them makes one want to become a Medusa head in order to turn the figures into stone, to freeze them, which is of course, what one does when one is an artist. Celan would have us see that this supposed frozenness, this act of petrification (an echo, perhaps, of the Laocoon group) can actually be a higher aliveness, a call to concentration. And he cites Benjamin in his essay on Kafka, quoting Malebranche: "Attention is the natural prayer of the soul."[44] And what inspires concentration, attention, higher awareness, liveliness more than the momentary pause and prayer of the work of art? A pause and prayer facilitated, as Musil well knew, by the extratemporal metaphoric coincidence of the I with its other: "Art, "Celan writes, "thus also the Medusa's head, the mechanism, the automaton, the uncanny so difficult to separate out and which in the final analysis is perhaps only *one* strangeness — Art lives on" (11). "The poem itself," he writes, "has only this one, unique, momentary present. . . ." The question, he continues, of the poem's origin or its destination "stays open," "does not come to an end" and searches for a place that doesn't exist, utopia, "the place where all tropes and metaphors want to be carried on ad absurdum" (10). This place and space of openness, utopia, this far-off land where tropes and metaphors proliferate, is made accessible through the stillness of the work of art. Its paradoxical aliveness reminds us of Ulrich and Agathe's description of the "mysterious, demoniacal quality of painted life" and its "exciting, vague, infinite echo" (*MwQ,* 1324), and also of Heidegger's concept of presence as elucidated in his essay on Van Gogh's shoes. In Heidegger's conception, the work of art has a presence, a radiant in-dwelling (related to Musil's concept of "living in" rather than "living for"?), which creates an energetic conduit between Being and Becoming, and thereby provides an opening — a "clearing" — for movement. Heidegger's idea of this "presentness in things," explains Steiner,

> has its own integral, "ecstatic" authority. To identify this nonpragmatic, nonutilitarian presence and ecstasy, Heidegger coins the verb *zu welten.* In and through the work of art, with its disinterestedly creative yet dependent relationship to wood, stone, or pigment, *with its total presentness in yet also out of historical time,* the world *weltet* (untranslatably, the world worlds). And it is just this mode of existentiality which turns out to be fundamental.[45]

It seems important, amid Heidegger's often rapturous discourse of essence and truth, to point out that the aesthetic experience referred to here is not one of finality, is not locked within frozen Being, but most certainly is directed outward toward Becoming, toward that which Steiner calls a "mode of existentiality." Celan, in a slightly less optimistic evaluation of the power of art, makes it clear that the things and places that the poem seeks do not actually exist anywhere, that they are not actually to be found; the perfect poem he speaks of, he clarifies, itself does not even exist;[46] Musil would probably concur. The value, rather, of the work of art, as suggested by Celan's essay, is to be found in the tension between change and stasis, in the way in which art continually renews itself, replaces and displaces itself, even in the face of the most treacherous forces of inhumanity. And this persistently alive journey of art, Celan writes, be it merely a matter of "re-routing, detours from you to you" (11), a circling akin to Musil's endless discourse, is a journey toward the self and toward the other, toward "blueprints of being [Daseinsentwürfe] perhaps, a sending oneself ahead toward oneself . . . a kind of a homecoming" (11). Celan ends with a beginning ("I am at the end," he writes, a page or so before really ending, "— I am back at the beginning." [10]), with an explanation of the title of his talk — "Meridian," a metaphor for "the connecting" (das Verbindende), for the connections and correspondences that the lonely poem forges. "I find," he writes, "what connects and leads, like the poem, to an encounter. I find something — something like language — immaterial, yet terrestrial, somewhat circular that returns to itself across two poles while — cheerfully — even crossing the tropics [tropes, too] —: I find . . . a *meridian*" (12).

And this "Begegnung" (encounter, meeting) that turns back toward itself while crossing over poles, which is in the form of a circling, should remind us — in an already fully glutted proliferation of echoes, likenesses, parallels, analogies, and versions, of Ulrich and Agathe's "Begegnung" (the title of drafts sketching their first meeting as adult "relations"), of the meeting of like but unlike; of the meeting of metaphor and its fateful, fleeting significance; of the meetings displacing meetings between words, chapters, versions, and ideas; "Daseinsentwürfe," drafts and sketches, not just of writing, but of being; between stillness and movement, meaning and new meaning, between Being and Becoming. A meridian, like the Other Condition, is a place for metaphors to meet, and might perhaps engender a mode of existence that communicates between traditionally polarized realms. While Celan, like the writer whom Büchner celebrates in his story, eventually chose silence and suicide over the fraught and imperfect medium of words or poetry, Musil's answer was to never come to closure, to never arrive at the final word, to constantly proffer more and more meetings and partings.[47] And insofar as every such meeting, every such parting requires an inaccuracy or a theft (Nietzsche might have meant precisely this when he wrote that the lie is the condition of life), the metaphoric process that vivifies stale meanings and forms allows us to begin to glimpse how something as seemingly harmless and insignificant as a still life or a "mere" metaphor is deeply and intrinsically related to questions of time, death, duration, meaning, love, artistic genres, perversion, crime, and the aesthetic requirement of doing, sometimes, what paradoxically isn't done.

Notes

[1] These versions, referred to as the "garden chapters" in the *Nachlass*, include the draft sections also titled "Conversations on Love," "Difficulties Where They Are Not Looked For," "Loving Is Not Simple," untranslated draft chapters such as "Attempts to Love a Scoundrel," and the different versions actually entitled "Breaths of a Summer's Day." The chapter "Moonbeams by Sunlight" is also conceptually and thematically related to these "Garden Chapters." In the English translation by Burton Pike some of the still-life material, which is included in a number of the "Breaths of a Summer's Day" chapters in the original *Nachlass*, is presented only in the version and section entitled "Loving Is Not Simple." While I will provide page numbers for the English text and use translations when they are from the same passages in the German, this chapter was written with the more comprehensive draft versions in mind and may refer to passages that are not present in the English edition. See *KA*: Genfer Ersetzungsreihen, Kapitelkommentar: Atemzüge eines Sommertags. Textgenese: "The last version of the 'Breaths' chapter represents a series of vast variations reaching back a long time. It reaches on the one hand back to the numerous preliminary sketches and further to the garden-chapter sketches of 1937/38 and to the chapter experiment, 'Attempts to Love a Scoundrel' of 1933/34. On the other hand, motifs and situations of the novel are narratively suspended in this, its last chapter: the conceptualization of death and entropy, / the journey of the siblings to the Mediterranean (incest) / the vision of the millennium (Agathe's dream) / the reintroduction, i.e. rehabilitation of the drive / the motif of qualitylessness. . . . [Menges1982, 250; Pietsch 1988, 118–149; Pekar 1989, 298; Fanta 2000, 522–526]." See also Karl Corino's description of Musil's last days and the context of the last version. Corino, *Robert Musil*, 1433–37.

[2] Rilke, "Der Panther im Jardin des Plantes, Paris,"in *Gedichte*, 447.

[3] Rilke, "Die erste Elegie" of "Die Duineser Elegien" (the first elegy of the Duino elegies), *Gedichte*, 690.

[4] *KA*: Transkriptionen & Faksimiles. Nachlass: Mappen. Mappengruppe V. Mappe V/5 "Arbeitsmappe." V/5/168 Korr VII 29/Arbeitsmappe 80.

[5] *KA*: Transkriptionen & Faksimiles, Nachlass: Mappen. Mappengruppe V. Mappe V/5 "Arbeitsmappe." V/5/169 Korr VII 30.

[6] *KA*: Transkriptionen & Faksimiles. Nachlass: Mappen. Mappengruppe V. Mappe V/5 "Arbeitsmappe." V/5/169 Korr VII 30.

[7] Refers to chapter draft "Es ist nicht einfach zu lieben," translated as "Loving Is Not Easy" in *MwQ*.

8 *KA*: Transkriptionen & Faksimiles. Nachlass: Mappen. Mappengruppe V. Mappe V/5. "Arbeitsmappe." V/5/166 Korr VII 27 / Arbeitsmappe 79.

9 Bryson, *Still Life*, 9.

10 KA: Lesetexte. Band 9: Gedruckte Reden. Rede zur Rilke Feier, 11.

11 *KA*: Lesetexte. Band 4: Der Mann ohne Eigenschaften. Die Vorstufen. Aus dem Nachlass Ediertes. Die Romanprojekte 1918–1926. Die Zwillingsschwester. S4 Anders-Agathe Reise.

12 *KA*: Lesetexte. Gedruckte Reden. Rede zur Rilke Feier, 14.

13 *KA*: Lesetexte. Band 19: Wiener und Berliner Korrespondenz 1919–1938. 1930. Robert Musil an Walther Petry, 25. April 1930.

14 Fanta, "Über den Ausgang der letzten Liebesgeschichte," 167.

15 *KA:* Lesetexte. Band 3: Der Mann ohne Eigenschaften. Die Fortsetzung. Fortsetzungsreihen 1932–1936. Erste Fortsetzungsreihe. 45. Hinter dem Gartengitter.

16 *KA:* Lesetexte. Band 3: Der Mann ohne Eigenschaften. Die Fortsetzung. Fortsetzungsreihen 1932–1936. Erste Fortsetzungsreihe. 45. Hinter dem Gartengitter.

17 Lessing, *Laocoon*, 109.

18 Lessing, *Laocoon*, 17.

19 *KA:* Lesetexte. Band 3: Der Mann ohne Eigenschaften. Die Forseztung. Zwischenfortsetzungen 1937–1939. Druckfahnen Kapitel 50: Agathe findet Ulrichs Tagebuch.

20 Sartre, *Nausea*, 89.

21 Sartre, *Nausea*, 95, 96.

22 Goethe, "Upon the Laocoon," 27.

23 *KA*: Lesetexte. Band 3: Der Mann ohne Eigenschaften. Die Fortsetzung. Zwischenfortsetzung 1937–1939. Druckfahnen-kapitel Mondstrahlen bei Tage.

24 *KA:* Lesetexte. Der Mann ohne Eigenschaften. Die Fortsetzung. Zwischenfortsetzung 1937–1939. Dritte Ersetzungsreihe 52. Atemzüge eines Sommertags.

25 Goethe, *Faust*, 67.

26 Goethe, *Faust*, 295.

27 *KA*: Transkriptionen & Faksimiles. Nachlass: Mappen. Mappengruppe VII. Mappe VII/9 "U/Ag Kap. Ausgehoben." VII/9/181 s4+. . .10 1 A-Ag Reise 27.

28 *KA*: Lesetexte. Band 3: Der Mann ohne Eigenschaften. Die Fortsetzung. Fortsetzungsreihen 1932–1936. Erste Fortsetzungsreihe. 49. Ulrichs Tagebuch.

29 Carson, *Eros*, 132. This quote is from Socrates. Further references to this work are given in parenthesis.

30 Proust, *Art and Literature*, 326–27.

31 Nietzsche, *Basic Writings*, 450.

32 Kant, "Critique of Judgment," 504–35, qtd. 506–7.

[33] Kant, "Critique of Judgment," 507.

[34] Kant, "Critique of Judgment," 508.

[35] For a subtle discussion of Musil's use of Ludwig Klages's philosophy as foundation of his Other Condition, see Preusser, "Masken des Ludwig Klages," 224–53.

[36] *KA: Lesetexte. Band 16: Frühe Tagebuchhefte 1899–1926. IV. Wien (1918–1926). 21: Die zwanzig Werke III (1920–1926). Wien/Brünn/Berlin, 1923.*

[37] *KA: Lesetexte. Band 16: Frühe Tagebuchhefte 1899–1926. IV. Wien (1918–1926). 21: Die zwanzig Werke III (1920–1926). Wien/Brünn/Berlin, 1923.*

[38] *KA: Lesetexte. Band 15: Fragmente aus dem Nachlass. Essaystische Fragmente. Das Essaybuch (1923–1927). Versuche einen andren Menschen zu finden.*

[39] Nietzsche, *Basic Writings*, 555.

[40] Steiner, *Real Presences*, 45.

[41] Nietzsche, *Will to Power*, 331.

[42] Celan, *Meridian*, back cover. Quotations from Celan will be noted in the text in parentheses. See also Cameron, "Note on 'The Meridian'": "Like the Hebrew prophets, Celan speaks, as he emphasizes, in the context of contemporary events. The event which leaves him 'no choice' in setting the 'acute accent' is, of course, the Holocaust. To establish this as the context, only a few oblique references are necessary, such as the remark about 'something in the air — in the air we have to breathe'"; http://www.pointandcircumference.com/celan/meridiannote.htm.

[43] In one note in the volume of the final draft, versions, and material cited above, Celan confesses that he himself shares this hostility, yet it should be noted that this hostility is directed against the rigidity and artificiality that art is prone to, not the living creaturely, breathing poetry that Celan counterposes to the automaton. "Büchner's hostility to art — permit the translator of Young Fate this confession — I share it." Celan, *Meridian*, 154.

[44] Celan, *Meridian*, 9.

[45] Steiner, *Martin Heidegger*, 133.

[46] Celan: "For I am talking about a poem that does not exist! The absolute poem — no, that certainly does not, cannot exist! But there is indeed in each poem, even in the most unassuming poem, this irrecusable question, this outrageous claim" (10).

[47] See Carson, *Economy of the Unlost*, 120, for a discussion of Celan's eventual silencing.

Conclusion

Aber man kann Ideale nicht leben, sie schlagen in Widersinn um. Anderseits ist es unerläßlich, dass wir Dinge erfinden, die es nicht geben kann, um das Leben zwischen den Dingen, die es gibt, erträglich zu gestalten. Aber was bedeutet es, dass die Ideen keinen andern Zweck haben, als das, was ist, mit etwas zu durchsetzen, das nicht ist? Ich verbringe mein Leben damit u[nd] weiß nichts davon.

[But one cannot live ideals; they turn into their opposite. On the other hand, it is indispensable that we invent things that cannot exist, in order to make life amid those things that do exist bearable. But what does it mean that ideas have no other goal than infusing that which is with what is not? I spend my whole life on this, and know nothing about it.]

— Musil, *Nachlass*

The most extreme form in which the question posed by the enigmaticalness of art can be formulated is whether or not there is meaning. For no artwork is without its own coherence, however much this coherence may be transformed by its own opposite.

— Adorno, *Aesthetic Theory*

Gesang, wie du ihn lehrst, ist nicht
Begehr, nicht Werbung um ein endlich Erreichtes;
Gesang ist Dasein . . .

[Song, as you teach it, is not
Desire, not seeking after something finally attained;
Song is existence . . .]

— Rilke, *Sonette an Orpheus*

HOW STRONG THE PULL toward closure is, toward "something finally attained," may be proved by the desire to somehow end on a decisive note, to weave all the bifurcating strands into some meaningful formula or design, a form fixed at least for the moment. The multiplicity of concatenations tend to drown each other out by creating a blanket of noise, just as competing fictive events and philosophical perspectives vie for temporary predominance. The listener or reader highlights one or two correspondences or connections, emphasizing those few tones and rhythms that seem to ring out more boldly than the rest, in order to approximate some sort of coherence. As we have seen, Musil exposes this metaphoric selecting out as an inaccurate representation of the real messiness of experience, which does not ever exactly repeat itself; but he also maintains that it is just this activity of seeing correspondence or creating temporary harmonies that brings "Schönheit und Erregung" (*MoE*, 573; beauty and excitement, *MwQ*, 625) into the world. We have also seen that Musil qualifies his praise of this metaphor-making still further by insisting that for the activity to be revolutionary and not stagnating there must be metaphoric transparency. The creative subject must be aware that the metaphors used to describe the world are only contingent and invented possibilities, not absolute solutions to the problem of describing or creating it. Creative possibilities must not, in other words, be allowed to ossify into finalities or static truths that would inhibit the creation of new ways of seeing new and different forms.

This is also true when it comes to interpreting a vast and multifaceted novel such as Musil's, particularly when it comes to speculation about the novel's potential conclusion. The dangers of reaching premature and absolute certainty about any of the novel's "truths" or meanings on the basis of individual statements or passages taken out of context are increased by the unfinished and nonlinear nature of Musil's laboratory of the thousand manuscripts. Since the results of the experiments are not and never will be in, we do not know which, if any, of the posited conclusions Musil might have chosen to end or settle on. We do not know if, indeed, he would ever have been able to come to closure at all. Might he have ended the novel in the chaos or mystical ecstasy of war, in the suicide or the reunion of the siblings, with Ulrich beginning to write a book,[1] with Moosbrugger as Messiah and Clarisse as his prophet? Would Musil's final word vindicate the Other Condition, or the Inductive Ethos, the Utopia of the Motivated Life, of Essayism, or of God as Empiricism? Or would he have chosen despair and cynicism? We cannot know; yet even in a cosmos of oscillating shifting perspectives we can trace the already existing pattern to find the probability: the only fitting answer to the question of conclusion is, thus, an *inconclusion*, a continual questing and questioning to match the internal churning telos of Musil's lifelong process. As presence is in constant philosophical and formal tension with an active generating of new ideas and forms within the novel, inconclusion entails both the inability to ever conclude and an eternally reverberating utopic conclusion (and origin) of in-dwelling. The novel can only end in nonending, in hovering outside time and aslant of narrative closure, in the aesthetic utopia of the Other Condition.

Yet many critics have declared the opposite, assuming that Musil intended the Other Condition to fail, disappoint, end,[2] to be replaced either by another utopia or a more realistic assessment of the demands of normal reality. It has, indeed, become a commonplace that Musil rejected the aesthetic utopia of the Other Condition. Reasons for this rejection

can generally be classed under the following three categories: the experiences of the Other Condition are not translatable into normal reality, it
does not last, and it is not socially viable. In accordance with these assessments, and as their usual source, Musil himself states on a number of
occasions that the Other Condition fails, cannot last, ends negatively, falls
apart. One late note, for example, reads:

> U[lrich]-Ag[athe] ist eigentlich ein Versuch des Anarchismus in der
> Liebe. Der selbst da negativ endet. Das ist die tiefe Beziehung der
> Liebesgeschichte zum Krieg. . . . Was bleibt am Ende aber übrig?
> Dass es eine Sphäre der Ideale u[nd] eine der Realität gibt? Rich-
> tbilder udgl? Wie tief unbefriedigend! Gibt es keine bessere Ant-
> wort?" (*MoE*, 1876).

> [U[lrich]-Ag[athe] is really an attempt at anarchism in love. Which
> even here ends negatively. That is the deep relationship between the
> love story and war. But what remains in the end? That there is one
> sphere of ideals and one of reality? Symbolic images and suchlike?
> How deeply unsatisfactory! Is there no better answer?]

Yet despite Musil's occasional direct statements suggesting failure, he
continues in fact to celebrate the Other Condition and the realm of utopian, unrealizable ideals, and, as in the passage above, continues to ask if
there may not be some other, more satisfying, answer besides its negation.
One is reminded of Plato's thought experiment of banishment of the arts
from his Republic and his hopeful summarizing dialogue (a sort of challenge to the poets who would come after):

> ". . . if our allegations met a poetic rebuttal in lyric verse or what-
> ever, would we be justified in letting poetry return?"
> "Yes."

(And a challenge to the critics and theorists as well):

> And I suppose we'd also allow people who champion poetry because
> they like it, even though they can't compose it, to speak on its behalf
> in prose, and to try to prove that there's more to poetry than mere
> pleasure — that it also has a beneficial effect on society in general.
> And we won't listen in a hostile frame of mind, because we'll be the
> winners if poetry turns out to be beneficial as well as enjoyable.[3]

With practically Musil-ian perspectival freedom of thought, Plato, the
writer, the fabulist, the artist, perhaps with conscious irony, considers and
weighs the possibility of what good could be gained by casting the arts
out of his utopia ("what's in the balance here is absolutely crucial — far
more so than people think. It's whether one becomes a good or bad

person"),[4] and Musil, the *Dichter* (creative writer) firmly committed to a life of intensely motivated aesthetic experiences likewise explores the possibility of giving up what is most sacred to him, weighing the ethical or even moral questions of good and bad and the beneficial or detrimental effects of the aesthetic perspective on society, asking: Is there really no better answer than abandoning all that has seemed the best and most meaningful? Musil understood that what was in the balance was absolutely crucial, that the relationship between aesthetics and ethics was volatile, "far more so than people think." True to Musil's dialogic process, and precisely because of the importance of the relationship, the questioning and answering would continue to posit reasons and exempla for and against, for and against, ad infinitum. And yet the polarizing dialectic is miraculously suspended by the coincidence of opposites of the Other Condition, the living work of art that contains all contradictions.

A number of notes suggest that Musil at one moment favored the Utopia of the Inductive Attitude or Ethos over the Other Condition as a more viable, social alternative; but this favoring does not ever constitute a wholesale rejection of the value and meaning of the latter. In one late note we see Musil's typical oscillation between possibilities and the legerdemain necessary to hold all of them up in the air indefinitely:

> Im Ganzen hängen die Mob[ilizierung] Kap[iteln], namentlich darin U[lrich], vom Ausgang der Utopie der induct[iven] Gesinnung ab, der noch nicht feststeht. Aber wahrscheinl[ich] kommt er hinaus auf: Kämpfen (geistig) u[nd] nicht Verzweifeln. Ahnen reduziert auf Glauben, u[nd] zw[ar] der induktive Gott; unbeweisbar, aber glaubwürdig. Als ein die Affekte in Bewegung haltendes Abenteuer. Leitvorstellung. Kreislauf des Gefühls ohne Mystik. Entdeckung Gottes à la Köhler, oder auf Grund anderer Vorstellungen: Realwerden Gottes. Ahnen, a[nderer] Z[ustand]: mag vielleicht ein anderer, besser Geeigneter aufnehmen. Wie man das den Leuten aufnötigen könnte: unvorstellbar. Entweder das gehaßte der Zeit überlassen. Oder dahin wirken, d[as] i[st] für ihn: Buch schreiben, also Selbstmord, also in Krieg Geh[e]n.[5]

> [In general the mob[ilization] chapters, and within them especially Ulrich, depend on the as yet undetermined outcome of the Utopia of Inductive Thinking. But apparently it will amount to: struggling (mentally) and not despairing. Intimation reduced to belief, belief in an inductive God. Unprovable but credible. As an adventure that keeps the affects in motion. Main idea. Circulation of the emotions without mysticism. Discovery of God in Köhler's fashion [Wolfgang Köhler, founder of Gestalt psychology], or on the basis of other ideas. God's becoming material. Intimation, O[ther] C[ondition]: someone else who is better suited might perhaps take these up. How

could one force this on people: unimaginable. Either leave what is hated to the age. Or work toward it [the utopia], that is for it: write a book, therefore suicide, therefore go to war. (*MwQ*, 1757)]

In another classically ambivalent comment, Musil writes, referring to the Inductive Attitude as possible forerunner:

> Von diesen ist die der induktiven Gesinnung in gewissem Sinne die ärgste Utopie!: das wäre, literarisch, der einzunehmende Standpunkt (der die beiden anderen Utopien rechtfertigt). Dieser Nachweis oder die dazugehörige Darstellung vollendet sich aber erst mit dem Ende (Krieg)... Die Reise ins 1000j[ährige] R[eich] stellt die beiden andern Utopien in den Vordergrund u[nd] erledigt sie, soweit wie möglich.

> [Of these, the utopia of inductive thinking is in a certain sense the worst! That would be the standpoint to be adopted from a literary point of view (which justifies the other two utopias). But this demonstration, or the representation that goes along with it, is only complete with the end (war)... The journey into the Millennium places the other two utopias in the foreground and disposes of them as much as possible. (*MwQ*, 1753)][6]

"As much as possible," refers, of course to the idea of conclusion and the deferral of ending, which seem to be the constants in this eternal swirl of occasional momentary certainty.

It is essential to remind ourselves that the process of writing the novel for Musil was experimental in earnest: Musil himself did not know what the conclusions would be. While the first parts were published and printed under his supervision, he released even these published parts only reluctantly and begrudgingly. In keeping with his idea of the Utopia of the Next Step, Musil would not consider the success or failure of something until able to evaluate the next step it engendered. Whatever he had conceived of, drafted, or arranged in words was ideally subject to alteration in response to whatever might come after. Ideally, the book would be continually rewritten in a backward and forward motion (*vor- und rücksichtig*), ad infinitum. Furthermore, it is important to avoid seeing Musil's novel in a linear fashion, wherein we mistake the provisional order of later draft chapters arranged by editors as the order in which he intended the book to be read or (more crucially) as the order in which he wrote or planned to leave the novel. While we may assess certain changes in his orientation and intentions over time, they are usually not definitive and can usually not be read in a strictly chronological order. While Musil meanders in search of different leads and follows many different strands, he continually circles back to first principles and first questions. Fascinations wax and wane, positions are posited and criticized, scenarios, plot developments, and beliefs are tried out and compared with others; moments of insight flare up and fade, convictions and feelings are passionately embraced and then allowed to dissolve into disinterestedness and dullness, only to appear again, fresh, new, just as attractive as they were at first. The Other Condition may temporarily fade or fail, but it always recurs.

If the Other Condition of experience were indeed definitively rejected by Musil as a possible answer to the problem of how to live, this would mean that he, at some moment in time, finally negated this possibility, which he had spent decades exploring, researching, and trying to capture in descriptions and essays, and that there is a clearly delineated path of decision-making on Musil's part, wherein we can see him embracing and rejecting one or another of the utopias or solutions he considers in his notes and drafts. Those who maintain that Musil rejected the Other Condition raise the question of *when* exactly this rejection is supposed to have occurred within linear time. For Musil was, as we know, working on perhaps the most beautiful description of the Other Condition the hour that he died. Was it, then, a deathbed conversion, conceived after he reread, one last time, the rapturous prose describing Ulrich and Agathe in their garden paradise? Even if he had doubted the Other Condition with his last breath, the larger circular pattern of oscillation between doubt and belief, significance and weariness, motivated life and despair suggests that he would have looked upon it differently had there been one more exhale.

If, furthermore, the aesthetic state of the Other Condition were really untranslatable into normal reality, how would it be possible for Musil to translate it for us as powerfully as he does? Indeed, one of the most central goals of modernist art was to find strategies to communicate otherwise non-intelligible and fleeting subjective experiences, strategies such as metaphor, image, rhythm — *formal strategies* — to approximately bridge the gap between inwardness and social communication. To suggest that the Other Condition remains utterly unintelligible and inconsequential[7] is to ignore this central motivation and practice of modernist literature and art, or to suggest that this attempt by modernist artists itself fails, that the novel itself fails to communicate such states and experiences. Musil's discussion of mysticism and magic is a metaphor for the aesthetic experience; the Other Condition, while clothed in occult robes and a certain otherworldliness, is a metaphor for art. While Musil himself makes it clear that when we recite a poem in the stock exchange both the poem and the stock exchange disappear, this is obviously not an argument for him against poems and their relevance in the face of stock exchanges. If the Other Condition fails, the novel fails; art fails; Musil's life and work were in vain.

I propose, once more, that we look beyond the occasional pronouncements of failure and beyond the paradigms of duration and practical utility incompatible with Musil's process and theme. Instead, we must look at the facts presented by Musil's text and his life. In so doing, we discover that the extratemporal metaphoric moment embodied by Musil in the Other Condition remains the reverberating core of a motivated conduct of life central to his project.

The Other Condition, most clearly explored in the mystical chapters describing Ulrich and Agathe's foray into crime, asocial behavior, and mysticism, is, as we know, a metaphorical mode in which one can do no wrong, in which the normal bonds between persons and things have been lifted, in which time and space are immeasurable. It is an aesthetic space, an ethical space, a space of experiment and simultaneously of contact with anciently familiar forms and traditionally familiar ecstatic experience. It is similar to the other utopias Musil discusses in many ways. So much so, in fact, that it is fair to say that to some extent they are all alternate versions of the Other Condition, non-exact metaphors for it, which share its essential metaphoric value as ciphers for living a motivated, significant life of heightened aesthetic awareness and ethical action in contrast to the *seinesgleichen geschieht* of everyday normalcy. Yet there is one important distinction to be made — one that parallels the tension traced in this study between originary phenomena and existentially generated image-making.

The Inductive Attitude is a way of being in the world whereby one meets each new experience as fresh and untested; it is also related to what Musil calls the Utopia of Empiricism or of the Age of Experience. It is thus the opposite of a deductive attitude, which draws meaning from an already existent idea, belief, or sense about the world, merely fitting what it finds to that already existent idea. The Inductive Attitude seems to correspond to the "existence" of existential philosophy, while at least one aspect of the Other Condition is made up of the "essence" posited as somehow *a priori* present and deductive. And yet, as we have seen, the Other Condition actually seems to simultaneously contain this taste and taint of originary essence and the more progressive characteristic of being a breeding ground or open space for aesthetic play. Despite his differentiation of the Inductive Ethos and the Other Condition, in other words, Musil actually attributes both inductive and deductive characteristics to the Other Condition. The Inductive Ethos, for its part, despite its slightly more practical and socially viable nature, is in many ways just as distanced from normal reality as its more mystic alternative. This may be a result of a fundamental imprecision on Musil's part. Perhaps specific and important details have been lost between the lines of what remain only Musil's personal notations; or perhaps he had not yet come to clarity about the differences between the various utopias. The fact remains that he never goes far beyond suggestions and inexplicit comparisons and that these comments are rife with internal contradictions. While, according to Patrizia McBride, Musil knew from the start that he would favor the

Inductive Ethos over the Other Condition, because the latter was immature and hostile to reality, he does not actually ever outgrow his commitment to aesthetics and does not come to see aesthetics as an adolescent
delusion. He continues, rather, to the end, to oscillate between a commitment to the non-realizable ideal of the Other Condition, implying a
rejection of so-called "real life," and an active intentional engagement in
what he called "making history," that is, creating reality, more along the
lines of the Inductive Attitude. These two actions together make up what
McBride calls an "aesthetic utopia," a utopia she calls a planned failure.
Had Musil really already decided the results of his experiment, we would
have to call his scientific method a meaningless game. We would also be
at a loss to understand why he continually engages in earnest analysis of
the complex question and why he continues to access the resources of the
Other Condition to describe what remain the most meaningful and influential aspects of perceived reality. Musil never gives up on utopian thinking or ideals just because the world may be unready for them, or because
their realization in the inductive case would turn them into their opposite
(as the freezing of any momentary passion or gesture into eternal stasis
becomes grotesque).

The Inductive Ethos that is supposed to be a more practical solution, furthermore, is really just as utopian as the Other Condition and,
if believing in the existential power of aesthetic experience is adolescent,
the Inductive Ethos is just as "immature." Once we have accepted that
the two utopias are closer to each other than they might at first seem, and
have admitted to what can only be described as Musil's fundamentally
imprecise designations, we see the commonality inherent in all of Musil's
utopias. Just as the perverse can be linked to the healthy via a string of
contagious analogies, Musil's varying solutions are all forms of what he
would call the Utopia of the Motivated Life. They are all types of exceptional moments that strive in vain to be lasting, and they all leave meaningful traces in static everyday reality. All avail themselves of essayistic
extratemporal experimentation. All the utopias are fleeting and dependent
on constant oscillation; all of them demand intensely heightened concentration and ethical consciousness; all present a problem when it comes to
the question of enacting them on the scale of mass rather than individually; all are therefore highly socially problematic. All keep the tension alive
between inductive and deductive, creation and discovery of forms, desire
and knowledge. And they remain, over decades, Musil's only models for
the answer of how to live the right life.

In one notebook entry of 1908 Musil cites Ellen Key, the Swedish
philosopher and feminist, who connects the ideas of a number of German
thinkers who have found different ways of expressing the ideal of something she calls "ethical-aesthetic self-creation."[8] Musil paraphrases, implying a connection between his own idea of the Other Condition and of the

Inductive Attitude and the individualistic concept of the *Übermensch*. We see the precise vivisector once again as indiscriminate metaphor-maker:

> Humanitätsideal Lessings und der natürlichen Religion, Leibnitz' Selbstvervollkommnungsgedanke, Göthes Selbstkultur, Schleiermachers Selbstdarstellung, Nietzsches Übermensch nur verschiedene Worte für das ethisch=ästhetische Selbst seien.[9]

> [Lessing's humanistic ideal and natural religion, Leibniz's concept of perfection of self, Goethe's self-culture, Schleiermacher's self-creation, Nietzsche's *Übermensch* are only different words for the ethical=aesthetic self.]

In an earlier note from 1905 Musil mentions coming across Key's essay: "Die Entfaltung der Seele durch Lebenskunst" (The development of the soul through the conduct of life) in a café, and being "powerfully moved" because it reminded him of his own past. He buys the book and avoids reading it, musing about why that might be: "Warum lese ich nicht in dem Essay? Warum knüpfe ich nicht an den Fäden, von denen ich so sehr bedauere, dass sie einst abrissen?"[10] (why do I not read the essay? Why do I not pick up the thread that I so regret having let go of once?). He answers that he had let fall an earlier resolution of which the essay reminded him, a state of being he then connects to the mystical "Valerie experience" and characterizes as a "Vertiefung der Persönlichkeit" (deepening of personality) and a commitment to "jeden Tag etwas Feines" (something fine every day[11]). He presumably overcomes his resistance or fear and does pick up the essay, for the following pages of the notebook are filled with paraphrases and comments on Key's ideas about "self-culture" and an aesthetically motivated conduct of life with ties to thinkers such as Goethe, Schiller, Thoreau, and Pater. Were these just youthful ideas that Musil later abandoned and attributed merely to ridiculed characters in the novel (such as Diotima, whose name is frequently associated with Key's in Musil's later notes)? Or did he maintain until the end of his life a commitment to the "Vertiefung der Persönlichkeit" and "jeden Tag etwas Feines"?

Later notes describing the utopias Musil continued to consider as viable answers suggest that he never abandoned these earlier ideas, despite being very much aware that their fulfillment required utopian potentialities not likely to be found in everyday reality or in average human beings. In a late note from a collection of sketches for an uncompleted chapter project on the Utopia of Motivated Life probably from around 1937 or 1938, Musil returns to his preoccupation with a heightened conduct of life, reminiscent of his rediscovery of the lost thread of the Valerie experience upon picking up the Key essay in a café. A good thirty years later he echoes his comment of 1905, when he had remembered that two and a half years earlier he had made (and temporarily abandoned) a "resolution" in response to a living thought. While the living thought — which in its most modest extent leads to art and, in its most extreme, to the Other Condition — will fade and seemingly "end negatively," it returns again and again, just as fresh as the first time:

Nachdem uns ein lebendiger Gedanke ergriffen hat, sind wir wie eine |beinahe| verdurstete Blume, auf die Regen gefallen ist.
"Nachdem uns ein lebendiger Gedanke ergriffen hat," haben wir fast immer den Vorsatz, ein interessanterer Mensch zu werden.
"Nachdem uns ein lebendiger Gedanke ergriffen hat," scheint uns, dass es kein größeres Laster gebe, als an Geld zu denken oder an Berufsfragen, an Notwendigkeiten oder an Sicherheiten \Gewiß'heiten . . .
Ein lebend gewesener Gedanke wird nur in neuem Zusammenhang wieder lebendig; d[as]h[eisst] er erfüllt ein neues Gebiet mit unserem Geist.
Auf das bescheidenste weitergeführt, geht es zu Kunst u.ä.; auf das unbescheidenste zu a[nderem] Z[ustand].
Ein lebender Gedanke ist einer, der zum Mittelpunkt einer augenblicklichen Kristallisation unseres ganzen Wesens zu werden scheint. Er ist bedeutend. (*KA*)[12]

[After we are seized by a living thought, we are like an |almost| parched flower upon which rain has fallen.
"After we are seized by a living thought," we almost always make the resolution to become a more interesting person.
"After we are seized by a living thought," it seems to us that there is no greater sin than thinking about money or career questions, of necessities or certainties . . .
Taken to its most modest extent, it arrives at art, etc.; to its most extreme extent at the O[ther] C[ondition].
A living thought is a thought that becomes the center of a momentary crystallization of our entire essence. It is significant.]

A few lines later Musil considers the question: "Was ist bedeutend" (What is significant or important), stating that Freud would answer that that which activates the drives is important. Then he asks: "Kann ich sagen: was die weltverändernde Tendenz des Trieblosen anreizt? Das hieße: das allgemeine, stimmungsmäßige, selbstlose, asoziale Verhalten verändert?" (Can I say: that which arouses the world-transforming tendency of those who are lacking in drive? That would be: that which transforms the general, conforming temper of selfless, asocial behavior?)[13] What might that rousing, activating instrument of transformation be, if not art, aesthetic experience, or aesthetic-ethical philosophy? For, as Pater writes in his famous conclusion to *The Renaissance*: "'Philosophieren,' says Novalis, 'ist *vivificieren, dephlegmatisieren*'" (philosophy is vivifying, de-phleg-matizing).[14] And *vivificieren, dephlegmatisieren* was precisely the aim of modernist art. A book that, as Kafka writes, breaks the frozen sea within us,[15] that unsettles certainty and creates what Musil refers to as the tear in the surface of the paper of habit or reality,[16] unmooring all previously arrived ideas, is a modernist text par excellence.

That this sort of heightened commitment to experiencing was not likely to be shared by all of Musil's fellow beings (whom he characterized in one classic contemptuous phrase as "the ant-people") was not, at least for Musil, a reason to reject the Other Condition at its source. While the Other Condition is initially antisocial, it did, however, also include the possibility of a social culmination, in the idea of the millennium in which the love of the two siblings Ulrich and Agathe would spread to a univer-sal love of all beings. Granted that this culmination is hardly realistically expected to occur within the pages of the novel, and that the Other Con-dition is mainly illustrated as somewhat escapist, we must note that the Inductive Attitude is also rather anti-social and is called by Musil a "Genie Moral" (genius morality).[17] Musil specifically notes the problem of incor-porating it among the masses. Lest we take this to be a criticism by Musil of the utopia *qua* utopia, we should note that he was a fierce individualist who saw collectivism as perhaps the greatest threat to the autonomy of the artist, whose endangerment would, in turn, pose the greatest threat to society, politics, and government. McBride mentions in an aside that Musil's tendency toward the "genius morality" "displays a troubling elit-ist streak" on Musil's part.[18] However, Musil's fascination with genius is hardly a minor anomalous error of judgment, but rather a fundamental part of his thought. Despite his generally liberal principals and politics of social justice, exemplified in the novel when Ulrich and Agathe attempt to overcome their disgust and temporarily love "ein Scheusal" (a scoun-drel) — to imagine communion with the homeless man who wanders outside their mansion[19] — he placed his primary hope for the future of humanity in the genius and his or her ability to resist the leveling of col-lective mass stupidity. The autonomous and elevated artist was, according to Musil, a fundamental requirement for a healthy society. An expansion of this special state to a mass of individually motivated persons is not out of the question, but certainly just as unlikely as that of the expansion of the love of two hermitlike mystics into a universal ecstasy. Yet the fact that an ideal is unrealizable is not, to Musil's mind, reason to cease dreaming of it, even if its actual realization would turn the ideal into its opposite. The question of how to hold a feeling fast is also raised by Pater's call to "burn always with this hard gem-like flame." One cannot burn always without burning up, just as one cannot keep an icicle from melting by holding on to it. Except in the realm outside time: except, as we have noted above, in art. And Musil's commitment to a life in art is evidence of a burning proportionately more than common, a more than common commitment to enhanced momentary consciousness and a rigorous ethical and aesthetic practice of Pater's "failure to form habits." Musil, although he recognized the challenge and perhaps the impossibility of translating such individual commitment into social reality, did not view it as in itself antisocial; in fact, the opposite was the case. Individual aesthetic commitment is rather, to Musil, the cornerstone of ethical social conduct.

One section of Musil's notes begins with the heading: "Der andere Zustand als Grundzustand der Ethik" (The Other Condition as foundational condition of ethics).[20] This heading is eventually followed by another related concept: "Versuch einer unstarren Moral" (Attempt at an unfrozen morality).[21] In another note, entitled: "Zur Grundhaltung" (on the basic stance), he writes:

> Es handelt sich nicht darum, den andern Zustand zum Träger des Gesellschaftslebens zu machen. Er ist viel zu flüchtig. Ich selbst kann mich heute kaum genau seiner erinnern. Aber er läßt Spuren in allen Ideologien, in der Liebe zur Kunst usw. und in diesen Abformen, das Bewußtsein von ihm zu wecken, das gilt es, denn darin beruht das Leben dieser Erscheinungen, die im Erstarren begriffen sind. (*KA*)[22]

> [It is not a matter of making the Other Condition the bearer of social life. It is much too fleeting. I myself can hardly remember it precisely today. But it leaves traces in all ideologies, in the love for art etc. and the important thing is to awaken the consciousness of it in all of these reflected forms, for the life of all of these phenomena, which are on the brink of petrifying, is waiting therein.]

That the Other Condition does not, as Musil notes elsewhere, offer "Vorschriften für das praktische Leben" (precepts for everyday life), is an argument not against it but rather in its favor. "Du kannst heiraten, leben, wie du willst usw. Auch die Utopien sind ja zu keinem praktikablen Ergebnis gekommen . . . D[as] i[st] auch: Gegen die Totallösung u[nd] System"[23] (You can marry, live as you wish, etc. Utopias, too, have not produced any practicable results . . . That also means: against the total solution and system, *MwQ*, 1736). In the face of totalitarian control and dogmatic final solutions, Musil proposes the Other Condition as a state of radical openness that maintains its power precisely because of its distance from normal reality. In a late note for the afterword to his still-unfinished novel he writes: "Es sind zu viele auf der Welt, die genau sagen, was getan und gedacht werden müsse, als dass mich nicht das Gegenteil verführen sollte — die strenge Freiheit"[24] (there are too many people in the world who say exactly what must be thought and done for me not to be seduced by the opposite. Strict freedom, *MwQ*, 1767).

As required in a cosmos of oscillation, however, freedom immediately longs for its opposite — for some border or boundary, some limit to its circling. Musil writes:

> Das Leben ist eine dauernde Oszillation zw[ischen] Verlangen u[nd] Überdruß. S[iehe] Kreislauf des Gefühls. Hat man eine Weile etwas getan, so will man sein Gegenteil . . . (Gefühle vertragen Dogmatisierung u[nd] vertragen keine). Das gilt von den Trieben, aber auch von den höheren Beschäftigungen. . . . Die Frage ist nun einfach: Gibt es etwas, das man dauernd tun kann? gibt es ein bleibendes Verhalten?[25]

> [Life is a continual oscillation between desire and weariness. Vid. circle of feeling! If one has done one thing for a while, one wants its opposite . . . (feelings demand dogmatization and cannot bear it). This is true of drives, but also of the higher activities. . . . The question is really simple: is there something one can do enduringly? Is there an enduring way of acting?]

In response to this seemingly hypothetical question, Musil notes the special case of the Other Condition: that it alone can "der Periodik von Aufbau u[nd] Zerstören Einhalt tun" (halt the periodic of creation and destruction). And yet, of course, this state is itself only fleeting and in constant oscillating tension with the reality of normal existence.

The Other Condition, as mode of significance and ongoing questioning, effectively and dramatically stands in opposition to the already established failure and horror of *seinesgleichen geschieht* and the insignificance of normal reality and un-motivated experience; it offers a more successful realm of living ethics, creative action, significance, and beauty. Although there are moments in notes when Musil says that the Other Condition could not have "worked" or that it was not "realizable," it is even more significant that he expresses the gravest possible doubts about reality itself and the world around him as a meaningful measure or touchstone for the viability or significance of the value of spirit, art, ideals, and intellectual or aesthetic activity. "'U[lrich]s system'" he admits in one note, "ist am Ende desavouiert" (is disavowed in the end), but, he continues, so is "das der Welt" (*KA*,[26] the world's). Art, and the realm of "spirit" (the German word, "Geist," includes the meanings mind, intellect, and culture) which Musil prized above all other considerations, was not to be judged on the basis of static reality, politics, state, or nation, but vice versa. Art was not to be bound by time, place, or immediate needs. In an aphorism he writes:

> Meine Ethik hat, was ich gern übersehe, ein "höchstes Gut," es ist der Geist. Worin unterscheidet sich das aber von der mir wenig sympathischen Vorstellung der Philosophen, dass die Vernunft das höchste Gut sei?" (*KA*)[27]

[My ethics has, although I like to overlook it, a "highest good." It is spirit. But how is this different from the idea of the philosophers, which is less pleasing to me, that reason is the highest good?]

And in other notes written from within the prison of the totalitarian age he continues his defense of spirit, art, and unrealizable ideals:

Ich will nicht nur sagen: die Sphäre der Kunst ist eine andere als die der Wirklichkeit. Sondern: die Kunst bildet die Wirklichkeit, indem sie ihr Para=Bilder liefert. Nicht Vorbilder; sie bleibt irreal (auch im Realismus). Sie ist von höchster Wichtigkeit u[nd] Ung-reifbarkeit[.]
Wer das nicht versteht, trocknet die Gesellschaft aus. Die Kunst soll nur mit größter Vorsicht gefördert werden[.]
Nicht sie muss zum Staat kommen, sondern der Staat zu ihr. Oder wenn das zu ausschweifend erscheint: man liebe sie, aber man erz-iehe sie nicht. (*KA*)[28]

[I don't just want to say: the sphere of art is a different one from that of reality. Rather: art creates reality by offering it para-images. Not models; it remains irreal (even in realism). It is of the greatest importance and cannot be grasped[.]
He who doesn't understand that desiccates society. Art can be culti-vated only with the greatest care[.]
Art must not come to the state, but rather the state to art. Or if that seems too excessive: one loves it, but doesn't train it.]

Wie kommen die Ideen in die Politik? Im großen gesehn, aus dem Geist. Der Geist hat die Idee der Freiheit, die der Humanität usw. lange ehe sie zu politischen Forderungen geworden sind. Die Poli-tik nimmt sie auf, bildet sie um u[nd] entfremdet sie ihnen selbst. (Wenn sie sie unterdrückt, verdurstet sie) Das Nationale, Soziale, Religiöse soll Kunst enthalten, nicht umgekehrt. Oder: Kunst ist immer national usw. Auch l'art pour l'art. (*KA*)[29]

[How do ideas enter into politics? For the most part, from the spirit. The spirit had the idea of freedom, of humanity etc. long before these became political requirements. Politics adopts them, reshapes them, and alienates them from themselves. (If it represses them, it dies of thirst.) Art should contain the national, social, reli-gious, not the other way around. Or: art is always national etc. L'art pour l'art, too.]

In another aphorism from the same period he refers directly to the situation of oppression by totalitarian dictatorship and the difficult role of spirit therein, concluding with an ambiguous sort of hope for spiritual victory in a time holding out little hope:

Die Freiheit des Geistes: Der Geist kann sich nur bis zu einem gewissen Grad unterordnen u[nd] angleichen, ohne sich aufzugeben.
Es ist eine ganz gute Prüfung, dass heute eine Art Sondergerichts-
barkeit über ihn verhängt ist. Der Geist braucht Freiheit u[nd]
Liebe /Freiwilligkeit/ um überhaupt zu funktionieren[.] (Man weiß
es schon als Schüler[.])
    Die Stabilität des Geistes durch 2 Jahrtausende.
    Der Geist ist moralisch unbestechlich; er kann zugrunde gehn,
aber er kann sich nicht ändern[.][30]

[The freedom of spirit: The spirit can be subordinated and assimi-
lated only to a certain extent without relinquishing itself. It is a very
good test, that today it has been saddled with a kind of kangaroo-
court mentality. The spirit needs freedom and love (free will), in
order to function at all[.] (We know this already as schoolchildren.)
    The stability of the spirit over two centuries.
    The spirit is morally incorruptible; it can go under, but it cannot
alter itself]

So-called reality was to be valued insofar as it supported or inhibited
the free functioning of spirit, imagination, and critical openness. Amann
writes:

In December of 1940, after more than two years in exile, after two
more years of continued work on the novel, without the slightest
possibility of living from his writing, in a situation wherein his work
was banned in the Third Reich and put under a publication ban in
Switzerland, he wrote . . . to Victor Zuckerkandl:
    Von mir läßt sich nicht mehr sagen, als dass ich noch immer den
MoE wie ein Paar Handschellen an mir hängen habe; ich bin auch
gar nicht weitergekommen mit dem Buch, doch hoffe ich: tiefer.
Und da Sie mir freundliche Worte über mich sagen, möchte ich
erwidern, dass es mir wirklich so am wichtigsten ist. Es ist so etwas
wie Selbstbehauptung der Dichtung gegenüber den allzu heftigen
Mächten der Wirklichkeit.[31]

[There is not much more to be said about me than that I still have
the MwQ hanging on me like a pair of handcuffs . . . And since you
say friendly words about me, I'd like to respond that this is precisely
what is really the most important thing to me. It is something like
a self-affirmation of literature against the all too-powerful forces of
reality. (*B*, 1254)]

Spirit must not alter itself or bend to the demands of normal reality, even
if it must go under, continue in exile, in something close to silence. But
how is spirit to be nurtured under less than ideal circumstances?

During his years of exile in Switzerland, Musil seems to have come close to suicide at a number of points, struggling with poverty, writer's block, and tormenting misery and guilt about not risking his (and Martha's life) by speaking out directly about the regimes of Austrian and German fascism.[32] Two of the three possibilities in the novel for conclusion if the experiment with the Other Condition were to fail (suicide, writing books, going to war[33]) are, in real life, effected by the author, while the third is just barely avoided. Although posited as alternatives to the Other Condition, these three possibilities are actually also in Musil's notes themselves ciphers for the Other Condition. They are not, then, real alternatives, but virtually substitutes with similar metaphoric value. The Other Condition is fundamentally related to writing books, to the aesthetic experience of creation and reception, and may also be related to a sort of metaphoric suicide (death of the individuated self, turning away from the world, apraxia of action); Musil makes it very clear, as well, that the "Other Condition = war." War in this sense is valued as a sort of communal experience where the boundaries between individuals are lifted and one has, for once, a sense of conviction and purpose, albeit an often foolish and dangerous one. And "all lines lead to war" is one of the recurrent comments in notes for the ending. Shall we do the math and surmise: all lines lead to the Other Condition?

Indeed, the First World War did come at the end of the historical year Musil depicts in the novel (and the Second World War during his last years of writing in exile). It is thus reasonable to imagine the advent of the First World War ending the novel, as it does in Thomas Mann's contemporary *Magic Mountain,* or at least being the next plot twist and not yet the ending (as it is in Proust's *Remembrance,* where the narrator's social whirlwind is interrupted for a time by the war). But this may not help us to understand what Musil might have meant by this ending. Would it be, as Gene Moore proposes, an expression of "the cultural suicide of the age" and by association the failure of Musil's dream of the Other Condition? Or would the ending in war connote something more positive?

As Amann demonstrates, Musil was almost obsessed with coming to terms with the mass enthusiasm surrounding mobilization at the outbreak of the First World War, a hysteria or ecstasy in which he himself participated, a madness that he deeply regretted, and one that he was well aware could easily come again. While on the one hand he characterized this hysteria as a serious and disturbing problem, he also saw within it an example of an impressive group ecstasy, one markedly in contrast to *seinesgleichen geschieht.* A wartime near-death experience, described in a diary note entitled, "Ein Soldat erzählt" (A soldier narrates), also figures as one of Musil's powerful early mystical experiences (along with the Valerie episode). Musil speaks of a "Feuertaufe" (baptism by fire) and writes that he was "in die unsichtbare Kirche aufgenommen" (initiated into the invisible church): "Ich glaube" (I believe,) he writes, "wie ein Mädchen, das der Herr angesehen hat" (like a virgin whom the lord has looked upon). . . . "zum Schluß dieser wenigen Augenblicke war eine neue Vorstellung in meinem Leib, die er nie zuvor beherbergt hatte: Gott" (at the end of those few moments there was a new presentiment in my body, one that had never found a home there before: God).[34] The meaning of war (or Other Condition) as cipher and symbol in Musil's notes thus cannot be simplistically read as an absolute negative. Tempered by Musil's more literal reflections on the reality of war and its devastating effects on culture and humanistic values, we find war and the Other Condition repeatedly equated in notes for the conclusion to the novel as symbols for a mode of an intensely motivated conduct of life. But how could this exceptional experience, embodied by war, by love, by intense aesthetic experience be carried over into normal reality? How, in other words, might the Other Condition accommodate itself to normal life or be commensurate with reality? The question cannot be answered without redefining reality in accordance with Musil's conception of it. Reality itself, we must remember, is a fiction created by our thoughts, actions, and experiments.

It is a fiction that never comes to a conclusion, one that is largely nonlinear, that bifurcates in all directions, that shifts and changes depending upon circumstances and infinite details, that pauses and accelerates, retreats and leaps forward, that stands still and speeds on. As Musil writes, describing Vienna/Kakania on the first page of his novel:

> Autos schossen aus schmalen, tiefen Straßen in die Seichtigkeit heller Plätze. Fußgängerdunkelheit bildete wolkige Schnüre. Wo kräftigere Striche der Geschwindigkeit quer durch ihre lockere Eile fuhren, verdickten sie sich, rieselten nachher rascher und hatten nach wenigen Schwingungen wieder ihren gleichmäßigen Puls. Hunderte Töne waren zu einem drahtigen Geräusch ineinander verwunden, aus dem einzelne Spitzen vorstanden, längs dessen schneidige Kanten liefen und sich wieder einebneten, von dem klare Töne absplitterten und verflogen. (*MoE*, 9)

> [Automobiles shot out of deep, narrow streets into the shallows of bright squares. Dark clusters of pedestrians formed cloudlike strings. Where more powerful lines of speed cut across their casual haste they clotted up, then trickled on faster and, after a few oscillations, resumed their steady rhythm. Hundreds of noises wove themselves into a wiry texture of sound with barbs protruding here and there, smart edges running along it and subsiding again, with clear notes splintering off and dissipating. (*MwQ*, 3)]

Musil's reality is a moving, changing, unpredictable and interactive aliveness, and it is itself destroyed, critiqued, rearranged, re-formed, and recreated within the Other Condition. In a passage already cited above,

Musil narrates this attempt to reconcile the Other Condition and reality, using in this instance the word pair, "metaphor and truth," and explicating why this reconciliation is not only probably impossible, but actually undesirable:

> Ohne Zweifel ist das, was man die höhere Humanität nennt, nichts als ein Versuch, diese beiden grossen Lebenshälften des Gleichnisses und der Wahrheit miteinander zu verschmelzen, indem man sie zuvor vorsichtig trennt. Hat man aber an einem Gleichnis alles, was vielleicht wahr sein könnte, von dem getrennt, was nur Schaum ist, so hat man gewöhnlich ein wenig Wahrheit gewonnen und den ganzen Wert des Gleichnisses zerstört. (*MoE*, 593)

> [No doubt what is called higher humanism is only the effort to fuse together these two great halves of life, metaphor and truth, once they have been carefully distinguished from each other. But once one has distinguished everything in a metaphor that might be true from what is mere froth, one usually has gained a little truth, but at the cost of destroying the whole value of the metaphor. (*MwQ*, 647)]

Metaphor itself is the driving force of possibilitarian energy, more meaningful than static reality or truth. And while it may seem specious to speak of metaphors as reality when there are bullets flying and real suffering in the world, we must remember that for Musil the making of metaphors is an ethical activity that literally resists the forces of oppression and the deadly triumph of time. For while death is sure and winter follows autumn, spirit remains.

Within the context of the age of totalitarianism and its aftermath it is understandable that a conscientious thinker would necessarily grapple with the possible dangers of ideals, grand narratives, and ideological systems. Musil himself was heartily opposed to political systems and structures that impeded individual autonomous thinking and expression — not only because of their tendency to cramp his literary style and personal comfort and safety — but also because he recognized the deep connection between cruelty, terror, and the crushing of critical individual agency. For him, however, this resistance was waged primarily by defending (not attacking) the sanctity of art, artist, and aesthetic experience, by defending what to him remained an essentially meaningful and still potentially influential entity and role. In a note about the two addresses he gave in Vienna and Paris on the subject of totalitarianism, collectivism, and the role of the artist, he wrote: "Alle 'Eisenbreiten' und Eisenfresser gehen von der Erscheinung aus, dass wir zu viel Kultur gehabt hätten, das heißt schon in einer Phase der Überkultur und ihres Verfalls gewesen wären, während wir in Wahrheit zu wenig Kultur hatten" (*KA*;[35] All bullies and braggarts begin with the assumption that we had too much culture, that, in other words, we were already in a state of excess culture and its decline, while in reality we had too little culture). His defense of aesthetics did not mean that he simplistically believed that the real physical and material needs and sufferings of humans should be ignored or belittled, but rather that culture itself was a primary defense against such sufferings. A conversation between Ulrich and Agathe touches upon the sort of callous aestheticism from which Musil consciously distanced himself, asking whether the suffering of a thousand people might be worth the creation of a poem of genius. Together the siblings answer that such a thought is adolescent, unfeeling, and absurd. When we look at Musil's nuanced response to National Socialism and Stalinism, we see a much more sophisticated and clearly engaged approach to the problem of aesthetics, ethics, politics, and physical suffering.

Klaus Amann, in *Robert Musil: Literatur und Politik* (Literature and politics), clearly and subtly elucidates Musil's complex relationship with political engagement, citing Musil's comment: "Es ist unmöglich, dass ein Dichter, der nicht bloß ein begabter Geisteskranker ist, keinerlei soziale Verantwortung fühlt; aber die Arten dieser Verantwortung sind sehr verschieden" (*KA*;[36] It is impossible that a writer who is not merely a talented insane person feels no social responsibility at all; but the kinds of responsibility are very different). If one reads, along with Amann, the multiple drafts and notes for speeches and essays before and during Musil's exile in Switzerland, it becomes clear that his response to the conforming powers of *Gleichschaltung* and ultimate brutal silencing was to bravely continue to do what he thought was his own chief responsibility: to maintain his perspectival critical stance even while others were becoming more and more polarized into sides, and to continue to write, both creatively and intellectually, half in despair, half in expectation of a later time, when the artist might again be free to be the conscience of the nation.[37]

When he exclaims, in one note, "Nieder mit dem Kulturoptimismus"[38] (down with cultural optimism), he is referring to the optimism of many of his fellow European intellectuals about the new Soviet Republic as well as the more obviously disingenuous propaganda of the Nazi regime. The trend of thought that led over the next half century to a suspicion of aesthetics, individuality, and essence was itself just as implicated in ideologies of control and false utopia as the fascisms and idealisms that it attacked. Musil recognized this paradox early on, and was only partly forgiven for his insight after many of his more ideologically correct colleagues were lost to the Gulag. Despite the most bleak outlook imaginable, despite deeply complex ambivalence, Musil remained to the end committed to what he viewed as the essential value of an autonomous cultural and intellectual life and to the importance of the aesthetic experiences of living in (not for), committed to the end to his task of writing the novel.

Since over the course of the mid to late twentieth century "being" and "essence" became guilty by association of the crimes committed by ideological rigidity, totalitarianism, and the abstraction of individual human realities into myths, modernist artists and writers struggled to come to terms with a pull toward affiliating themselves with one or other system or ideology or toward rejecting systems of total belief altogether. This has often led to nihilism or to an extreme crisis of language, communication, or fatalism about the possibility of shared experience or meanings. Musil chose resistance to affiliation, but without subscribing to the wholesale despair of other thinkers and artists who increasingly abandoned the high modernist search for methods or strategies to impart subjective feelings and establish workable grounds for communal meaning. This refusal to affiliate with either the grand narrative of Soviet Russia, National Socialism, or even democracy might seem to make Musil a proto-postmodernist, an early exponent of deconstructive skepticism, except that he did not abandon the realms of belief and meaning altogether; nor did he abandon the notions of genius and individualism, or his belief in the redemptive role of art and artists. Instead, he constructed his own aesthetic and ethical cosmos, which maintains spirit — in the sense of intellect, creativity, and critical and utopian thinking — as its highest good. Any visit to the realms of the Other Condition is by definition temporally limited, which ensures that it does not ossify into cliché or system. But the fact that one moment has passed or faded does not mean that another call to intensity will not come again, two years, thirty years, a hundred years later. It is, in fact, bound to recur, at least in some metaphoric form.

It goes without saying that we must have uninspired moments and non-motivated experiences, that *seinesgleichen* must occur on a regular basis, that all moments cannot be genius moments, that we sometimes have to act as if things repeat themselves and pragmatically live an unexamined life; but is it absurd to suggest that we do this as little as possible? Pater, Thoreau, Nietzsche, Emerson, and Musil all call for a life of wakefulness, of a success measured by the ability to "maintain" as much as possible, as Pater writes hopefully, "this ecstasy."[39] In the face of normal, chronological, progressive, measured time, essential, mystical, aesthetic extra-temporality — the experience of presence and in-dwelling — serves as a quickening informing an existentially motivated Heideggerian being-toward-death. This is perhaps why in "Breaths of a Summer's Day" and the other garden chapters the garden is described in oscillating images of death and birth, spring and winter.

Moments of fleeting timelessness actually encapsulate and reveal the border of death and the triumph of time. In the face of the unavoidable reality of chronological time, the reality of death, and the physical horror of war, the realizations gained through dwelling in extra-temporal metaphoric moments may endure as guideposts toward a conduct of life informed by intensity, significance, and a commitment to aesthetic-ethical experimentation. As such, the Other Condition, like any small chapterlet of Musil's novel, like any exceptional and separated moment of life, is naturally artificially separated from the other reality of *seinesgleichen geschieht*. In formal terms, a sense of boundary, be it consciously set in a work of art or as the possibility of the surprise of death, creates a sense of focus, an intensity of significance. Perhaps Musil was musing on the tension between open-ended infinity and the ever-present boundary of death when he noted this comment by Ludwig Tieck:

> Alle echte Kunst ist nur ein Fernrohr unserer inneren Sinne. . . . Aber, wenn wir etwas schaffen wollen, müssen wir unserem Tiefsinn eine willkürliche Grenze setzen; so entsteht alle Wirklichkeit, alle Schöpfung, dass die Liebe sich auch in der Liebe ein Ziel, einen Tod setzt: die liebende Angst zieht sich plötzlich in sich zurück und übergiebt ihr Liebstes der Gleichgültigkeit, der Existenz, sonst könnte nie etwas entstehen.[40]

> [All genuine art is only a telescope of our inner senses. . . . But if we want to create something, we must set an arbitrary border around our deepest sense; all reality, all creation arises in this way, love too sets a goal for itself in love, a death; the loving anxiety retreats back into itself and surrenders its most beloved to casualness, to existence, otherwise nothing could come into being.]

Musil's comments on this Tieck quote reveal his characteristic thinking in analogies and the way in which this question of border can be explored on many levels, from the final frontier of death to that of every other sort of otherness:

> Der Tod als conditio sine qua non der Schöpfung. Die Grenze als Bedingung für das Begrenzte, denn jede Grenze ist ein Tod. Man wird sofort sagen: nur für die Wahrnehmbarkeit des Begrenzten. Gut bleiben wir auf subjektivem Boden. Die Angst vor dem Tode ist die bereits vorhandene Latenz der Auflösung. Und dies conditio sine qua non des Ich-Gefühls. . . . Hier ist zu bemerken, dass der Tod nicht die einzige Grenze für das Leben darstellt, sondern jedes Nicht-Ich eine solche ist. (*KA*)[41]

> [Death as a condition sine qua non of creation. The border as requirement for that which is enclosed, for every boundary is a death. One will immediately say: only for the apperception of that which is enclosed. We do well to remain on subjective ground. Fear of death is the already present latency of the denouement. And this condition [is the] sine qua non of the I-feeling. [. . .] Let us just note here that death is not the only boundary for life, but rather every not-I constitutes one.]

The other (every not-I) constitutes a border that may be temporarily lifted (and transgressed by metaphor), just as the works and concerns of normal existence can be interrupted and obviated by exceptional vision. And the march of time is intermittently suspended in the merging of metaphoric opposites, enabling a vision that will necessarily fade or be replaced by another different, even antithetical one. That "war," as Musil writes in a late novel draft, "lasts a month and sex a night," is not an argument against the reality of either. That Musil does not depict the duration of these moments of exceptional experience is precisely the point, for "real essences," in a post-Einsteinian universe, are neither solid nor consistent: real essences are in flux; they change depending upon the conditions, the atmosphere, on our relative relationship to them, depending, most of all, upon their association or temporary metaphoric relationship with other essences. Musil's answer to the impossibility of holding the moment in the real world, of maintaining a sense of conviction, desire, love, or beauty, can indeed be glimpsed in the reflection of the more unabashedly aesthetic solutions of Proust's novel.

The extratemporal aesthetic moment, despite all techniques of deferral, despite all infinite expansion of exceptional moments, is always shadowed by the insistent march of literal linear and narrative time. Marcel discovers, after returning from a long convalescent exile during the First World War, that all of his friends have grown so suddenly old that he believes at first that he has arrived at a masquerade party where the guests are wearing powdered wigs and face makeup. When he realizes that it is not a masquerade, he is dumbstruck. "For I knew," Marcel relates — pointing to the inevitability of death, "what these changes meant, what they were the prelude to." The only response to this shock of fleetingness, surely experienced by Musil himself, could be the creation of a lasting work of art, the writing of the book that Musil, like Proust, would spend the rest of his postwar life writing — the book he was working on the day he died — the novel, the work of art that threatens and promises to take over, to live beyond life itself. Any of its motivated, beautiful, temporarily meaningful moments mean more than the dead insignificant reality of *seinesgleichen geschieht*.

Which must be why Proust himself, on his death bed, furiously dictated his experiences of dying to his secretary, to be transposed into the still-unfinished novel as the death scene of another character! Even — or perhaps especially — in death, literature was more important than life. "Little patch of yellow wall, little patch of yellow wall," mutters a perishing character in Proust's novel, sucking in his very last glimpses of beauty before a Vermeer painting: "And finally," Proust writes, "the precious substance of the tiny patch of yellow wall. His giddiness increased; he fixed his eyes, like a child upon a yellow butterfly which it is trying to catch, upon the precious patch of a wall." For there in this little patch of color, not, after all, in remembering the people he had loved or lost or been betrayed by, not in reviewing the fleeting heroic actions, the failures and successes of idle scenarios or delusive desires, but there, in a metaphoric transubstantiation in which paint becomes an image of a wall becomes prose becomes the uncatchable, elusive, fluttering yellow butterfly that is mortality, there is the extratemporal moment, the experience of the Other Condition, the aesthetic state of in-tensity, in-dwelling, in-finity, and in-conclusion, something incalculably worth preserving in a world of more solid, practical, lasting things, in a world of dead words and deadly and brutal ideologies.

Musil's fierce defense of the individual's experience and expression requires that the temporary experience of the Other Condition remains free and non-committed to any over-arching program or system. As Albrecht Schöne points out in his essay linking the formal structure of the subjunctive mood with Musil's ethical and aesthetic process, utopians would be the first kind of person to be thrown out of any established Utopia; Musil's thought, therefore, must be categorized as utop*ian*, that is, a constantly provisional revisional consideration of alternate visions, emphatically not as a striving after a closed, completed, Utopia. Like the traverser of Emerson's circles, the utopian who finds herself having arrived at any given center will soon begin to draw a new circle around its circumference, a circle that will also, in time, be overcome. This is the grammar of the extra-temporal metaphoric moment that is the basic building block, the internal coherence, of Musil's theory and practice. The aesthetic experience of the Other Condition, in other words, simultaneously provides the key to the enigma, suggesting answers to the question of whether or not there can be meaning, while continuously ensuring the undigestibility of the work of art. And the autonomy of the work of art ensures the autonomy of the creative thinking individual and his or her potential to participate effectively in the continual negotiation and shaping of shared realities.

In answer, then, to Renoir's probably consciously naive question: Why should beauty be suspect? we can easily call forth the terribly real specters of holocaust and genocide on the one hand and, on the other, the superficial emptiness of the materialist simulacrum; but the aesthetic need not be a whitewash of horrors or of treacherously ugly realities hidden behind a mask of falsely harmonic ideals, need not be escapism and frivolity that ignores and thereby blasphemes the suffering of millions. For Musil, as we have seen, a devotion to the aesthetic involves an even greater commitment to ethical responsibility than would a slavish devotion to some already forged political ideology, which in itself would signal the beginnings of terror. Adorno, who famously wondered whether there could be poetry after Auschwitz, momentarily condemns art in his book *Aesthetic Theory*, noting, like Musil, the deceptive process of metaphor-making. He writes

that even in "the process of selecting, trimming, renouncing. . . . [art] pro-
longs guilty domination in artworks, of which they would like to be free,"
concluding that "form is their immorality." But in his characteristic self-
contradicting dialectic, he then emphatically counters his condemnation,
condemning instead those who deny art its autonomous internal telos.
This metaphoric deception, he argues now, does not mean "the total
condemnation of art." Indeed, he goes on, seeming to speak as much to
the more treacherous thought police of the Nazi/Stalin era as to those
milder ideologues of contemporary political correctness: "Whosoever
rails against art's putative formalism, against art being art, does so in the
name of cliques that, in order to retain better control of the oppressed,
insist on adaptation to them."[42]

Revolutionary art, as Musil knew, is neither the agent of oppression
nor a soporific. Adorno, however, differentiates between traditional art,
which is supposedly always implicated in tyranny and oppression, and
avant garde art, which supposedly struggles more honestly to come to
terms with its demons. But even if this latter self-critical role has, indeed,
become more conscious in the last century, all real art, as an abstraction
and rearrangement of static reality, has *always* been revolutionary, critical, and utopian. While art may reinforce and repeat time-honored ideals and values, received ideas, and socially constructed models of beauty
and goodness, it almost always simultaneously unravels these and presents
new forms that critique and create new ways of looking at the world.
Art, which has always been formal as well as a bearer of content or
ideas, always aesthetic as well as didactic, has always had the potential to
unmoor accepted values and visions of the world. In an address he dared
to present in Vienna in 1934,[43] Musil wrote that "Kunst" (art) — and
it should be understood that he meant an autonomous art uninhibited
by the interests of ideologies or practical goals — "die Kunst . . . erhält
das Noch-nicht-zu-Ende-Gekommene des Menschen, den Anreiz seiner
Entwicklung am Brennen" (*KA*;[44] Art . . . preserve[s] people's sense of
not yet having come to closure: it keeps their impulse for progress alive,
P, 260). And as such, autonomous art, sometimes misleadingly called "art
for art's sake," is arguably the most fundamental basis of a society of critical open discourse, freedom, and utopian imaginings.

The impossibility of reconciling the aesthetic insights of the Other
Condition with the reality of everyday existence, then, might seem like
a failure, as we see Musil struggling at times within the novel to make
the two realms commensurable. And yet we simultaneously see him
strain — in a life more and more threatened by the external demands of
competing political interests and physical deprivations — to keep the aesthetic realm inviolable, separate, and autonomous not only as a precondi-
tion for a fruitful aesthetic generativity of forms and ideas but also as the
basis for a healthy and productive social and political system.

As Musil struggles in his notebooks to express his outrage about the regimes of terror, it becomes clear that he equates the totalitarian terror of violence with stupidity and barbarism, with the very enemies of art, culture, and critical thought. Art, Musil argues, is not the enemy of humanity, as some would make it, but an essential product of a protected humanism, ensured only by the basic social prerequisites of freedom of thought and speech, honesty, bravery, and critical openness. In one note Musil elucidates his criteria for creative production, for the nurturing and protection of culture and spirit, as follows:

> Freiheit, Offenheit, Mut, Unbestechlichkeit, Verantwortung und Kritik, diese mehr noch gegen das, was uns verführt als gegen das, was uns abstößt. Auch die Wahrheitsliebe muss dabei sein, und ich erwähne sie besonders, weil das, was wir Kultur nennen, wohl nicht unmittelbar dem Kriterium der Wahrheit untersteht, aber keinerlei große Kultur auf einem schiefen Verhältnis zur Wahrheit beruhen kann.[45]

> [Freedom, openness, courage, incorruptibility, responsibility, and criticism, criticism even more against what seduces us than against what repels us. These concepts must even include the love of truth, and I mention this especially because what we call culture is not directly subservient to the criterion of truth, but no great culture can rest on a distorted relationship with truth.]

Art, separate from life, must nevertheless be nurtured by life, then, in order to freely create and to provide life with models for more authentic living. So while the internal telos of Musil's unfinished and unfinishable novel, as moving, living expanding map of his life in art, does not come to a final conclusion on the question of how to reconcile metaphor and reality, this very "failure" constitutes its enduring faithfulness to its own ethical and aesthetic laws, whether or not they conform to external commands, expectations, or requirements. If this book succeeds, Musil wrote to a friend upon the publication of book 2 of his novel, it will have been wrong.[46]

A passage in Musil's collection of short prose, *Nachlass zu Lebzeiten* (Posthumous papers of a living author), presents us with the stone sarcophagus portraits of an old married couple in ancient Rome. They recline under a tree, Musil writes, propped up on their elbows, as if on a picnic. They look into each other's eyes.

> Es fehlt nur der Korb mit Käse, Früchten und Wein zwischen ihnen. . . . Und sie lächeln einander an, lang, sehr lang. Du siehst weg, noch immer, ohne Ende.
> Dieser treue, brave, bürgerliche, verliebte Blick hat die Jahrhunderte überstanden, er ist im alten Rom ausgesandt worden und kreuzt heute dein Auge.

Wundre dich nicht darüber, dass er vor dir andauert, dass sie nicht wegsehen oder die Augen senken; sie werden nicht steinern dadurch, sondern menschlich.[47]

[The only thing lacking is the basket with cheese, fruit, and wine. . . . and they smile at each other; for a long, long time. You look away: and they continue to look at each other, without end.

This true, upright, bourgeois, beloved look has lasted for centuries; it was transmitted from ancient Rome and it passes in front of your eyes today.

Do not be amazed that the look endures before your gaze, that they do not look away or lower their eyes; this does not make them stonier; it makes them, rather, more human].

These crumbling traces of dead ancient Romans are like the siblings Ulrich and Agathe, or perhaps more like the married couple Robert and Martha Musil, reclining in a garden in Vienna or in Switzerland, caught in an eternal momentary glance, while the trees around them grow, come into leaf, flower, fruit, fall, and rot, again and again; while the world around them declines, explodes, and transforms. And the enduring glance of this pair, like and unlike, dead but alive, is itself a metaphor for something else, something essential, something that never can be definitively or finally frozen, a metaphor for art. Enigmatic and unresolvable. Fleeting and infinite. Like Musil's life work. An enduring success, despite the flickering failure of any other worlds.

Notes

1 For example, Bernstein, in his chapter on Musil in *Five Portraits*, writes that a "purely aesthetic solution" like the "sub-Proustian strategy" of ending the novel with Ulrich deciding to "write about his failed attempt to find *das rechte Leben* in a book we retroactively understand is the very novel we have just finished reading" would have had "no appeal for Musil, in part because," Bernstein states, Musil "was unconvinced about the redemptive power of art." Bernstein, *Five Portraits*, 53. We ultimately do not know whether Musil would or would not have ended his novel with Ulrich sitting down to write the novel we have just read, but there is no substantial reason to exclude this option as one of the three looming possibilities (writing books, suicide, going to war). A draft for an afterword written in Ulrich's voice and addressed to the postwar generation suggests that this conceit was not completely out of the question.

2 See the introduction.

3 Plato, "Republic," 49–80, qtd. 80.

4 Plato, "Republic," 80.

5 *KA*: Transkriptionen und Faksimiles. Nachlass: Mappen. Mappengruppe II. Mappe II/2 "Nr 23–" Notizen zur Reinschrift 23–36.II/2/16 NR 33 3. Studie zum Problem-Aufbau 3.

6 *KA*: Transkriptionen & Faksimiles. Nachlass: Mappen. Mappengruppe II. Mappe II/8 "II R Fr" Fragen zur Reinschrift von Band II. II/8/257 II R Fr 29 7.

7 See McBride, *Void of Ethics*, 105–6. The supposed impossibility of making the insights of the Other Condition intelligible to normal consciousness is one of McBride's central reasons for claiming that the Other Condition fails.

8 Key is paraphrasing Karl Lamprecht here.

9 *KA*: Kommentar & Apparate. Register. Autoren und Werke. K: Key, Ellen.

10 *KA*: Lesetexte. Band 16 Frühe Tagebuchhefte 1899–1926. I. Brünn/Stuttgart/Berlin (1899–1908). 11: Schwarzes Heft (1905–1908). Stilistische Studien und Projekte, 1905.

11 *KA*: Lesetexte. Band 16 Frühe Tagebuchhefte 1899–1926. I. Brünn/Stuttgart/Berlin (1899–1908). 11: Schwarzes Heft (1905–1908). Stilistische Studien und Projekte, 1905.

12 *KA*: Transkriptionen & Faksimiles. Nachlass: Mappen. Mappen Gruppe II. Mappe II/7 "Ü6" "Üx; x=6." II/7/67 Ü6–4 3.

13 *KA*: Transkriptionen & Faksimiles. Nachlass: Mappen. Mappen Gruppe II. Mappe II/7 "Ü6" "Üx; x=6." II/7/67 Ü6–4 3.

14 Pater, *Renaissance*, 188.

15 Kafka, *Briefe, 1900–1912*, 36.

16 "'Und plötzlich zerreißt das Papier!'fiel Agathe ein. 'Ja. Das heißt: irgendeine gewohnheitsmässige Verwebung in uns zerreißt'" (*MoE*, 762; "And suddenly the paper tears!"Agathe broke in. "Right. That is, some tissue of habit in us tears," *MwQ*, 827).

[17] See, for example, "Schema für die Behandlung der Utopie d. induct. Gesinnung (Scheme for handling the Utopia of the Inductive Attitude), where Musil notes: "Es liegt vor[:]Grundsätzliche Trennung: Induktive Gesinnung für die wenigen a) 'Induktive Gesinnung für die vielen b) a) kommt hinaus auf U[lrich]s Geniemoral, die er auf die Menschheit ausdehnt" (Basic separation: Inductive Attitude for the few a) Inductive Attitude for the many b) depends on U[lrich']s genius morality, that he extends to humanity). *KA*: Transkriptionen & Faksimiles. Nachlass: Mappen. Mappengruppe II, Mappe II/8 ÏI R Fr" Fragen zur Reinschrift von Band II. II/8/257 II R Fr 29 7.

[18] McBride, *Void of Ethics*, 167.

[19] Amann, *Musil: Literatur und Politik*, 19, on Musil's generally positive political involvements with Social Democracy.

[20] *KA*: Lesetexte. Band 15: Fragmente aus dem Nachlass. Essayistische Fragmente. Das Essaybuch 1923–1927. Versuche einen anderen Menschen zu finden.

[21] *KA*: Lesetexte. Band 15: Fragmente aus dem Nachlass. Essayistische Fragmente. Das Essaybuch 1923–1927. Versuche einen anderen Menschen zu finden.

[22] *KA*: Lesetexte. Band 15: Fragmente aus dem Nachlass. Essayistische Fragmente. Das Essaybuch 1923–1927. Versuche einen anderen Menschen zu finden.

[23] *KA*: Transkriptionen und Faksimiles. Nachlass: Mappengruppe II. Mappe II/7. "Üx; x-6. II/7/100" U 6/I Studie zu Krisis und Entscheidung 1.

[24] *KA*: Lesetexte. Band 14: Gedichte, Aphorismen, Selbstkommentare. Selbstkommentare aus dem Nachlass. Zum Roman Parerga und Paralipomena 1921–1937. Zum Nachwort und Zwischenvorwort.

[25] *KA*: Transkriptionen & Faksimiles. Nachlass: Mappen. Mappengruppe II. Mappe II/8. "II R Fr" Fragen zur Reinschrift von Band II. II/8/235 2 II R Fr 26 9.

[26] *KA*: Transkriptionen & Faksimiles. Nachlass: Mappen. Mappengruppe II. Mappe II/8. "II R Fr" Fragen zur Reinschrift von Band II. II/8/16 II Band 4/ Sua 3 4. The Passage, entitled "Agathe Ulrich Conclusion," includes the statement: "Nicht Ulrich, sondern die festen Stützen sind desavouiert. Ein Höhepunkt: anderer Zustand — normaler Zustand. Kommt nicht zur Entscheidung" (Not Ulrich, but the solid foundations are disavowed. A high point: other condition — normal condition. Comes to no decision). *KA*: Lesetexte. Band 3: Der Mann ohne Eigenschaften. Die Fortsetzung. Fortsetzungsreihen 1932–1936. Eine Art Ende. 12. Agathe Ulrich Schluss.

[27] *KA*: Lesetexte. Band 14: Gedichte, Aphorismen, Selbstkommentare. Aphorismen aus dem Nachlass. Germany. Seite 10.

[28] *KA*: Transkriptionen & Faksimiles. Nachlassmappen: Mappengruppe VI. Mappe VI/1 "Aufsätze" SDS- und Paris-Vortrag, Exerpte VI/1/25 SDS II 4.

[29] *KA*: Transkriptionen & Faksimiles. Nachlass: Mappen. Mappengruppe VI. Mappe VI/1 "Aufsätze" SDS- und Paris-Vortrag, Exerpte VI/1/39 SDS IV 2 2.

[30] *KA*: Transkriptionen & Faksimiles. Nachlass: Mappen. Mappengruppe VI. Mappe VI/1 "Aufsätze "SDS- und Paris-Vortrag, Exerpte VI/1/40 SDS IV 2 3.

[31] Amann, *Musil: Literatur und Politik*, 143.

[32] See Amann, *Musil: Literatur und Politik*, 68: "His 'testament' probably from about the same time, a text of harrowing desolation and an expression of stark despair, demonstrates that the fact of absolute lack of means 'had brought [him] several times to the brink of suic[ide].'" The "testament," entitled by Musil "Ich kann nicht weiter" (I can't go on), referred to by Amann here is a painful account of how Musil came to the financial and spiritual crisis he found himself in around 1933. *KA*: Transkriptionen & Faksimiles. Nachlass: Mappen. Mappengruppe II. Mappe II/1 "Handmaterial." II/1/141 Ich kann nicht weiter. For commentary on this text see *KA*: Werkkommentare. Band 14: Gedichte, Aphorismen, Selbstkommentare. Selbstkommentare aus dem Nachlass. Zum Roman. Parerga und Paralipomena 1921–1937. Textgenese. Vorrede.

[33] Musil served in the First World War and this was the war he began writing about in the novel. As the world inched closer and closer towar the Second World War, however, a sense of overlap is unavoidable here.

[34] *KA*: Transkriptionen & Faksimiles. Nachlass: Mappen. Mappengruppe IV. Mappe IV/2 "AN" "Anfänge und Notizen" IV/2/199 AN 271 14 Ein Soldat Erzählt I 6. See "That Was Not a Farce, But the Collapse of a Wall," my translator's foreword to Musil's "Vinzenz and the Mistress of Important Men."

[35] *KA*: Lesetexte. Band 14: Gedichte, Aphorismen, Selbstkommentare. Aphorismen aus dem Nachlass. Germany, Seite 4.

[36] *KA*: Transkriptionen & Faksimiles. Nachlass: Mappen. Mappengruppe VI. Mappe VII/1 "Aufsätze" SDS- und Paris-Vortrag, Exerpte. VI/1/74 Vortrag Paris Entwurf A 3 Vortrag Paris Entwurf B 1.

[37] Bringazi calls attention to Musil's connection between "Geist" (intellect, spirit, intellectual) and "Jude" (Jew) in his *Mythen der Nation*. The "Geist" and the Jew, Musil writes, ". . . have statelessness in common, that they don't have, anywhere in the world, their land" (Musil, *T*, 907).

[38] *KA*: Lesetexte. Band 9: Reden. Vortragsmanuskripte aus dem Nachlass. Rede auf dem "Internationalen Schriftstellerkongress für die Verteidigung der Kultur" in Paris. Berichtigung eines Berichts.

[39] Pater, *Renaissance*, 189.

[40] Musil transcribed this quotation from a letter of Ludwig Tieck which he found in Ricarda Huch's *Blütezeit der Romantik* (*KA*: Register. Autoren und Werke. Ricard Huch. Blütezeit der Romantik). His transcription can be found in his notebook 11, *KA*: Lesetexte. Band 16: Frühe Tagebuchhefte 1899–1926 I. Brünn/Stuttgart/Berlin (1899–1908). 11: Schwarzes Heft (1905–1908). Stilistische Studien und Projekte, 1905.

[41] *KA*: Lesetexte. Band 16: Frühe Tagebuchhefte 1899–1926 I. Brünn/Stuttgart/Berlin (1899–1908). 11: Schwarzes Heft (1905–1908). Stilistische Studien und Projekte, 1905.

[42] Adorno, *Aesthetic Theory*, 144.

[43] Musil noted that the greatest success of this speech was that he had spoken at all ("Der Erfolg dieses meines Vortrags hat hauptsächlich darin bestanden, dass ich überhaupt gesprochen habe"). *KA*: Lesetexte. Band 9: Reden. Vortragsmanuskripte aus dem Nachlass. Der Dichter in dieser Zeit. Einleitung Basel.

[44] *KA*: Lesetexte. Band 9: Reden. Vortragsmanuskripte aus dem Nachlass. Der Dichter in dieser Zeit. Rede anlässlich des zwanzigjährigen Bestehens des SDÖS am 16.12.1934 in Wien.

[45] *KA*: Lesetexte. Band 9: Reden Vortragsmanuskripte aus dem Nachlass. Rede auf dem "Internationalen Schriftstellerkongress für die Verteidigung der Kultur" in Paris. Vortrag Paris.

[46] The following quote was first brought to my attention by Stefan Kutzenberger in his talk on Musil reception at the Lancaster Robert Musil Conference: "Recontextualizing Robert Musil the Author without Qualities," in 2007: "Ein Erfolg dieses Romans würde dem Bild der Zeit, das er selbst entwirft, widersprechen. Das Ausbleiben des Erfolges würde vielleicht die Überzeugungskraft des Autors in Frage stellen, gleichzeitig aber die Konzeption des Romans bestätigen. Was soll ich mir wünschen? Natürlich wünsche ich mir doch die Wirkung, auf die Sie hoffen. Aber ich glaube nicht daran. Später, vielleicht, später sicherlich." Musil, quoted in Rasch, *Über Robert Musils Roman*, 20. (A success for this novel would contradict the picture of the times which it itself paints. The absence of success would, perhaps, call the author's powers of persuasion into question, but, at the same time, attest to the novel's conception. What should I hope for? Naturally I wish for the response that you anticipate. But I don't believe in it. Later, perhaps, much later.)

[47] Musil, *Sämtliche Erzählungen*, 304.

Works Cited

Adorno, Theodor. *Aesthetic Theory*. Edited by Gretel Adorno and Rolf Tiede-
mann. Newly translated, edited, and with a translator's introduction by
Robert Hullot-Kentor. U of Minnesota P, 1977.
———. "Extorted Reconciliation: On Georg Lukács' Realism in Our Time."
In *Notes to Literature*, edited by Rolf Tiedemann, 216–40. New York:
Columbia UP, 1991.
Agamben, Giorgio. *The Man without Content*. Translated by Georgia Albert.
Stanford, CA: Stanford UP, 1999.
Amann, Klaus. *Robert Musil: Literatur und Politik*. Reinbek bei Hamburg:
Rowohlt, 2009.
Bab, Julius. *Das Leben Goethes*. Ludwigsburg: Verlag Waidelich, 1949.
Bangerter, Lowell A. "Experimental Utopias: The Man without Qualities."
In *Robert Musil's The Man without Qualities*, edited by Harold Bloom,
5–20. Philadelphia: Chelsea House, 2005.
Baudelaire, Charles. "The Painter of Modern Life." Translated by Jonathan
Mayne. In *The Norton Anthology of Theory and Criticism*, edited by Vin-
cent B. Leitch. New York: Norton, 2001, 792–802.
Bell, Clive. *Art*. New York: Capricorn Books, 1958.
Benjamin, Walter. *The Arcades Project*. Translated by Howard Eiland and
Kevin McClaughlin. Cambridge, MA: Belknap/Harvard UP, 1999.
———. *Aura und Reflexion: Schriften zur Ästhetik und Kunstphilosophie*.
Frankfurt am Main: Suhrkamp, 2007.
———. *Illuminations*. Edited by Hannah Arendt. Translated by Harry Zohn.
New York: Schocken Books, 1969.
Bernstein, Michael André. *Five Portraits: Modernity and the Imagination in
Twentieth Century German Writing*. Evanston, IL: Northwestern UP, 2000.
———. *Forgone Conclusions: Against Apocalyptic History*. Berkeley: U of CA
P, 1994.
Bloom, Harold, ed. *Robert Musil's The Man without Qualities*. Philadelphia:
Chelsea House, 2005.
Bouveresse, Jacques. "Genauigkeit und Leidenschaft: Das Problem des Essays
und des Essayismus im Werk von Musil." Translated by Rosemarie Zeller.
Musil-Forum 29 (2007): 1–56.
Bringazi, Friedrich. *Robert Musil und die Mythen der Nation*. Frankfurt am
Main: Lang, 1998.
Bruno, Giordano. *Giordano Bruno: His Life and Thought with an Annotated
Translation of His Work "On the Infinite Universe and Worlds."* Trans-
lated and edited by Dorothey Waley Singer. New York: Schuman, 1950.

Bryson, Norman. *Still Life: Looking at the Overlooked*. London: Reaktion Books, 1990.

Cameron, Esther. "A Note on 'The Meridian.'" In *Against Time: Essays on Paul Celan, 1976–2004*. Point and Circumference.com, 2004. Web.

Carson, Anne. *Economy of the Unlost*. Princeton, NJ: Princeton UP, 1999.

———. *Eros the Bittersweet*. Champaign, IL: Dalkey Archive Press, 1998.

Celan, Paul. *The Meridian: Final Version — Drafts — Materials*. Edited by Bernhard Böschenstein and Heino Schmull. Translated by Pierre Joris. Stanford, CA: Stanford UP, 2011.

Clark, Ronald W. *Einstein: The Life and Times*. New York: Harper Collins, 1984.

Corino, Karl. "Der Dämon der Möglichkeit: Vom Scheitern Robert Musils." In Lüdke and Schmidt, *Literaturmagazin 30: "Siegreiche Niederlagen"; Scheitern, die Signatur der Moderne*, 62–71.

———. *Robert Musil: Eine Biographie*. Reinbek bei Hamburg: Rowohlt, 2003.

Deleuze, Gilles. *Proust and Signs*. Translated by Richard Howard. Minneapolis: U of Minnesota P, 2000.

Dostoevsky, Fyodor. *The Idiot*. Translated by Constance Garnett. New York: Macmillan, 1923.

———. *Notes from Underground*. Translated by Richard Pevear and Larissa Volokhonsky. London: Everyman, 2004.

Emerson, Ralph Waldo. *Early Addresses*. Cambridge, MA: Harvard UP, 1972.

———. *Essays, 1st Series*. Philadelphia: Altemus, 1892.

———. *Journals and Miscellaneous Notebooks: 1841–1843*. Cambridge, MA: Harvard UP, 1960.

———. *The Later Lectures of Ralph Waldo Emerson: 1843–1871*, vol. 1. Athens, GA: U of Georgia P, 2010.

Fanta, Walter. "Competing Editions and the 'Telos' of the Narrative." In Payne, Bartram, and Tihanov, *Companion to the Works of Robert Musil*, 371–94.

———. "The Genesis of the Man without Qualities." In Payne, Bartram, and Tihanov, *Companion to the Works of Robert Musil*, 251–84.

———. "Über den Ausgang der letzten Liebesgeschichte bei Robert Musil." In *Die Lust im Text: Eros in Sprache und Literatur*, edited by Doris Moser and Kalina Kupczynska. Vienna: PRAESENS VERLAGSgesmbh, 2009, 159–73.

Fanta, Walter, ed. with Klaus Amann and Karl Corino. *Klagenfurter Ausgabe: Kommentierte digitale Edition sämtlicher Werke, Briefe und nachgelassener Schriften. Mit Transkriptionen und Faksimiles aller Handschriften*. Annotated Digital Edition of the Collected Works, Letters and Literary and Biographical Remains, with Transcriptions and Facsimiles of All Manuscripts. Robert Musil-Institut, Alpen-Adria Universität Klagenfurt, Austria, 2009.

Fontana, Oskar Maurus. "Was arbeiten Sie? Gespräch mit Robert Musil." *Die Literarische Welt* 2/18 (30. April, 1926): 1.

Freed, Mark M. *Robert Musil and the Non-Modern.* New York: Continuum, 2011.

Freud, Sigmund. *Totem and Taboo: Resemblances between the Psychic Lives of Savages and Neurotics.* Translated by A. A. Brill. London: Routledge, 1919.

Gebauer, Gunter. *Wittgensteins anthropologisches Denken.* Munich: C. H. Beck, 2009.

Genette, Gérard. *Narrative Discourse.* Translated by Jane E. Lewin. Ithaca, NY: Cornell UP, 1980.

Goethe, Johann Wolfgang von. *Faust: A Tragedy.* Translated by Bayard Taylor. Boston: Houghton-Mifflin, 1883.

———."Upon the Laocoon". In *Goethe's Literary Essays,* 22–35. Translated by J. E. Spingarn. New York: Harcourt Brace, 1921.

Goltschnigg, Dieter. *Mystische Tradition im Roman Robert Musils: Martin Bubers "Ekstatische Konfessionen" im "Mann ohne Eigenschaften."* Heidelberg: Stiehm, 1974.

Grill, Genese. "Ecstatic Experience, Crime, and Conversion in Robert Musil's 'The Man without Qualities.'" PhD diss., CUNY Graduate Center, NY, 2001.

———. "That Was Not a Farce, but the Collapse of a Wall." Foreword to Musil's "Vinzenz and the Mistress of Important Men." *Fiction* 16, no. 1 (1999): 81–86.

———. "The Other Musil: Robert Musil and Mysticism." In Payne, Bartram, and Tihanov, *A Companion to the Works of Robert Musil,* 333–54.

———. "Versuche ein Scheusal zu lieben: Zwillingsriten in Robert Musils *Der Mann ohne Eigenschaften.*" In *Musil an der Schwelle zum 21. Jahrhundert,* edited by Marie-Louise Roth and Pierre Béhar, 187–200. Bern: Peter Lang, 2005–.

Hadot, Pierre. *The Veil of Isis: An Essay on the History of the Idea of Nature.* Cambridge, MA: Harvard UP, 2006.

Harrison, Thomas. "Robert Musil: The Suspension of the World." In Bloom, *Robert Musil's The Man without Qualities,* 21–50.

Holquist, Michael, ed. *The Dialogic Imagination: Four Essays by M. M. Bakhtin.* Translated by Caryl Emerson and Michael Holquist. Austin: U of Texas P, 1982.

Hüppauf, Bernd. *Von sozialer Utopie zur Mystik: Robert Musils "Der Man ohne Eigenschaften."* Munich: W. Fink, 1971.

Jonsson, Stefan. *Subject without Nation: Robert Musil and the History of Modern Identity.* Durham, NC: Duke UP, 2000.

Josipovici, Gabriel. *What Ever Happened to Modernism?* New Haven, CT: Yale UP, 2010.

Kafka, Franz. *Briefe, 1900–1912.* Edited by Hans-Gerd Koch. Berlin: S. Fischer, 1999.

Kant, Immanuel. "From Critique of Judgment." Translated by Werner S. Pluhar. In *The Norton Anthology of Theory and Criticism,* edited by Vincent B. Leitch, 504–35. New York: Norton, 2001.

Kenner, Hugh. *The Pound Era*. Berkeley: U of California P, 1973.

Kermode, Frank. "Modernism, Postmodernism, and Explanation." In *Prehistories of the Future: The Primitivist Project and the Culture of Modernism*, edited by Elazar Barkan, 357–74. Stanford, CA: Stanford UP, 1995.

———. *The Sense of an Ending: Studies in the Theory of Fiction*. Charlottesville: U of Virginia P, 1967.

Kern, Stephen. *The Modernist Novel: A Critical Introduction*. Cambridge: Cambridge UP, 2011.

Kroner, Richard. "What Is Really Real?" *Review of Metaphysics* 7, no. 3 (March 1954): 351–62.

Lessing, Gotthold Ephraim. *Laocoon: An Essay upon the Limits of Painting and Poetry*. Translated by Ellen Frothingham. New York: Dover, 2005.

Lüdke, Martin, and Delf Schmidt, eds. *Literaturmagazine 30: "Siegreiche Niederlagen"; Scheitern, die Signatur der Moderne*. Hamburg: Rowohlt, 1992.

Mallen, Enrique. "Stealing Beauty." *Guardian Unlimited: On-line Picasso Project*. Web, 2006.

McBride, Patrizia C. "On the Utility of Art for Politics: Musil's Armed Truce of Ideas." *German Quarterly* 73, no. 4 (Autumn, 2000): 366–86.

———. *The Void of Ethics: Robert Musil and the Experience of Modernity*. Evanston, IL: Northwestern UP, 2006.

Mehigan, Tim. *The Critical Approaches to Robert Musil's Man without Qualities*. Rochester, NY: Camden House, 2003.

Moore, Gene. *Proust and Musil: The Novel as Research Instrument*. Austin: U of Texas P, 1978.

Musil, Robert. *Briefe: 1901–1942*. Edited by Adolf Frisé with help from Murray G. Hall. Reinbek bei Hamburg: Rowohlt, 1981.

———. *Diaries: 1899–1941*. Translated by Philip Payne. Edited by Mark Mirsky. New York: Basic Books, 1998.

———. *Klagenfurter Ausgabe: Kommentierte digitale Edition sämtlicher Werke, Briefe und nachgelassener Schriften. Mit Transkriptionen und Faksimiles aller Handschriften*. (Annotated Digital Edition of the Collected Works, Letters and Literary and Biographical Remains, with Transcriptions and Facsimiles of All Manuscripts.) Edited by Walter Fanta, Klaus Amann, and Karl Corino. Robert Musil-Institut, Alpen-Adria Universität Klagenfurt, Austria, 2009.

———. *Der Mann ohne Eigenschaften*. Edited by Adolf Frisé. Reinbek bei Hamburg: Rowohlt, 1970.

———. *The Man without Qualities*. Translated by Burton Pike and Sophie Wilkins. 2 vols. New York: Knopf, 1995.

———. *Precision and Soul: Essays and Addresses*. Edited and translated by Burton Pike and David S. Luft. Chicago: U of Chicago P, 1990.

———. *Sämtliche Erzählungen*. Hamburg: Rowohlt, 1979.

———. *Tagebücher, Aufsätze, Essays und Reden*. Edited by Adolf Frisé. Reinbek bei Hamburg: Rowohlt, 1955.

———. *Tagebücher.* Edited by Adolf Frisé. 2 vols. Reinbek bei Hamburg: Rowohlt, 1976.

———. "Vinzenz and the Mistress of Important Men," act 1. Translated by Genese Grill. *Fiction* Vol. 15, no. 2 (1999).

———. "Vinzenz and the Mistress of Important Men," acts 2 & 3. Translated by Genese Grill. *Fiction* Vol.16, no.1 (2000).

Nabokov, Vladimir. *Lectures on Russian Literature.* Edited by Fredson Bowers. New York: Harcourt Brace, 1981.

Neymeyr, Barbara. *Utopie und Experiment: Zur Literaturtheorie, Anthropologie und Kulturkritik in Musils Essays.* Heidelberg: Universitätsverlag Winter, 2009.

Nietzsche, Friedrich. *Basic Writings of Nietzsche.* Translated and edited by Walter Kaufmann. New York: Random House, 2000.

———. "On Truth and Lying in a Non-Moral Sense." In *The Norton Anthology of Theory and Criticism*, edited by Vincent B. Leitch. Translated by Ronald Speirs, 874–84. New York: Norton, 2001.

———. *The Gay Science: With a Prelude in Rhymes and an Appendix of Songs.* Translated by Walter Kaufmann. New York: Random House, 1974.

———. *Untimely Meditations.* Edited by Daniel Breazeale. Translated by R. J. Hollingdale. Cambridge: Cambridge UP, 1997.

———. *The Will to Power.* Translated and edited by Walter Kaufmann. New York: Random House, 1967.

Pater, Walter. *The Renaissance: Studies in Art and Poetry.* Berkeley: U of California P, 1980.

Payne, Philip, Graham Bartram, and Galen Tihanov, eds. *A Companion to the Works of Robert Musil.* Rochester, NY: Camden House, 2007.

Perloff, Marjorie. *Wittgenstein's Ladder: Poetic Language and the Strangeness of the Ordinary.* Chicago: U of Chicago P, 1996.

Pike, Burton. "Literature as Experience." In Bloom, *Robert Musil's The Man without Qualities*, 75–92.

———. "Negative Freedom in *The Man without Qualities.*" Unpublished talk delivered at "Recontextualizing Robert Musil," International Robert Musil Society Conference, Lancaster, England, in 2007.

———. "Unfinished or without End?" In Payne, Bartram, and Tihanov, *A Companion to the Works of Robert Musil*, 355–70.

Plato. "From The Republic, Books II–X." Translated by Robin Waterfield. In *The Norton Anthology of Theory and Criticism*, edited by Vincent B. Leitch, 49–80. New York: Norton, 2001.

———. *Timaeus.* Translated by Benjamin Jowett. Rockville, MD: Serenity Books, 2009.

Porchia, Antonio. *Voices.* Translated by W. S. Merwin. Port Townsend, WA: Copper Canyon Press, 2003.

Preusser, Heinz-Peter. "Die Masken des Ludwig Klages: Figurenkonstellation als Kritik und Adaption befremdlicher Ideen in Robert Musils Roman *Der Mann ohne Eigenschaften.*" *Musil Forum* 31 (2009–10): 224–53.

Proust, Marcel. *Marcel Proust on Art and Literature: 1896–1919*. Translated by Sylvia Townsend Warner. New York: Basic Books, 1997.

———. *Remembrance of Things Past*. Translated by C. K. Scott Moncrieff. 2 vols. New York: Random House, 1934.

Rancière, Jacques. *Aesthetics and Its Discontents*. Translated by Steven Corcoran. Malden, MA: Polity, 2011.

Rasch, Wolfdietrich. *Über Robert Musils Roman "Der Man ohne Eigenschaften."* Göttingen: Vandenhoeck & Ruprecht, 1967.

Richardson, Robert D. *Emerson: The Mind on Fire*. Berkeley: U of California P, 1995.

Ricoeur, Paul. *The Rule of Metaphor*. Translated by Robert Czerny, with Kathleen McLaughlin and John Costello, SJ. Toronto: U of Toronto P, 1977.

———. *Time and Narrative*. Vol. 3. Translated by Kathleen Blamey and David Pellauer. Chicago: U of Chicago P, 1950.

Rilke, Rainer Maria. *Die Gedichte*. Frankfurt am Main: Insel, 2006.

Roth, Marie-Louise. *Robert Musil: Ethik und Ästhetik*. Munich: P. List, 1972.

Ryan, Judith. *The Vanishing Subject: Early Psychology and the Modernist Novel*. Chicago: U of Chicago P, 1991.

Sartre, Jean Paul. *Existentialism is a Humanism*. Trans. Carol Macomber. New Haven: Yale UP, 2007.

———. *Nausea*. Translated by Lloyd Alexander. New York: New Directions, 2007.

Schelling, Ulrich. "Das analogische Denken bei Robert Musil." In *Robert Musil: Studien zu seinem Werk*, edited by Elisabeth Albertsen, Karl Corino, and Karl Dinklage, 170–99. Reinbek bei Hamburg: Rowohlt, 1970.

Schmidt, Jochen. *Ohne Eigenschaften*. Tübingen: Niemeyer, 1975.

Schöne, Albrecht. "Über den Gebrauch des Konjunktivs bei Robert Musil." *Euphorion* 55 (1968): 196–220.

Sebastian, Thomas. *The Intersection of Science and Literature in Musil's "The Man without Qualities."* Rochester, NY: Camden House, 2005.

Singer, Dorothy Waley. *Giordano Bruno: His Life and Thought with an Annotated Translation of His Work "On the Infinite Universe and Worlds."* New York: Schuman, 1950.

Sokel, Walter. "Agathe und der existenzphilosophische Faktor im Mann ohne Eigenschaften." *Beiträge zur Musil-Kritik* (1983): 111–28.

———. "Robert Musil und die Existenzphilosophie Jean-Paul Sartres: Zum 'existenzphilosophischen Bildungsroman' Musils und Sartres." In *Literaturwissenschaft und Geisteswissenschaft: Festschrift für Richard Brinkmann*, edited by Jürgen Brummack, 658–91. Tübingen: Niemeyer, 1981.

Steiner, George. *Grammars of Creation*. New Haven, CT: Yale UP, 2002.

———. *Martin Heidegger*. Chicago: U of Chicago P, 1991.

———. *Real Presences*. Chicago: U of Chicago P, 1991.

Tadie, Jean-Yves. *Marcel Proust: A Life*. Translated by Euan Camerson. New York: Penguin, 2001.

Thiher, Allen. *Understanding Robert Musil.* Columbia: U of South Carolina P, 2009.

Thoreau, Henry David. *Walden and Resistance to Civil Government.* New York: Norton, 1992.

Tiedemann, Rolf. "Dialectics at a Standstill." In *The Arcades Project,* by Walter Benjamin, 929–45.

Wagner-Egelhaaf, Martina. *Mystik der Moderne: Die visionäre Ästhetik der deutschen Literatur des 20. Jahrhunderts.* Stuttgart: Metzler, 1989.

Weinstein, Philip M. *Unknowing: The Work of Modernist Fiction.* Ithaca, NY: Cornell UP, 2005.

Wellmer, Albrecht. *The Persistence of Modernity: Essays on Aesthetics, Ethics, and Postmodernism.* Translated by David Midgley. Cambridge, MA: MIT Press, 1991.

Willemsen, Roger. *Das Existenzrecht der Dichtung: Zur Rekonstruktion einer systematischen Literaturtheorie im Werk Robert Musils.* Munich: Wilhelm Fink, 1984.

Wilson, A. N. *God's Funeral: The Decline of Faith in Western Civilization.* New York: Norton, 1999.

Wolf, Norbert C. *Kakanien als Gesellschaftskonstruktion: Robert Musils Sozioanalyse des 20. Jahrhunderts.* Cologne: Böhlau Verlag, 2012.

Woolf, Virginia. "Modern Fiction." In *The Common Reader: First Series,* 146–54. Orlando, FL: Houghton Mifflin Harcourt, 2002.

———. *Mrs. Dalloway.* Oxford: Oxford UP, 2000.

Worringer, William. "From Abstraction and Empathy." In *Art in Theory, 1900–2000,* edited by Charles Harrison and Paul Wood. Malden, MA: Blackwell, 2009.

Index

a priori morality, 20, 29, 34, 67, 94, 106–7, 163

a priori reality, 4, 9, 20, 49, 96, 100, 109–10, 113, 116, 163

abstraction: as artistic method, 3–4, 10, 13, 22, 32, 50, 65, 69–72, 78, 87, 89, 94–96, 98–100, 114, 116, 125–27, 135–36, 146–49, 180; as process of thinking, 3–4, 8–10, 22, 32, 80–83, 100, 109, 113–14, 125–27, 134–35, 147–49, 176

action, and inaction: in life, 9, 18, 21, 22, 28, 33, 36, 38, 41, 47, 51, 68, 89, 94, 112, 120, 124, 126, 131, 145, 150, 163, 169; in novels, 2, 33, 35, 36, 43, 60, 71–73, 119, 121–26, 131–32, 136–37, 142, 145, 150

Adorno, Theodor, 179

Adorno, Theodor, works by: *Aesthetic Theory*, 18, 157, 179–80; "Extorted Reconciliation," 12

aesthetic experience, 1, 3, 9, 17, 24, 35, 38, 40, 64, 65, 67, 73, 78, 79, 94, 98, 101, 128, 138, 152, 160, 162, 164, 166, 172–74, 176, 177, 179

aesthetics, 5, 7, 18, 25, 35–38, 51, 64, 65, 78, 79, 82, 87, 98, 100, 103, 114, 138, 145–46, 157, 158–82, 183; and ethics, 1–3, 5, 9, 10, 13, 15, 16, 19, 38, 52, 58, 73, 79, 87, 91, 107, 121, 138, 160, 164–82; and modernism, 3, 6, 7, 9, 12, 18, 19, 25, 35–37, 55, 100, 114

Agamben, Giorgio, works by: *The Man without Content*, 13

allocentricism, and egocentricism, 28, 32, 35, 38, 67, 124

als ob (as if), subjunctive thinking, 36, 43, 98, 110–14, 179

Amann, Klaus, works by: *Klagenfurter Ausgabe* (Klagenfurt edition; as editor, with Karl Corino and Walter Fanta), 1–2; *Musil: Literatur und Politik* (Musil: literature and politics), 13, 171, 172, 175, 185

anderer Zustand. *See* Other Condition

Apollo and Dionysus, 63, 68, 101

appetitive and non-appetitive way of life, 28–32, 35, 37, 47, 120, 124, 145, 149

archetypes, 49, 51, 54, 69, 94, 106, 127

Archimedian point, 27, 31

Aristotle, 32, 111

art for art's sake, 87, 170, 180. *See also* autonomy

Augustine, 37, 110, 111

autonomy, of art, artist and thinker, 6, 11, 12, 18, 87, 167, 174–80. *See also* art for art's sake

Bab, Julius, works by: *Das Leben Goethes* (Goethe's life), 30

Bakhtin, Mikhail, 9–10

Bangerter, Lowell, works by: "Experimental Utopias," 8, 115–16

Baudelaire, Charles, 108

Baudelaire, Charles, works by: *Flowers of Evil*, 108; *Painter of Modern Life*, 114

Becoming, 30, 113, 115, 150, 151, 152

Being, 2, 3, 19, 50, 101, 111, 113, 115, 122, 151, 152, 163, 176

Bell, Clive, works by: *Art*, 94, 98

Benjamin, Walter, 109, 151

Benjamin, Walter, works by, *Arcades Project*, 93; *Aura und Reflexion* (Aura and reflection), 108–9; *Illuminations*, 94, 108, 151

Berlin, Isaiah, idea of negative freedom, 40–41

Bernstein, Michael André, works by: *Five Portraits*, 183; *Foregone Conclusions*, 36

Bouveresse, Jacques, works by: "Genauigkeit und Leidenschaft: das Problem des Essays und des Essayismus im Werk von Musil" (Precision and passion: the problem of the essay and of essayism in Musil's work), 13

Breitinger, Johann Jakob, 111

Bringazi, Friedrich, works by: *Robert Musil und die Mythen der Nation* (Robert Musil and the myths of the nation), 185

Bruno, Giordano, 26, 27

Bruno, Giordano, works by: *De l'infinite universi et mondi* (On the infinite universe and worlds), 26–27

Bryson, Norman, works by: *Still Life: Looking at the Overlooked*, 126

Buber, Martin, works by: *Ecstatic Confessions*, 12, 53–54

Büchner, Georg, works of: "Lenz," 151–52

Cameron, Esther, works by: "A Note on the Meridian," 155

Carson, Anne, works by: *Economy of the Unlost*, 155; *Eros the Bittersweet*, 142–44

Celan, Paul, 152

Celan, Paul, works by: *The Meridian*, 150–52, 155

Chardin, Jean-Baptiste-Siméon, 144

Clark, Ronald W., works by: *Einstein: The Life and Times*, 27

coincidence of opposites, 3, 35, 68, 126, 151, 160, 178

collectivism, 6, 167, 174

conceptualization, 3, 4, 5, 6, 7–9, 10, 12, 49–79, 85–87, 99, 103, 109, 111, 114, 148, 149

conduct of life, 17–18, 36–38, 51, 57–58, 63, 64, 68, 74, 163–65, 173, 176

consummation, 30, 80, 119, 121, 127, 132, 137, 143, 147–50

Copernicus, 36

Corino, Karl, works by: "Der Dämon der Möglichkeit: Vom Scheitern Robert Musils" (The demon of possibility: on the failure or Robert Musil), 13; *Klagenfurter Ausgabe* (Klagenfurt edition; as editor, with Klaus Amann and Walter Fanta), 1–2; *Robert Musil: Eine Biographie* (Robert Musil: a biography), 153

creative subject, 2–3, 51, 86–87, 95, 100–103, 106, 110–13, 149–50, 158

crime, criminal acts, taboo, 10, 24, 49–54, 72, 72, 94, 100, 108, 150, 153, 158, 163

culture, defense of, 3, 6, 169, 173–75, 181

Cusa, Nicholas of, 26

Cusa, Nicholas of, works by: *de docta ignorantia*, 25–26

dead and living words, 9, 10, 25, 29, 52, 53, 56, 87, 101, 102–3, 105, 137, 167, 179

death, 10, 12, 17, 21, 41, 72, 73, 93, 101, 119–21, 126, 127, 130, 131, 132, 139, 140, 150, 153, 172, 174, 176, 177, 178, 179

deferral, 5, 10, 15, 24, 31, 35, 41–42, 51, 119–32, 150, 161, 178

Deleuze, Gilles, works by: *Proust and Signs*, 12, 78

desire, indifference, drives, lack of desire, 20, 38, 66, 73, 78, 80, 120, 125, 126, 135, 136, 140, 142, 143, 144, 145–49, 157, 164, 166, 169, 178. *See also* appetitive and non-appetitive way of life; disinterestedness

disinterestedness, 9, 10, 17, 119–20,
145–49
Döblin, Alfred, 97, 104–5
Dostoevsky, Fyodor, 5, 68
Dostoevsky, Fyodor, works by: *The
Idiot*, 39–40; *Notes from Underground*, 34, 41–42, 61–62, 85–86
drafts, revisions, and variations, 1, 2,
10, 16, 19, 23, 33, 35, 36, 55, 60,
72, 74, 77–78, 95, 98, 110, 119–
32, 152, 153, 155, 163, 175
duration, 1, 6, 10, 19, 22, 26, 35–36,
43, 44, 52, 54, 69, 70, 78–82,
93, 95, 101, 108, 113, 114–16,
124–26, 136–53, 162, 164, 169,
178–82

Eckhart, Meister, and idea of *ohne
Eigenschaften* (qualitylessness), 47
ecstatic experience, 17, 30, 38, 40, 46,
53–54, 146–47, 163
egocentricism. *See* allocentricism
Einstein, Albert, 24, 26, 27, 36, 178
Eliot, T. S., 106
Eliot, T. S., works by: "Ben Johnson,"
117; "Tradition and the Individual
Talent," 117; *The Waste Land*, 106
Emerson, Ralph Waldo, 5, 17, 25, 34,
35, 37, 68, 91, 112, 113, 176
Emerson, Ralph Waldo, works by:
"Circles" (in *Essays*), 36–37, 42–43,
179; *The Early Lectures*, 17; *Journals*, 57; *The Later Lectures*, 17;
"The Poet" (in *Essays*), 57, 102
emotion (also feeling), 21, 22, 24, 28,
47, 124, 131, 146, 148, 169, 176;
in contrast to logical thinking, 21,
136, 148, 176; fleetingness of, 28,
35, 40, 47, 50, 82–83, 124, 137,
141–45, 162, 167, 169; specific
and non-specific, 80–83, 123–27,
149
empiricism, 24, 51, 57, 82–85, 91, 96,
103, 111, 158, 163
Escher, M. C., 23
essayism, 13, 24–25, 158
essence, 4, 9, 10, 11, 20, 22–24, 34,
49, 67–68, 76–79, 83, 94–95, 100,

106, 112, 125, 133, 134, 152,
163, 166, 175–76, 178
eternity, eternalization, 10, 19, 22, 23,
27, 28, 29, 34, 37–38, 41–42, 54,
68, 72, 78–79, 91, 93–95, 102–3,
108, 113–15, 120–27, 132, 142,
150–52, 158, 161, 164, 182
ethics, 1, 3, 4, 9, 10, 15, 19, 37–38,
40, 51, 67, 87, 121, 137, 138,
160, 163, 164, 168–70, 174,
175, 176, 179, 181; as contrasted
with morality, 29, 51–52, 64, 68,
70–71, 79, 87. *See also* aesthetics,
and ethics
exceptional conditions, moments,
states, 1, 4, 17, 19, 39, 40, 51, 68,
70–71, 73, 74, 78, 79, 80, 99, 101,
109, 119, 164, 173, 177, 178
existentialism, 1, 3, 9, 35, 36, 38, 50,
51, 56, 67, 68, 83, 86, 87, 91,
94–95, 100, 106, 110, 120, 149,
163, 164, 176
experimentation, 1, 2, 5, 6, 7, 8, 9,
11, 16, 18, 19, 22, 23, 24, 25, 36,
37, 38, 39, 42–43, 49, 50, 52, 53,
64, 68, 72, 73, 74, 75, 79, 93, 95,
96, 105, 108, 110, 111, 113, 121,
136, 139, 158, 159, 161, 163,
164, 172, 173, 177
extratemporal metaphoric moment,
realm, 38, 72, 78, 80, 108, 132,
151, 163, 176, 178, 179. *See also*
metaphor, as deferral
extratemporality, 10, 22, 30, 59,
78, 101, 164. *See also* time,
timelessness

failure, 1–11, 12, 23, 35–36, 38, 39,
40, 44, 159–64, 169, 172, 179–82
Fanta, Walter, works by: "The Genesis
of *The Man without Qualities*,"11;
Klagenfurter Ausgabe (Klagen-
furt edition; as editor, with Klaus
Amann and Karl Corino), 1–2;
"Über den Ausgang der letzten
Liebesgeschichte bei Robert Musil"
(On the conclusion of the last lover
story in Robert Musil), 132

fascism, Austrian and German, 16,
18, 94, 171–72, 175. *See also Gleichschaltung*; National Socialism;
totalitarianism
Feeling. *See* emotion
fetishism, 31, 124, 126
finishing and not finishing, 1, 2, 4, 5,
10, 13, 19, 23, 25, 32, 36, 41–44,
46, 51, 93, 96–97, 103, 111, 113–
15, 119–20, 143, 158, 181
Fontane, Oskar Maurus, works by:
"Was Arbeiten Sie? Gespräch mit
Robert Musil" (What are you working on? Conversation with Robert
Musil), 80
formal arrangement, 1, 3, 10, 55, 59,
71, 72, 74, 94, 95, 96, 101, 103,
114–15, 125, 180
fragmentation, 2, 5, 7, 23, 24, 25, 26,
73, 106, 113, 134
Frazer, James, works by: *The Golden
Bough*, 115
Freed, Michael, works by: *Robert
Musil and the Non-Modern*, 5
Freud, Sigmund, 48, 166
Freud, Sigmund, works by: *Totem and
Taboo*, 100
Fühmann, Franz, 12

Gebauer, Gunter, works by: *Wittgensteins anthropologisches Denken*
(Wittgenstein's anthropological
thought), 100–101, 116
Genette, Gérard, works by: *Narrative
Discourse*, 12
genius, 94, 124, 167, 175–76, 184
genius moments, 39, 40, 70–71, 73,
176
gestalt, gestalt psychology, 4, 12, 23,
37, 160
Gleichschaltung, 17, 175; definitions
of, 45–46. *See also* fascism; National
Socialism; totalitarianism
God, gods, 10, 20, 37, 56, 57, 82, 83,
89, 93, 97, 102–3, 110–11, 115,
119, 120, 121, 123, 124, 140,
144, 158, 160, 173; death of, 27,
64–65, 83

Goethe, Johann Wolfgang von, 30,
35, 47, 94, 165; and *Urpflanze*,
40, 94
Goethe, Johann Wolfgang von, works
by: *Elective Affinities*, 141–42;
Faust, 120, 140–41; "Upon the
Laocoon," 138–40
Gogol, Nicolai, 20–21
Goltschnigg, Dieter, works by: *Myst-
ische Tradition im Roman Robert
Musils: Martin Bubers "Ekstatische
Konfessionen" im "Mann ohne
Eigenschaften"* (Mystical tradition
in Robert Musil's novel: Martin
Buber's "Ecstatic Confessions"), 12
Gottsched, Johann Christoph, 111
Grill, Genese, works by: *Ecstatic Expe-
rience, Crime and Conversion in
Robert Musil's "Der Mann ohne
Eigenschaften,"* 46; "The Other
Musil: Robert Musil and Mysti-
cism," 13, 116; "That was not a
Farce," 185; "Versuche ein Scheu-
sel zu lieben" (Attempts to love a
scoundrel), 116

Hadot, Pierre, works by: *The Veil of
Isis*, 101–2, 109–10
harmony, 1, 4, 39, 40, 46, 51, 63, 67,
85, 105, 113, 150, 158, 179
Harrison, Thomas, works by: "Suspen-
sion of the World," 9, 14, 89
Heidegger, Martin, 151–52, 176
Hofmannsthal, Hugo von, works by:
Lord Chandos Brief (Lord Chan-
dos's letter), 3–4, 55
Hölderlin, Friedrich, 69
Holquist, Michael, works by: "Intro-
duction" to *The Dialogic Imagina-
tion*, 9–10
Hornbostel, Erich von, 97–98, 107
Huch, Ricarda, works by: *Blütezeit der
Romantik* (Flowering of the age of
Romanticism), 185
Hüppauf, Bernd, works by: *Von sozi-
aler Utopie zur Mystik: Robert
Musils "Der Mann ohne Eigen-
schaften"* (From social utopia to

mysticism: Robert Musil's "The Man without Qualities"), 12

Ideals, 40, 150, 157, 159, 164, 169, 170, 174, 179, 180
ideology, 11, 13, 17, 18, 26, 87, 168, 174–76, 179, 180
incest, 51, 93, 107–8, 113, 121, 126, 127, 128, 132, 149, 150, 153, 167, 182. *See also* consummation
individualism, 3, 8, 9, 18, 21, 37, 41, 49, 51, 55, 68, 86, 94, 96, 164–65, 167, 168, 172, 174, 175, 176, 179, 179
inductive attitude, inductive ethos. *See* Utopia, of Inductive Attitude
infinity, 2, 8, 19, 20, 22, 23, 24–27, 30, 34, 35, 39, 41–42, 64, 69, 100, 103, 124–26, 173, 177, 178, 179, 182
irrationality, 8, 65, 95, 108, 115
Isis and Osiris, 54, 93, 113, 115, 116

Jonsson, Stefan, works by: *Subject without Nation: Robert Musil and the History of Modern Identity*, 5, 9, 11
Josipovici, Gabriel, works by: *What Ever Happened to Modernism?*, 13–14
Joyce, James, 106
Joyce, James, works by: *Finnegan's Wake*, 106

Kafka, Franz, 151, 167
Kant, Immanuel, 17, 24, 34, 51
Kant, Immanuel, works by: *Critique of Aesthetic Judgment*, 87, 145–46
Kaufmann, Walter, works by: notes to translation of Nietzsche's *Dawn*, 32
Kenner, Hugh, works by: *The Pound Era*, 106
Kermode, Frank, works by: "Modernism, Postmodernism, and Explanation," 104, 116; *Sense of an Ending*, 13
Kern, Stephen, works by: *The Modernist Novel*, 11

Key, Ellen, works by: *Die Entfaltung der Seele durch Lebenskunst* (The development of the soul through the conduct of life), 164–66, 183
Klages, Ludwig, 13, 112, 155
Klages, Ludwig, works by: *Kosmogonischer Eros* (On cosmogonic Eros), 146–49, 155
Köhler, Wolfgang, 160
Kretschmer, Ernst, 43, 48
Kroner, Richard, works by: "What Is Really Real?," 117
Kutzenberger, Stefan, 186

Lamprecht, Karl, 183
language crisis, 3–5, 8–9, 24, 50, 55–58, 70, 89–90, 94, 95, 100, 104–6, 109, 152, 176
Leibniz, Gottfried Wilhelm, 165
Lessing, Gotthold Ephraim, 165
Lessing, Gotthold Ephraim, works by, *Laocoon*, 136–38, 141–42
Lévy-Bruhl, Lucien, works by: *Les fonctions mentales des sociétés primitives*, 99, 100
living *in* and living *for* something, 28–35, 42, 124, 151, 175
living thought, 166. *See also* dead and living words
logos, 102, 120, 142
Lüdke, Martin, works by: introduction, with Delf Schmidt, to *Siegreiche Niederlagen: Scheitern, die Signatur der Moderne* (Triumphant defeat: failure, the signature of modernism), 12, 13
Lukács, Georg, critique of Musil, 12

Mach, Ernst, 9, 50
Magic, 9, 13, 46, 53, 54, 63, 69–70, 93–94, 96–98, 100, 102, 104–9, 110, 114–15, 116, 120, 125, 128, 132, 135, 162
Maimonides, Moses, works by: *Guide for the Perplexed*, 34
Malebranche, Nicolas, 151
Mann, Thomas, works by: *The Magic Mountain*, 172

McBride, Patrizia, works by: "On the Utility of Art for Politics," 13; *The Void of Ethics: Robert Musil and the Experience of Modernity*, 5, 6–7, 13, 38, 163–64, 167, 183

meaning, meaninglessness, 3, 5, 7, 9, 10, 16–17, 18–20, 23–29, 35, 38–41, 50, 51, 52, 53–56, 57, 64–65, 71–72, 77, 78, 79, 82, 87, 88, 89, 90, 100–102, 111–12, 114, 120, 136, 150, 152, 153, 157, 160, 163, 164, 166, 174, 176, 178, 179

metaphor: as abstraction, 30, 32, 40, 54, 56, 57, 64, 66, 70, 74, 78–79, 80, 85–87, 100, 102, 114, 135, 143–44, 147, 158, 176, 178, 179–80; as bringer of "beauty and excitement," 3, 59, 65, 76, 82, 114, 174; as cliché, 9, 38, 53, 55, 56, 58–59, 63, 68–69, 77–78, 89, 143; as commonality, correspondence, not distinguished from analogy, likeness, simile, metonymy, etc., 12, 20, 46, 59–60, 74, 76, 77, 89, 100, 107–8, 128–30, 142, 151; as compared to incest, 107–8, 128, 132, 149; as deferral of action and as extratemporal moment, 10, 20, 23, 30, 32, 35, 36, 37, 43, 60, 61, 70, 72–73, 74, 79–80, 89, 108–9, 119–35, 143, 151, 163, 176, 178, 179, 182; as disordering of tenor/ vehicle relationship, 20, 22–23, 128, 130, 133, 150; as form and process of constructing knowledge, 26, 80, 101, 143, 148; as infinite subjunctive generator of alternative living ideas, 3, 10, 19, 20, 22, 27, 35, 36, 38, 43, 49, 53, 56, 57, 59, 60, 62, 63, 64, 66, 68–69, 80, 82, 86–87, 89, 102. 110–11, 114–15, 119–35, 143, 149, 151–53, 179; as inherently inaccurate repre- sentation of reality, 3, 9, 20, 50, 53–55, 57, 60, 76, 77, 89, 102, 111, 114, 143–44, 158, 165, 174, 178. 179–80; as means of perceiv- ing reality and the world, 3, 9, 20, 22, 23, 26, 35, 53–55, 57, 60–61, 63, 64, 66, 70, 74, 77, 85–87, 89, 94, 102, 107 108–9, 111, 114–15, 128, 143; as modernist technique for describing ineffable essence and experience, 1, 3, 4, 5, 9, 24, 43, 54, 55–56, 72–73, 76, 77, 78–79, 80, 99, 102, 107–8, 114–15, 126, 162, 179, 182; novel as metaphor for life, 20, 27, 43, 60–61, 110, 135; reconciliation of metaphor with reality or truth, 12, 174, 181; as synecdoche, 20, 35, 70, 126, 134, 150; as world-making, 1, 2, 3, 9, 11, 23, 35, 43, 49, 54, 63–64, 66, 85–87, 89, 93–94, 103, 107, 110–15, 128, 151–53, 174, 179. *See also* abstraction; conceptualiza- tion; poetic image

metaphoric transparency, 9, 53, 54, 64, 70, 111, 149, 158

metaphoric value (*Gleichniswert*), 23, 77–78, 163, 172

millennium (*tausendjähriges Reich*), 6, 35, 40, 50, 140, 153, 161, 167

mimesis, 3, 32, 73, 94, 98–99, 107, 108–9, 111, 149

modernism, 3, 5, 8, 11, 12, 13, 34, 38, 50, 55, 72–74, 89, 93–100, 102, 104–6, 110, 114, 120

moment(s), 17, 19, 20, 24–26, 27, 29, 34–37, 39, 43, 44, 59–61, 68–74, 81, 99, 101–2, 108–9, 113–14, 120, 125, 132, 135, 136–42, 147–51, 162, 163, 164, 166, 168, 173, 176–79. *See also* exceptional conditions, moments, states

Moore, Gene, works by: *Proust and Musil: the Novel as Research Instru- ment*, 13, 172

morality, 8, 17, 24, 29, 34, 36, 37, 40, 51–52, 64, 65, 68, 70–71, 73, 79, 87, 107, 115, 119, 123, 124, 145, 147, 149, 150, 160, 167, 168, 171, 180, 184. *See also a priori* morality; ethics, as contrasted with morality; genius multiverses, 2, 20, 22, 26–27, 36, 46, 110–11, 115, 126

Musil, Robert, works by (besides *Der Mann ohne Eigenschaften*): "Ansätze zu neuer Ästhetik" (Toward a New Aesthetic), 18, 96, 103, 114, 116, 117; "Atemzüge eines Sommertags" (Breaths of a Summer's Day, *Nachlass* versions in *MoE*), 10, 119–40, 153, 154, 176; "Aufzeichnung zur Krisis des Romans" (Notes on the crisis of the novel), 16; "Aus einem Rapial" (Arrows from a quiver), 32; "Der Dichter in dieser Zeit" (The creative writer at this time), 180, 185, 186; "Döblins Epos" (Döblin's epic), 97, 104, 116, 117; "Ein Soldat Erzählt" (A soldier narrates), 172–73, 185; "Isis und Osiris" (Isis and Osiris), 93, 115–16; "Literat und Literatur" (Literati and literature), 97–98, 116, 117; *Nachlass zu Lebzeiten* (Posthumous papers of a living author), 117, 181–82; "Paris Vortrag" (Paris: address), 174, 184, 185, 186; "Rede zur Rilke Feier" (Rilke eulogy), 127, 128; "Schwarze Magie" (Black magic), 114–15, 117; "Über die Dummheit" (On stupidity), 15, 36; "Vinzenz und die Freundin bedeutender Männer" (Vinzenz and the Mistress of Important Men), 11, 57, 90, 185

mysticism, 2, 4, 7, 8, 10, 11, 12, 17, 18, 23, 24, 30–31, 34, 35, 37–38, 47, 51, 53–54, 67, 72, 75, 77, 79, 89, 96, 99, 102, 103, 104, 106, 108, 112, 113, 116, 123, 132, 141, 146, 150, 158, 160, 162, 163, 165, 167, 172, 176

Nabokov, Vladimir, works by: *Lectures on Russian Literature*, 20

naming, 50, 54, 56–57, 63–67, 69, 83–84, 90, 100, 102, 105–6, 123, 139

narrative, 1, 5, 16, 22, 23, 25, 32–33, 36–37, 43–44, 59–61, 64–65, 70–75, 119–26, 135–42, 153, 158, 178

National Socialism, 16, 18, 45, 94–95, 171–72, 175–76, 180. *See also* fascism; *Gleichschaltung*; totalitarianism

Negative freedom, and positive freedom, 40–41

Neymeyr, Barbara, works by: *Utopie und Experiment: zur Literaturtheorie, Anthropologie und Kulturkritik in Musils Essays* (Utopia and experimentation: on literary theory, anthropology and cultural critique in Musil's essays), 11, 13

Nietzsche, Friedrich, 2, 3, 5, 9, 13, 17, 30, 35, 38–39, 41, 50, 56, 60, 64, 68, 89, 101–2, 111, 113, 152, 165, 176

Nietzsche, Friedrich, works by: *The Birth of Tragedy*, 11, 17, 65; *Dawn*, 32, 46; *Gay Science*, 27, 37, 47; *Genealogy of Morals* (in *Basic Writings*), 33, 145–46, 148–49; "On Truth and Lying," 54–59, 66, 67, 85–87; *Untimely Meditations*, 51; *Will to Power*, 102, 111–13, 150

Nihilism, 9, 22, 63, 64, 66, 101, 102, 176

non-appetitive way of life. *See* appetitive way of life

non-linearity, 1, 2, 10, 17, 22, 25–39, 43–44, 51, 60–61, 71–72, 73–75, 119, 126, 151, 161, 162, 173, 178

normal condition, 17, 18, 22, 26, 36, 39–40, 43, 59, 60, 63, 66–68, 70–71, 73, 74, 99, 109, 119, 130, 144, 158, 159, 162, 163, 168, 169, 171, 173, 176, 178, 183, 184

Novalis (Friedrich von Hardenberg), 147, 166–67

Novel, as genre, 9–10, 11, 16–17, 22–23, 25, 31–32, 36, 43, 52, 56, 60–61, 71–74, 79, 96–97, 119–20, 126, 135–43, 178

originary phenomenon, originary
ideas, 4, 10, 29, 33–34, 49, 67–68,
69, 76, 77, 78, 89, 91, 94–96,
106–7, 113, 120, 146–48, 163
Other Condition (*anderer Zustand*), 1,
4, 7, 13, 17, 18, 29, 35, 37–39, 43,
53, 68, 80, 101, 108, 111, 113,
115, 128, 132, 146, 152, 155,
158–82, 183, 184

Pater, Walter, 2, 165, 176
Pater, Walter, works by: *Studies in the
History of the Renaissance*, 166–68,
176
patterns, 42, 49–82, 94, 100, 147,
158, 162
Perloff, Marjorie, works by: *Wittgen-
stein's Ladder*, 12
perspectivism, 1, 2, 4, 8, 19, 23, 35,
37, 39, 52, 89, 91, 111–12, 113,
148–50, 158–59, 175
Petry, Walther, 128
Picasso, Pablo, 100
Pike, Burton, 32, 47, 103, 153
Pike, Burton, works by: "Literature
as Experience," 13; "Negative
Freedom in the Man without
Qualities,"40–41; "Unfinished or
Without End,"24
Plato, 67, 94, 94–95, 113, 117
Plato, works by: *Phaedrus*, 142–43;
Republic, 157; *Timaeus*, 109–11
poetic image (also symbol), in contrast
to concept, 4, 9, 10, 19, 20, 23,
25, 38, 48, 53, 54, 55, 62, 76, 78,
94, 95, 96, 109, 115, 126, 133,
137, 138, 146–48, 159, 162, 170,
179. *See also* metaphor
politics, 3, 6, 9, 10, 11, 13, 18, 29,
31, 88, 94–95, 111, 149, 170–82,
184
polytheism, as model for individual
seeing, 37
Porchia, Antonio, works by: *Voices*, 52
possibilitarianism, possibility, 1, 2, 11,
13, 20, 22, 23, 24, 27, 34–36, 38,
39, 41–43, 51–53, 55, 59, 64, 66,
68, 72, 75, 77, 78, 86, 87, 95, 98,

100, 103, 106, 107, 110–15, 121,
124–26, 131, 132, 138, 145, 149,
150, 158, 160, 174
postmodernism, 3, 5, 8, 11, 12, 34,
102, 104, 116, 176
Potemkin, Grigory, 46
Pound, Ezra, works by: *The Cantos*,
106
Preusser, Hans Peter, works by:
"Masken des Ludwig Klages"
(Masks of Ludwig Klages), 13, 155
primitivism, 10, 23, 50, 53, 54, 69,
89, 93–100, 103–8
progress, purpose, 2, 15–16, 17, 19,
22, 26, 27, 29–32, 35–37, 39,
41–43, 44, 47, 56, 64, 67, 68, 71,
72, 94, 96, 119–26, 136, 142, 172,
176, 180
Proust, Marcel, 5, 65, 108, 125
Proust, Marcel, works by: "Chardin"
in *Marcel Proust on Art and Literature*, 144–45; *Remembrance
of Things Past*, 5, 56, 57, 59, 60,
65, 71, 72, 78–79, 90, 125, 172,
178–79, 183

qualitylessness, 10, 11, 38, 55

Rancière, Jacques, works by: *Aesthetics
and Its Discontents*, 11, 12
randomness, 63, 68, 72, 79, 100–101
Rasch, Wolfdietrich, works by: *Über
Robert Musils Roman* (On Robert
Musil's novel), 186
rationality, reason, 8, 10, 12, 19, 25,
27, 35, 40, 51, 65, 86, 90, 94, 95,
102, 103, 104, 115, 148, 170
reality, 1, 3, 8–10, 15, 17, 18, 20–23,
27, 34–36, 43, 49, 51–53, 54,
57–60, 64, 65–68, 71–82, 86–87,
89, 94–96, 99–113, 121–23, 126,
133, 133, 135, 136, 143, 145,
149, 150–51, 158–62, 163–75,
177–78, 180–81. See also *a priori*
reality
religion, 30, 68, 75, 76, 97, 98, 105,
165, 170
Renoir, Pierre August, 179

repeatability, 9, 25, 49–54, 57, 61,
63–64, 67–76, 78–87, 94, 100,
105, 107, 147–48, 158, 176, 180
Rice, Dharman, 47, 102, 116
Richardson, Robert D., works by:
Emerson: the Mind on Fire, 17
Ricoeur, Paul, works by: *Rule of Meta-
phor*, 60; *Time and Narrative*, 60
Rilke, Rainer Maria, 127–28
Rilke, Rainer Maria, works by:
"Archaic Torso of Apollo" in
Gedichte (Poems), 37; *Duino Ele-
gies*, 120; *The Notebooks of Malte
Laurids Brigge*, 91; "Der Panther"
(The panther), in *Gedichte*, 119;
Sonnets to Orpheus, 157
Ritual, 23, 53–54, 93–94, 96–97,
107–8, 110
Roth, Marie-Louise, works by:
Robert Musil: Ethik und Ästhetik
(Ethics and aesthetics), 12, 13,
115–16
Ryan, Judith, works by: *The Vanishing
Subject*, 73–74

Sappho, 106
Sartre, Jean Paul, 5, 68
Sartre, Jean Paul, works by: *Existen-
tialism is a Humanism*, 83; *Nausea*,
56, 71–72, 89–90, 101, 137–38
Schelling, Ulrich, works by: "Das anal-
ogische Denken bei Robert Musil"
(Analogical thinking in Robert
Musil), 46
Schiller, Friedrich, 165; idea of free
play, 11
Schleiermacher, Friedrich, 165
Schmidt, Delf, works by: introduction,
with Martin Lüdke, to *Siegreiche
Niederlagen: Scheitern, die Signatur
der Moderne*, 12, 13
Schmidt, Jochen, works by: *Ohne
Eigenschaften* (Without qualities),
47
Schnitzler, Arthur, works by: "Der
Reigen" (The round), 19
Schopenhauer, Arthur, 98–99,
145–48

Schopenhauer, Arthur, works by:
World as Will and Idea, 147–48
Schöne, Albrecht, works by: "*Zum
Gebrauch des Konjunktivs bei Robert
Musil*" (On the use of the sub-
junctive mood in Robert Musil),
110–11, 113, 179
Schrödinger, Erwin, 27
science, 4, 5, 8, 9, 15, 24, 25, 26, 51,
53, 74, 83, 85, 86, 95, 104, 111,
113, 164
Scriabin, Alexander, works by: "The
Mysterium," 97
Sebastian, Thomas, works by: *The
Intersection of Science and Litera-
ture*, 9, 12, 13, 89
seinesgleichen (the selfsame), 4, 10, 20,
40–41, 49–53, 68, 72, 74, 89, 109,
123, 163, 169, 172, 176, 177, 178
Shakespeare, William, 120
Singer, Dorothy Waley, works by:
*Giordano Bruno: His Life and
Thought with an Annotated Trans-
lation of His Work "On the Infinite
Universe and Worlds,"* 46
Skeat, Walter W., works by: *Etymologi-
cal Dictionary*, 106
Socrates, 141, 142–44, 154
Sokel, Walter, works by: "Musil und
die Existenzphilosophie Jean-Paul
Sartres" (Musil and Jean-Paul Sartre's existentialism), 89–90, 91
Sophocles, 142
Soviet Republic, Stalinism, 175–76,
180. *See also* fascism; totalitarianism
spirit (*Geist*), 13, 160, 166, 169–71,
174, 176, 181, 185
Stein, Gertrude, works by: *Tender Buttons*, 105
Steiner, George, works by: *Grammars of Creation*, 69–70; *Martin
Heidegger*, 151–52; *Real Presences*,
150
Stendhal (Marie-Henri Beyle), 145–46
Stendhal (Marie-Henri Beyle), works
by: *On Love*, 146
still life/*nature morte*, 7, 10, 70,
119–53

subjectivity, 3, 4, 8, 16, 24, 26, 34, 36, 49, 52, 55, 56, 73–74, 85, 89, 94, 96, 102, 111, 112, 113, 114, 123, 146, 148, 162, 176, 177
subjunctive. *See als ob*
suicide, 56, 152, 158, 160–61, 172, 183, 185

Tacitus, works by: *The Annals*, 115
Tadie, Jean-Yves, works by: *Marcel Proust: A Life*, 65
Tieck, Ludwig, 177, 185
Thiher, Allen, works by: *Understanding Robert Musil*, 6, 10
thing in itself (*Ding an sich*), 49, 111–12
Thoreau, Henry David, 165, 176
Thoreau, Henry David, works by: *Walden and Resistance to Civil Government*, 91
Tiedemann, Rolf, works by: "Dialectics at a Standstill,"109
time, timelessness, 5, 10, 19, 20, 22, 23, 25, 26, 27, 30, 32, 34–40, 43, 52, 59, 60, 61, 67, 69, 70–72, 74, 78, 79, 108–9, 111, 113, 114, 119–27, 131, 133, 136–44, 148, 149, 150, 151, 153, 158, 162–63, 167, 174, 176, 178. *See also* extra-temporality
totalitarianism, 6, 10, 13, 15, 18, 168, 170–71, 174, 176, 181. *See also* fascism; *Gleichschaltung*; National Socialism
transcendentalism, 35, 38, 68, 112, 132, 145

uncertainty, 11, 16, 17, 66, 105–6, 113
utopia, 1, 6, 7, 8, 11, 33, 40, 43, 53, 91, 102, 111, 113, 115, 149, 151, 158–68, 175, 176, 179–80; of Empiricism, or God as Empiricism, 53, 82, 158, 163; of Essayism, 13, 158; of Inductive Attitude, Ethos, God, Sensibility, 82, 111, 158–67, 184; of the Motivated Life, 67, 158, 164–66; of the Next Step, 11, 33, 111, 161; of the Other Condition (see *Other Condition*)

Valerie experience (affair with the Frau Major), 30, 165, 172
Variations. *See* drafts

Wagner-Egelhaaf, Martina, works by: *Mystik der Moderne* (Mysticism of modernism), 89
war, 13, 32, 53, 56, 120, 159–60, 172–73, 176, 178; First World War, 6, 60, 94, 172–73, 178, 185; as novel ending, 7, 8, 56, 158, 159–61, 161, 172, 183; Second World War, 13, 172–73, 185
Weinstein, Philip M., works by: *Unknowing, the Work of Modernist Fiction*, 11
Wellmer, Albrecht, works by: *The Persistence of Modernity*, 11, 12
Wilde, Oscar, works by: "The Decay of Lying," 56
Willemsen, Roger, works by: *Das Existenzrecht der Dichtung: zur Rekonstruktion einer systematischen Literaturtheorie im Werk Robert Musils* (Literature's right to exist: toward a reconstruction of a systematic literary theory in Robert Musil's work), 7
Wilson, A. N., works by: *God's Funeral*, 51
Winckelmann, Johann Joachim, 137
Wittgenstein, Ludwig, 4, 12, 100–101, 116
Wolf, Norbert Christian, works by: *Kakanien als Gesellschaftskonstruktion* (Kakania as social construction), 11
Woolf, Virginia, 5
Woolf, Virginia, works by: "Modern Fiction," 73, 101; *Mrs. Dalloway*, 72
Wordsworth, William, 69
Worringer, Wilhelm, works by: *Abstraction and Empathy*, 98

Zuckerkandl, Victor, 44, 171